The Inside-Out Approach

THE INSIDE-OUT APPROACH

Mastering the Four Ways of Screenwriting

Will Bligh

Eucalyptus

Eucalyptus Publishing Australia

Text copyright © Will Bligh, 2025

The moral rights of the author have been asserted.

All rights reserved.

No part of this publication may be reproduced, stored in a retrieval system, or transmitted, in any form or by any means, without the prior permission in writing of the publisher, nor be otherwise circulated in any form of binding or cover other than that in which it is published and without a similar condition including this condition being imposed on the subsequent purchaser.

ISBN 978-0-6489193-1-5 (paperback)
ISBN 978-0-6489193-2-2 (hardcover)

A catalogue record for this book is available from the National Library of Australia

I'm learning to crawl, so one day I can walk.

I'm learning to think, so one day I can talk.

I'm learning to share, so one day I can grow.

I'm learning what's true, so one day I will know.

I'm learning to fall, so one day, I can touch the sky.

Acknowledgements

The origins of this book are routed in my PhD from the University of Technology, Sydney. The commitment of my research supervisors, Dr Alex Munt and Margot Nash, was vital in realising my academic and creative work. The Faculty of Communication granted me a stipend to support my research and various travel grants that were instrumental in providing crucial feedback from experts and access to relevant archives.

Writing this book was an extended process of finding the core ideas of the inside-out approach and the four modes of writing. From the early days of developing my PhD to the latter stages of proof-reading chapters, my wife Esther has been a constant support in writing this book. Her patience and insights have made completing my research and this manuscript possible. The final editing of this book has fallen on Dominic Coutts who has graciously revised multiple drafts of this work. His clarity and thoroughness have been essential.

To Janosch and Nina

Contents

1. Introduction 1

PART ONE: Character Identification

2. Écriture 17
   - FOUNDATIONS   22
3. Identity 24
4. Growth 31
5. Schema 39
   - PRACTICE   50
6. Creating an Identity 55
7. How to Write Character Actions 65

PART TWO: Structuring Action

8. A Thought Machine 77
   - FOUNDATIONS   82
9. Narrative 83

10. Hypotheses 90

11. Suspense 99

    PRACTICE   108

12. Finding Dramatic Structures 109

13. Creating Character Journeys 122

PART THREE: Mapping Emotions

14. Emotional Context 135

    FOUNDATIONS   142

15. Primal Emotions 143

16. Moral Emotions 152

    PRACTICE   164

17. Writing for a Market 165

18. Archetypical Film Experiences 176

PART FOUR: Visual Writing

19. Roles and Responsibilities 195

    FOUNDATIONS   206

20. A Writer-Director Approach 207

21. Collective Vision 214

22. Subjective Treatment 226

PRACTICE   242

23. Writing a Hitchcock Film 243

24. Case Study of Meet John Doe 250

25. Finding Images 272

26. Conclusion 281

Notes   288

Bibliography   300

Index   314

Appendix I: Analysis of North by Northwest   328

Appendix II: Creative Practice   336

Illustrations

Alfred Hitchcock and Kim Novak: *Vertigo* 7

A climactic scene: *Angle and the Badman* 34

The protagonist being tempted: *Scarlet Street* 37

A character's guilt: *The Man with the Golden Arm* 57

A publicity poster: *The Birds* 167

A screwball comedy: *His Girl Friday* 172

Suspense and horror: *Night of the Living Dead* 182

The little tramp: *The Gold Rush* 188

Examples of subjective treatment: *Charade* 234

A case study: *Meet John Doe* 253

Chapter One

Introduction

The biggest impediment for a screenwriter is not talent, time or money but false assumptions about how to write—in other words, working the 'wrong' way. This book attempts to re-access fundamental assumptions about how to write a screenplay by focusing on why films engage and move audiences and offers an approach to understanding the best screenwriting practices and how to write using these practices.

To help highlight what false assumptions exist, I will introduce a fictional character, Pete, who wants to be a screenwriter and loves movies but has no writing experience. The first thing Pete does is type into an internet search engine "how to write a screenplay," which returns results describing how to format a screenplay. Explaining a screenplay's format, no matter how superficially important, won't improve his screenwriting. The history of film is another fascinating topic that Pete would love to read but probably won't help his writing. This type of information is irrelevant to learning the craft of screenwriting, even though it appeared in Pete's searches.

Pete comes across a website that has the five golden rules of screenwriting. Pete gets excited after reading this, as he is very good at following rules. The problem for Pete is that following rules without understanding how they work may help him initially but will significantly limit how and what he can write. Pete really needs to understand how films engage and develop experiences for viewers. He needs knowledge of how movies create different types of experiences for an audience so he can fully realise his screenplay.

Rules close down a creative process by immediately limiting options because they describe a particular way of thinking about screenwriting. Rules are not meant to be broken (otherwise, it's not a rule). On the other hand, principles don't have a right and wrong, aren't black and white, but just describe how a film and screenplay work for a viewer. Rules are principles with a heap of assumptions baked in.

Robert McKee described the difference between rules and principles:

> A rule says, "You *must* do it *this way.*" A principle says, "This *works* and has through all remembered time." The difference is crucial. Your work needn't be modelled after the "well-made" play; rather, it must be *well-made* within the principles that shape our art. Anxious, inexperienced writers obey rules. Rebellious, unschooled writers break rules. Artists master the form.[1]

McKee is acknowledging the importance of principles of an art form in writing a screenplay. These principles underlying cinema's form need to be manifested in Pete's script.

But screenwriting principles have a problem: they don't tell you how to write. If I told Pete a mountain of screenwriting principles, he'd probably sit in front of his word processor with a panicked look on his face, unable to type a word. Principles alone are not useful for a screenwriter as they can't be applied to writing a screenplay. Without the additional knowledge of how to apply principles, any book is not practical and therefore doesn't answer the question, how to write a screenplay?

The principles outlined in this book explain how a writer must think to create particular audience experiences. There is no right or wrong with applying any of these principles, but rather what a writer needs to be aware of. For example, viewers expect the central character **not** to die halfway through a film. A writer needs to be mindful of this expectation but doesn't necessarily need to fulfil it. In *Psycho* (1960), the protagonist is killed a third of the way through the film. The audience is shocked by the crime, the brilliant editing, and the fact the protagonist is dead. Hitchcock has left the audience without a main character! In the next scene after the murder, Norman Bates (played by Anthony Perkins) cleans up the apartment to remove any evidence. This scene is three minutes long, far longer than necessary to communicate what Bates is doing. The experience for the audience is that they are becoming engaged with Bates' plight, so he becomes the new main character. Principles foreground the central concerns of a viewer and allow writers to manipulate these concerns.

Continuing with Pete's journey, while surfing the web, he comes across exactly what he has been looking for: Marcel Digby's step-by-step approach to screenwriting for idiots! Marcel, a self-proclaimed screenwriting guru, claims to have a sure-fire method for writing a blockbuster. Pete can't believe his luck. Surely, if he carefully follows Marcel's steps, he can write a really 'good' screenplay...

There is no one way to write a screenplay. Part of *becoming* a screenwriter is working out the best way for you to write. A writer's creative process may share some similarities with other writers, but it has to suit their skills and preferences. For example, someone with a design background may initially work more visually than someone with a theatre background. Providing a step-by-step description (or any prescriptive approach), at its best, will not work for everyone and, at its worst, is too general even to offer insights into the craft. *Becoming* a screenwriter is a process of finding the best way to work that develops desirable results.

Different screenwriting processes using the same skills will result in significantly different scripts. There are many processes available to a writer, and the creative process of choice should be a personal way of writing that works for that writer. A process does not need to be unique, but the scripts produced using a chosen approach should be as individual as the writer is.

Pete has read every screenwriting manual he can get his hands on. He has read *heaps* of books on the topic. He travelled from library to library, finding everything he could to become a genuine screenwriter and gaining a lot of knowledge. Pete has noticed a trend in screenwriting books describing plot templates backed up by classic films fitting these structures. Pete loves these structures because they explain what the main character should be doing in each section of a narrative. Two examples of established screenwriting structures are *The Hero's Journey* (a twelve-part structure)[2] and *Sequencing* (an eight-part structure)[3]. He plans to 'fill in' the structure with his story, invent new scenes where necessary, and he'll have a bona fide 'good' screenplay. Pete thinks this has to be the answer to writing his screenplay.

However, there is a problem with this approach. It is a false assumption to think that stuffing your story ideas into a predefined structure and 'voila' you have created a successful script. It doesn't work because the process of analysing a successful film or screenplay does not resemble the act of actually writing one. This kind of analysis provides neither skills nor a writing process. The film director and teacher, Alexander MacKendrick, described using plot templates for writing as creating a "dead thing."[4] He explained that a plot structure divorced from character and theme is lifeless and lacks creative vitality.[5] In other words, the plot needs to come from the characters and not the other way around. This point will be explored thoroughly throughout this book.

MacKendrick did add that plot templates have value for "dismantling, vivisecting and exploring the structure and engine of an already existing dramatic structure"[6]. So, once you have a draft of your screenplay, these types of pre-defined structures can be beneficial in determining problems with the overall dramatic shape of a script. Therefore, plot templates potentially have a place within the process of rewriting (this also will be explored in this book).

All writers have different strengths and weaknesses and a unique perspective on the world. There isn't a single way to write a screenplay. Best practices don't lie in rules or structures but rather in applying techniques based on principles. For every rule or structure that is listed in screenwriting books, there are an array of films that break these concepts. A way to transcend rules is to go deeper and describe why the rules exist in the first place and why

Introduction

particular structures are popular. To explain these *whys*, this book will examine how an audience thinks when they view a film.

Pete has become disillusioned as he still doesn't know 'how to write a screenplay.' But fear not, Pete, this book will draw inspiration from Alfred Hitchcock and a heap of academic literature to explain how to write a film. Pete does a little double-take. "Did you just say Hitchcock? But he isn't a screenwriter!" Oh yes, he is Pete, but more on this later. Hitchcock will provide inspiration throughout this book in terms of how to approach screenwriting. Not only is he one of the greatest film directors, but he also wrote and talked extensively about his creative process, including his screenwriting practices.

For the first piece of inspiration, I will turn to a description by Raubicheck and Srebnick of what makes a Hitchcock film:

> The essence of the Hitchcock narrative paradigm, if we can identify it as such, is the successful integration of the tension and suspense of the mystery or adventure with the exploration of character and building of relationships that occur simultaneously. The writers understood that if they were to be successful in their part of "making" the picture with him, the director required an engaging screenplay that developed characters, created complex human connections for them, and suggested the turbulence of the protagonist's inner world.[7]

I will show that narrating the character's inner world engages viewers. This is not only true of Hitchcock's films but of all films. Characters play a crucial role in engaging an audience and will be shown to be the unifying concept for screenwriting.

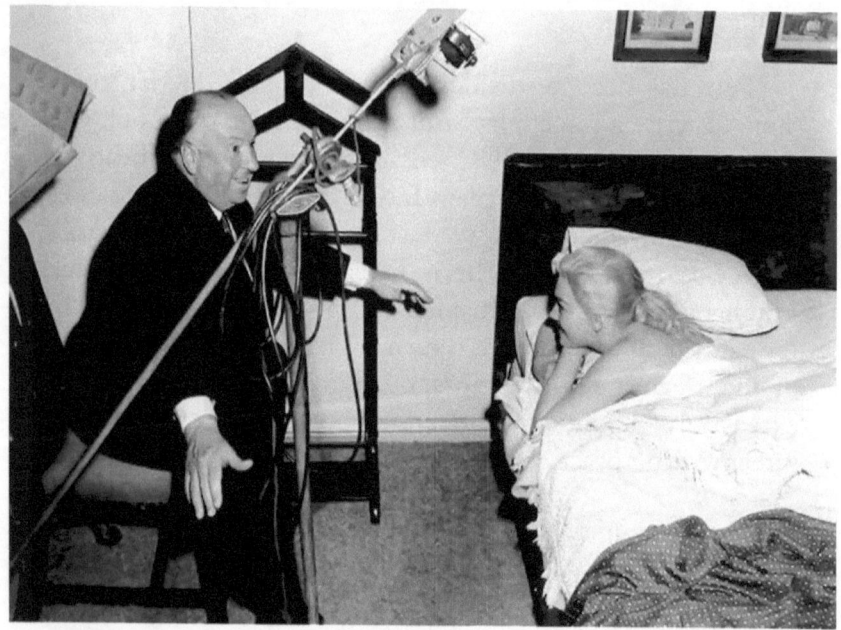

Alfred Hitchcock and Kim Novak on the set of Vertigo *(1958). Hitchcock is famous as a film director but also worked as a co-writer on many of his screenplays, even though he wasn't always credited.*

My central proposal in this book is that the best strategy for writing a screenplay is to realise the characters' inner journeys as the foundation on which all other aspects of a film experience are built. I call this strategy the *Inside-out* approach. This approach creates portraits of fictional people by narrating what each character is thinking and feeling, which will be shown to be the central concern of a film audience.

Inside-out recognises that plot, themes, and emotional affect are a function of character. Audiences engage with characters not because of what they do but why they do it. *Inside-out* draws on an audience's engagement with characters as a foundation for structuring a screenplay. This approach requires a writer to enter into each character's experience rather than conceiving a script solely by thinking it through.

The *Inside-out* approach recognises that a screenwriter is akin to a filmmaker, where a story requires visualisation during the writing process. *Inside-out* is an approach to screenwriting that can be applied in various ways. Its focus is on the audience and their experiences, where a screenplay represents not only a film but also the film experience. *Inside-out* understands a screenplay, written in words, is a representation of a film, written with images, which guides the audience's thought process.

Principles for cinema help write a screenplay because they describe how a film functions for a viewer. Human psychology forms the basis for most of the principles the *Inside-out* approach applies, as they explain an audience's reaction to a narrated story. *Inside-out* is focused on understanding the process of a viewer's cognition and emotions to provide principles and techniques for a screenwriting process.

The characters' inner worlds are fundamental to viewer engagement and elicitation of emotion. Because *Inside-out* approaches screenwriting from a cognitive perspective, it explains how the characters come 'alive' in films by rendering their internal worlds and consequently can result in a satisfying emotional journey for an audience. A writer's awareness of what audiences think and feel can be acquired using the principles outlined in each part of this book. The techniques presented offer practical help for writing film stories and focus on getting viewers to think and feel a certain way.

Inside-out examines the tension between a screenwriter's and an audience's point-of-view to gain insight into how to develop different types of experiences. I have foregrounded two perspectives: *Outside-in*, or how an audience thinks and feels while watching a film, and *Inside-out*, or how a screenwriter constructs a film audience's thinking and feeling. The principles governing how viewers mentally construct their experiences (i.e. *Outside-in*) will help to explain how a screenwriter forms a film audience's experience (i.e. *Inside-out*).

Many of the ideas I introduce come from academic literature and serve to provide a robust, understandable explanation for why film functions in a specific way. I hope the text is easily digestible and explains how and why this screenwriting approach works. Most importantly, it provides a solid foundation on which to argue this approach to screenwriting. Rather than accepting the screenwriting ideas on trust, this literature allows readers to make up their own opinions on the value of the arguments presented. I encourage readers to question any assumptions I have made, to debate my arguments, and to test this strategy with their own writing.

However academic literature is not enough for a practical book such as this. References from dramaturgical sources, filmmakers (most prominently Hitchcock) and screenwriters anchor my arguments within a world of tried and tested recommendations. Hitchcock's suggestions are grounded in the real-world application and live through his films. Again, questioning this type of practical advice is important, as it is a way of consuming and integrating this knowledge into your

Introduction

own processes.

A secondary source of practical knowledge comes from my own experiences of writing and viewing films. This takes the form of suggested practices to help apply already established foundations. My suggestions provide useful techniques for realising screenwriting ideas and are included for you to evaluate their relevance within your writing process.

The *Inside-out* approach is not fixed but rather organic, as there is no pre-defined system for applying techniques, and the central activity of a screenwriter is to find out how to best structure a script. The openness of this process is due to screenwriting being an art and originality being considered a central aim for any screenwriter. *Inside-out* defines a screenwriter as a creator of original experiences for the cinematic medium.

Mindsets

A problem, when screenwriters follow an approach based on rules, is that it blocks creativity and can make them worse writers than before they learnt these rules. However, rules for a particular structure (or plot templates) can be helpful when refining a screenplay. So when a writer is *not* creatively 'opening up' the story to possibilities but is logically distilling the story's possibilities by clarifying a character's journey and strengthening the experience for an audience, plot templates can be a godsend. Fundamentally, the *Inside-out* approach recognises two phases of screenwriting: discovering the story and refining the narrative. What makes these two phases distinct is that they require a screenwriter to participate in different kinds of thinking. Discovering the story is an open mindset where creativity abounds, and all possibilities are on the table. During this phase, any rules and structures may impede a creative process. The second phase, where a screenwriter refines the narrative, is a more restrictive mindset where restructuring and defining a story's narrative may be influenced by pre-existing narrative templates or other screenwriting principles. The discovery of a story is a process of determining what experiences the story will explore, how the audience will feel during the film and what the story is about, both for the audience and the screenwriter. Refining the narrative is about strengthening these experiences and finding ways to support and amplify each character's journey for a viewer.

These two phases are distinct because a writer can't be in both phases at once. A screenwriter is either opening up possibilities or refining existing ideas. I will further divide these phases into four separate mindsets. The 'opening up' phase can be achieved through *Character Identification* and *Visual Writing*, while the 'closing down' phase can be realised using *Structuring Actions* and *Emotional Mapping*. All four mindsets are different ways for a screenwriter to think and, when applied, offer practical ways to write. The *Inside-out* approach applies these mindsets to realise each character's inner journey.

Applying the four mindsets is like changing gears in a car: each perspective is like a single gear where a writer's thinking can only be in one mindset at a time. A writer can rapidly change between gears (i.e. mindsets) as required. A gear is chosen for the terrain a car is traversing; likewise, a mindset is chosen for how a screenwriter needs to work. When a writer shifts their perspective during the writing process, it depends on the problems a screenwriter faces and the techniques being applied.

Each mindset provides a foundation for a *way of writing*, offering a particular ethos within a screenwriting process. Each *way of writing* also requires related practical insights that explain how to apply this mindset. The practical insights explain how a way of thinking is generally used, offer specific techniques to achieve the aims of the mindset and highlight things to be aware of when writing this way.

The four *ways of writing* are a framework for thinking about and performing screenwriting, which any approach can apply. Therefore, these *ways of writing* provide a context for this book's central focus, *Inside-out*. They represent the four essential modes of screenwriting that promote a cinema experience for a viewer. There is no correct order to apply these modes, only that they must all be applied during a screenwriting process.

For *Character Identification*, a writer asks 'how the story's characters think and feel' to create an original work, develop interesting characters and find compelling moments. It introduces several new core concepts: character identification as a writing process, a definition of a character's identity, the notion of *duality of actions*, and explores why viewers align with certain characters. However, writing this way often develops a lot of loose ends and false leads and can lack clarity because it is not necessarily concise.

Structuring Actions is a way of writing where a writer asks 'how the audience thinks'. This mindset creates concise and clear writing, can set up suspense and focuses on finding the strongest actions. As well as discussing established ideas, the reader will learn about the term, *character context*, which represents a film spectator's thought process, and introduces a new category of suspense called *suppression*. A problem with this mindset is that it is the most comfortable way of writing, which can privilege this way of writing over the other three. Because it is not a creative way of working, results are created through logic and therefore tend to be cliche and predictable.

A writer applying *Emotional Mapping* is asking 'how the audience feels', which can provide an aim for the other three ways of writing. It develops a clear shape for the structure (both on a scene level and as a whole) and promotes a genre and marketing approach. I will introduce the concept of *fiction identification* that locates an audience's emotional engagement at points of character conflict, and define an alternative to genre categories based on *fiction identification*. This mindset is a type of compass for a writer that focuses on the audience's emotions but requires the actual narrative to be created through other ways of writing.

The final mindset, *Visual Writing*, asks of a writer 'how to write visually' and is a practical way of writing that helps reflect a visual medium. Even though this mindset can create new ideas visually, it does not define a particular practical process. How a writer visually writes needs to be found. I define a complimentary strategy to *Inside-out* called the writer-director approach. This way of writing promotes moving away from the standard Master-Scene format used by the industry for screenplay formatting to other media that can better represent visual ideas.

A screenwriter needs to be aware of the strengths and weaknesses of the four ways of writing, as they each have a distinct role within any screenwriting process. They work together and can negate their shortcomings. Neglecting any of these mindsets within a creative practice will ultimately weaken the screenplay produced.

This book is meant to be read with a pragmatic attitude. Readers should engage with ideas with an eye to improve

Introduction

their screenwriting and be willing to continually test the given techniques. This book is structured so that each *way of writing* builds on the previous ways, so skipping any sections may lead to holes in arguments. In many respects, this book is a homage to Hitchcock and I encourage the reader to further explore one of the greats of cinema. Two of Hitchcock's movies, *The 39 Steps* (1935) and *North by Northwest* (1959), are commonly referenced throughout this book and I strongly recommend that readers watch these films in preparation for relevant discussions.

The book is structured around the four *ways of writing*. The first part, *Character Identification*, is about how screenwriters should think and feel when writing a character's journey based on how audiences think about characters. The next part of the book, *Structuring Action*, explores how the audience thinks about characters in action and how writers can structure their thinking. A screenwriter's construction of an 'internal character structure' provides the foundation for the plot, themes and emotional effect. The third part, *Mapping Emotions*, examines why an audience's thinking about characters emotionally affects them and how a screenwriter can use this knowledge to help structure a screenplay. The final part, *Visual Writing*, explains how to visually communicate a character's internal journey. The process of manifesting an internal character structure is done with the knowledge of how the visual grammar of a film communicates to an audience. Throughout this book, characters in a movie play a crucial role in engaging the audience and will be shown to be the foundations allowing a screenwriter to develop particular types of cinematic experiences.

Each part is divided into a foundation and a practice. The foundation sections describe a mindset (or how a screenwriter thinks to achieve this way of writing) based on principles from academic, dramaturgical and filmmaking sources. The practice sections examine how to apply this mindset to your writing and are based on filmmaking sources with suggestions from my experience. Each *way of writing* describes techniques for screenwriting and suggests how they best apply to your screenwriting. Techniques can be considered tools, while principles explain how these tools work on an audience. At the end of each part is an example of the application of relevant techniques as well as a process for the reader to apply some of the ideas to their work. This book aims to inspire new and advanced writers alike.

PART ONE
CHARACTER IDENTIFICATION

Chapter Two
Écriture

Published in *The New York Times* on 4th March 1979, an article by French film director François Truffaut—entitled "Hitchcock: His True Power is Emotion"—described Hitchcock's *écriture* (French for hand-writing)[1]. Truffaut explained:

> [Hitchcock's] direction thus refuses simplistic recording of the action and adopts an "écriture" which consists of focusing on the character through whose eyes things will be seen (and felt by us, the public). This character will constantly be filmed from the front, and in close-up, so that we will identify ourselves with him. The camera will precede him in each of his movements while keeping his size constant within the image, and when he discovers something troubling, the camera will delay for a few seconds more (even too much more) on his face and look in order to heighten our curiosity. When he will be afraid, we will share his fear, and when he will be relieved, we will feel the same … but not before the end of the film.[2]

For Hitchcock, *écriture* focused on the audience's understanding of the fictional characters' internal world through the composition of imagery.

Truffaut's definition of *écriture* offers insight into Hitchcock's use of character to engage with and move audiences. *Écriture* highlights moment-to-moment awareness from the director of a viewer's experience. It suggests using a character's subjective perspective for storytelling where the film engages with more than action — it's telling the story of a character's experience, which consequently identifies a viewer with their plight. Hitchcock was focused on the character and spectator's thoughts and emotions while being aware of the narrative's role in creating a strong affect. The long-time Hitchcock collaborator and production designer Robert Boyle said the director was "most interested in feelings and was the most subjective director I know"[3]. Hitchcock often tied the audience through subjective visuals to a particular character to develop an emotional response. The association between the character and the audience is central to understanding how Hitchcock was able to move his audiences as effectively as cinema history suggests.

This first *way of writing* aims to discover a story through the characters. A writer needs to identify with all of the fictional people in the story and understand what motivates them, creating a unique internal dynamic within each character. This way of writing is about developing a character's inner world for an audience. Truffaut's description of Hitchcock's "handwriting" suggests a way to engage the audience by communicating this internal world. A writer needs to feel for the protagonist he is writing about, as well as understand the psychology of how each character thinks. A process of *character identification* is when a writer, in an imaginative sense, *becomes* the characters within a story. Whether the hero or villain, sidekick or mentor, a writer must embody each character, their emotional state, and their psychology.

By fully understanding and embodying different roles, a writer can embark on a process of discovery where each character leads the action. Real people act on emotions, and characters are no different. When a writer lets the protagonist emotionally and psychologically make decisions, the story will take surprising turns and open up possibilities for how the narrative can unfold. Discovering actions through the characters allows a writer to learn who they are and what motivates them. This first way of writing will define a personal type of 'hand-writing' for a screenwriter based on a deep understanding of character and offers a creative writing process, which opens up possibilities for the story.

Knowing and relating to the story's fictional personas is central to working this way. This personal and deep relationship will allow a writer's characters to appear genuine to the audience. It enables each role to act in a way that is believable and surprising. If a writer doesn't feel this kind of deeper connection, the fictional people and the story will become cliche. Creating by thinking logically about a character and story does not create originality. Instead, this first way of writing requires that a writer fully commit to the protagonist's inner world and understand what motivates him or her. This mindset is not necessarily logically understood by the writer but is driven by feelings and a sense of who a character is. There are unlimited ways a writer can find a character to which he or she relates. Screenwriting, in this sense, explores ideas about the individuals in a story and presents opportunities to 'find out' how they think and feel.

How does a screenwriter use characters to develop the audience's experience? How a writer and viewer think about characters are two processes that have an in-depth examination in this book. The first process involves a screenwriter creating film experiences using characters. A writer must engage with the protagonist's struggles and dilemmas and narrate the story to foreground this plight. It is a way of writing that focuses on who the characters are, their dreams, their desires, and what they are trying to achieve, and doing so through action shown on-screen. To create these internal worlds in a film, screenwriters need to identify with each persona in a screenplay.

The second process is the identification of an audience with the screen characters. To practically write in this manner, a screenwriter needs to understand how the viewer's thought process leads to identification. Identification is the "key relationship between the audience and character."[4] Edward Branigan wrote that a viewer's internal focalisation—where the "spectator's task is to identify the story world with the mental understanding of a specific character"—is an act of identification.[5] Branigan is referring to a type of cognitive (or mental) identification. Zillman notes a popular assumption is "the idea that our *emotional engagement* with fiction, and in particular film fiction, is somehow rooted in something like 'identification' with an empathetic response to the characters of fiction" (my italics).[6] Establishing identification as a central process for creating a viewer's experience plays a significant role in developing any screenplay.

These two processes will be connected through a cognitive understanding of character. This book argues that the audience engages with what and how each fictional individual is thinking. The actions that a screenwriter presents on screen need to represent a character's thinking and relate to a way of thinking for a writer. This way of writing focuses on understanding the characters' internal world and presenting their thought processes through actions on screen.

A screenplay is always written for an audience. Therefore, a writer needs to understand how an audience thinks about characters. There is a synergy between the act of writing and the act of a viewer interpreting that writing. This synergy described in cognitive terms will provide the conceptual framework for the first way of working. The rest of Part One is divided into two sections: *foundations*, which define a conceptual framework for this way of working and *practice*, describing how to apply these ideas.

All four ways (or modes) of writing are distinct in that they require a screenwriter to participate in different mindsets. For the first way of writing, a writer discovers the story with an open mindset where creativity abounds, and all possibilities are considered. Structured thinking can potentially impede the creative process during this writing mode and, therefore, should be minimised. The discovery of a story is a process of determining what the story is about both for the screenwriter and the characters.

FOUNDATIONS

The following three chapters lay the groundwork for a screenwriting practice by presenting theories and ideas relating to how writers and the audience think about characters. This conceptual framework is based on dramatic principles to underpin a practice for writing. Understanding these principles and how audiences think is not about defining rules but developing a mindset reflecting a film's dramatic form. These principles need to become second nature to writers so they can be open to creating rather than needing to be consciously engaged with any cognitive procedure.

There are three chapters in this framework: the first two ('Identity' and 'Growth') define how a screenwriter thinks about characters, while the third ('Schema') links this thinking to the cognitive process a viewer enacts while watching a film. Dramaturgical principles are introduced to explain how characters in films function dramatically. This section will describe how these principles mentally affect a viewer to form a dramatic *identity* for a character. Focusing on an audience's cognitive process will inform how writers apply these principles.

Chapter Three
Identity

Dramaturgy is the craft of dramatic composition and offers a means to orientate practice through logical thinking. The playwright, dramaturg, and scholar Leon Katz wrote, "The goal of dramaturgy is to resolve the antipathy between the intellectual and the practical ... fusing the two into an organic whole."[7] From a dramaturgical perspective, every decision a filmmaker makes for a movie has the function of constructing an experience for a viewer.

Characters typically have a motivation to achieve something. The notion that main characters in a film "should have an important dramatic goal to achieve" has been popularised by screenwriting manuals and has become a staple of screenwriting education.[8] Linda Seger writes:

> [T]he spine of the character is determined by the relationship of motivation and action to the goal. Characters need all of these elements to clearly define who they are, what they want, why they want it, and what actions they're willing to take to get it.[9]

Likewise, David Mamet highlights the protagonist's motivation as what engages an audience with a story.[10]

An *objective* is what a character is aiming to do in a scene. For example, 'to rob a bank' is an *objective* made up of a series of actions (e.g. a man covers his face, pulls out a gun, walks into a bank, etc). It describes why the character is doing these actions in the scene and has an intention. An *objective* is often inferred by the audience from the actions at the beginning of a scene (i.e. a viewer constructs an intention for why a character is acting) and provides a context for the remaining scene actions. Because an audience interprets a character's actions within a scene for meaning, and each action builds on the next to narrate an *objective*, actions "only have significance in relation to each other."[11] Providing a clear intention for a character communicates a coherent interpretation for each action, clarifies the scene, and produces stronger drama for the audience. An *objective* is always doable by a character, can be shown on-screen, and is aimed at a real object within the scene (e.g. money, a love interest, etc). For example, even when an *objective* is to convince someone to do something, the object is the person being convinced and can be visually shown in a film.

Scene *objectives* for a character have a deeper motivation called a *goal*. A *goal* is what a character desires or wants in a film, is abstract (not doable), and provides a rationale for each *objective*. For example, a scene in a movie may show a character robbing a bank, which is the scene's *objective* (i.e. it is doable and can be shown). The opening scenes of this film show the character's terminally ill brother, who could not afford a medical operation. So the *goal* for the main character (which is for most of the film) is 'to obtain money'. Perhaps in earlier scenes, this character tried other strategies for getting the money, like borrowing from other family

Identity

members. The *goal* of finding money to save his brother is not doable. It describes why he is doing something, not how he will do it. He can get the cash in various ways, and his decisions during the film will be shown as scene *objectives*. As the narrative reveals information about a character, a *goal* becomes more apparent to a viewer. Having a clear *goal* for the protagonist provides a context for interpreting *objectives* in scenes.

Goals provide unity for a character (i.e. a character acts consistently based on their *goal*) and create a type of audience expectation as viewers comprehend a character's *goal*. From a writing perspective, a character's *goal* provides clarity and direction for each scene *objective*, while scene *objectives* establish a context for actions. A protagonist's *goal* represents a through-line for the whole drama, where all their actions in each scene inherently fulfil this *goal*.

The deepest motivation, which relates to a character's psychology, is called a *motive*. The *motive* describes a moral or ethical justification for actions. It represents the underlying type of person, while a *goal* shows how this character will fulfil their attitude towards life. Therefore, *motive* is the rationale for the character's *goals*. A *motive* is who the character is, while a *goal* is what a character desires (or a way to fulfil this *motive*). *Motive* explains why the character wants something; the *goal* is what the character wants, and the *objective* is how the character attempts to get this want. Though the *motive* and *goal* develop an audience's understanding of a character, a *motive* is not inherently dramatic, while a *goal* is (this point will be discussed in depth).

In the scene where a man is robbing a bank (an *objective*), how a viewer interprets this scene depends on how the man's *motive* has been set up. The audience would assume his *goal* is to obtain money (as banks store money). If this scene appears at the movie's beginning and, therefore, no explicit setup has occurred for the man, his *motive* is assumed to be to live a comfortable and luxurious life. The audience will construct an interpretation and expectations based on the information they receive in the story. Alternatively, this bank robbing scene could appear later in a different movie where the man is set up to have a sick brother who requires expensive medication. When the man goes to rob the bank, the reasons are very different to having no setup. The underlying *motive* for the man can be completely different even though the same bank robbing scene is shown.

In the film *The Full Monty* (1997), the main character, Gary Schofield (played by Robert Carlyle), wants to earn money to pay his ex-wife the child-support he owes her. If he doesn't find the cash, he won't be able to see his son anymore. The relationship with his son shows Gary's *motive* and adds emotional depth to the film. He is often seen at a job-seekers' centre to look for work, representing one possible strategy for Gary to 'find the money' (his *goal*). He hits upon the idea to put on a strip show, and the audience joins this journey for most of the film. Each scene follows Gary as he attempts to organise the strip show (e.g. finding people to be involved, learning dance moves, etc). During these scenes, a viewer knows why he wants to earn the money, which affects the audience's experience and expectations. By the time they do the show, the local community has embraced the idea, the venue is full, and the performance is successful.

Frank Hauser sums up the importance of a writer entering into every moment of a drama:

| Recognise that the struggle is more important than the

Identity

outcome. Whether the characters accomplish what they set out to accomplish is not critical. What is important is that their intentions are clear—that they go about their struggles, encounter obstacles, and make moment-to-moment choices about what to do to achieve their goals. Their choices in the face of clear and compelling circumstances are what make them interesting; characters either change their circumstances or are changed by them.[12]

An *illusion of consciousness* is achieved onscreen by setting up a character's *motive* for a *goal* and having that character pursue that *goal* through actions. It gives the audience the illusion that a character is a thinking and feeling person with a consistent way of acting. A character's *identity* is defined by *motives* (perhaps implied) and whatever *goals* this character is pursuing. This *identity* remains consistent throughout the story and is challenged when something impedes this *goal*.

A character is only as strong as the resistance they overcome[13], which creates the illusion of willpower. Alexander MacKendrick asserts that a "dramatic character is definable only in relation to other characters or situations that involve tension".[14] The stronger a character's adversary in a film, the more threatening the obstacle to a character's *goal*; thus, greater conflict arises, and a better drama ensues. The common expression "drama is conflict"[15] summarises the essence of any drama and has been presented in many books for screenwriters or playwrights.[16] The stronger the obstacle to a character's *goal*, the more engaging the conflict for a viewer.

Giving a character a challenging *goal* to achieve provides a more captivating experience for an audience, while the contrary is also true (i.e. an easy task is less engaging to watch). Conflict often occurs when two characters in a story have opposing *goals*. The interaction of characters with potentially other forces—e.g. the sinking ship in the movie *Titanic* (1997)—can create the necessary hindrance in achieving their individual *goals*. For the audience, conflict is when characters come alive because their desires and beliefs are challenged, their determination is conceived, and their internal desires are played out externally in a film.

Character *identity* describes how audiences think about characters. An *identity* is formed in the viewer's mind when they watch a character's actions and develop an expectation about how the character will act in the future. Expectations describe how viewers think characters will act in future scenes, and a writer needs to be aware of what expectations their character's actions have developed. Expectations are the foundations for how viewers think about characters and events in films, which writers are constantly setting up and manipulating using different techniques. Actions performed by a character are understood within the context of these expectations. Audiences will update their expectations about a character during a film based on new information, typically through actions.

TO SUMMARISE:

- A *motive* is why a character wants something. A *motive* is not inherently dramatic and can be left ambiguous when writing a drama. Setting up a *motive* in a narrative adds a moral dimension to the character.

- A *goal* is what a character wants in a story. It is a type of expectation typically set up near the beginning of a film.

- An *objective* is what a character is doing in a scene. An *objective* is how the character aims to achieve a *goal* and can vary from scene to scene. While a *goal* is abstract (e.g. to get rich), an *objective* is always doable (e.g. to rob a bank).

- An *identity* is how the audience thinks about dramatic characters. An *identity* remains consistent throughout a film and consists of *motive(s)* and *goal(s)*. Defining a character's *identity* when screenwriting foregrounds the audience's thinking.

- Character *conflict* occurs when a scene *objective* meets an obstacle, either another character's actions or an event (e.g. a ship sinking). Because the *objective* is an attempt to fulfil a *goal*, *conflict* creates a struggle for a character's *identity* and develops an *illusion of consciousness*.

Chapter Four

Growth

Typically, characters in films change and grow from their experiences. This change often comes from inner turmoil or conflicting decisions the main character faces. Since *identity* describes fixed traits (i.e. a *motive* and a *goal*), how should a screenwriter think when characters change?

Thompson has suggested that characters possess "a set of clear traits, and our first impressions of those traits will last through the film—that is, the characters act consistently."[17] A problem with this definition is that acting consistently potentially reflects a character's *identity* yet doesn't recognise change. Another way of thinking is that character traits describe a "relatively stable or abiding personal quality", which allows for slight changes; however, some traits can potentially cease to exist as a character evolves during a film.[18] It has also been suggested that the act of an audience recognising a character does not deny the possibility for change "since it is based on the concept of continuity, not unity or identity."[19] Yet *motives* and *goals* are based on unity and represent a consistent trait for characters performing actions within a film.

Growth

The potential for characters to change typically exists from the story's beginning. When the protagonist changes, it should not come as a shock to an audience but rather emerge out of something they have seen him or her struggle with. How a screenwriter wants to narrate a character's journey will dictate how overt this change is for a viewer. *Inside-out* views this change as important to a story and is part of the dramatic *identity* of a character.

Change can be represented by two conflicting *goals*. A *want* is an attempt by a character to achieve a *goal* that is actively sought after in a movie. A *need* is an unrealised, ignored *goal* or desire that exists as part of a character. The popular screenwriting terms 'wants' and 'needs' have been adopted by numerous manuals to describe how to portray a character's inner turmoil. Because a *want* conflicts with a *need*, the *need* is challenged during a story by what a character does. There is typically a pivotal moment in a film where characters must choose between their *want* and *need*.

A writer sets up a character by having a *want* that is actively pursued, while a *need* is communicated but passive. As the story progresses and a character's *want* is challenged, they realise the importance of their *need*. Because a *want* and *need* conflict, a character must choose between their *goals*. By the film's end, the characters often have changed by understanding the importance of their *needs*, choosing their *needs* over *wants*, and showing how they have transformed due to their choice.

Foster-Harris emphasises that "all main characters … must each have his or her own internal struggle else the characters never live. *Conflict creates character*" (my italics).[20] As conflict creates character, so too "conflict grows out of character," and the "intensity of the conflict will be determined by the strength of will of the three-dimensional individual who is the protagonist."[21]

A protagonist's *need* is often what a film becomes about, and this *need* faces the most significant obstacles to success. It is common in cinema to set up a romance by establishing a secondary *goal* as a *need* for romantic love. In *The 39 Steps* (1935), "the love relationship became a main focus of the story, as it is in so many of Hitchcock's films, leaving the secret plans... as an insignificant afterthought."[22] In *Notorious* (1946), Hitchcock notes, "The whole film was really designed as a love story. I wanted to make this film about a man who forces a woman to go to bed with another man because it's his professional duty. The politics of the thing didn't much interest me."[23] There tends to be a pivotal moment in these films that reflects the importance of this avoided goal (i.e. *need*) where the hero and heroine "often [acknowledge] something that we, the audience, have known all along."[24]

Growth

In Angel and the Badman *(1947), John Wayne's character, Quirt, wants to revenge his foster father's death by killing Laredo Stevens. Quirt's love interest, Penelope, wants to live a non-violent life as she is a quaker. The story is about how Quirt changes and finds romantic love.*

Not all characters are complex. A writer doesn't want to distract from the main story by making every side character have an internal conflict. Sometimes, characters are just bit-players and exist to serve the protagonist's journey. The police in *The 39 Steps* are uncomplicated characters with a single active goal: to capture the (suspected) murderer Richard Hannay. These more superficial characters are less compelling for a spectator and, therefore, tend not to be the focus of a story.

Sometimes, writers choose not to give their protagonist's *needs*. This situation typically produces a superficial character who is only after one thing. A classic example in *Raiders of the Lost Ark* (1981) is Indiana Jones, a comic-book-like character representing a 'boys-only adventure' type of experience for a viewer. One could argue that his *need* is to find romantic love through Marion since he once had a relationship with her. However, Indiana's romantic interests are played more for humour than a serious *need*, as no meaningful actions support this expectation. The final scene showing Marion holding Indiana's arm supports the closure of her *need* more than his.

All *wants* and *needs* are *goals* with internal sources reflecting desires and are always focused on achieving something external to the characters. Both types of *goal* relate to the characters' actions in a story and usually find *external conflict* due to obstacles opposing these actions. When a character's *want* and *need* oppose each other during the story, *internal conflict* within the character develops. The character's journey becomes about choosing between these two desires. Each *want* and *need* has an implied *motive*, which can be set up to create a strong moral dimension. All characters must intend to achieve a specific *goal*, whether to aid the villain in his evil plans or fight the enemy in a war film.

A character's *internal conflict* implies a need for transformation and allows their choices to influence what they will become. Egri states: "'Growth' is a character's reaction to a conflict in which he is involved. A character can grow through making the correct move, as well as the incorrect one—but he *must* grow if he is a real character."[25] The growth of a character occurs through their two *goals*. Encounters create internal and external conflict, reshaping the character's attitudes and providing dramatic experiences for viewers. If a character undergoes growth or change, it is a progression from a character's active *goal* to the passive or avoided *goal*. An alternative to growth is when a character chooses to continue with the *want* and ignore the *need*, which typically has a negative repercussion for the character. A story can be viewed as an exploration of the relationship between these two goals of the protagonist.

A classic example of *wants* and *needs* is in Baz Luhrmann's MTV-inspired *Romeo and Juliet* (1996). The two protagonists have the same *want* (to be with each other) and *need* (to be loyal to their families). Their two families hate each other, and when Romeo kills Juliet's cousin, Tybalt, it creates strong *internal conflict* for both characters. When they decide to follow their *wants* to be together, the story ends in tragedy, with both *wants* and *needs* being unsuccessful.

A writer sets up a main character's *want* and *need*, so a screenplay has clear and compelling through-lines for the narrative. These *goals* effectively make the writing inherently more dramatic and engaging for an audience. Notably, an audience doesn't necessarily need a rational reason for a character to have a particular *goal*; however, for the screenwriting to be dramatic, one must clearly understand their *goal* (i.e. why a character is acting in a scene). For example, in *Seven* (1995), the audience knows that the killings are linked; however, a psychological explanation of why the serial killer is committing murders is redundant. The *motive* is assumed to be that he is deeply disturbed, which is not something viewers will generally identify with. What is essential, from a dramatic perspective, is that the character has a clear *goal* and is a formidable opponent, which develops conflict. In *Batman Begins* (2005), screenwriters Christopher Nolan and David Goyer give a back-story about what drove Bruce Wayne to become 'Batman'. Usually, this type of back-story is not required in Batman films, and the audience accepts he just wants to stop crime. However, his history sets up Bruce Wayne as having a fear he is trying to overcome, adding psychological depth and an explicit *motive*.

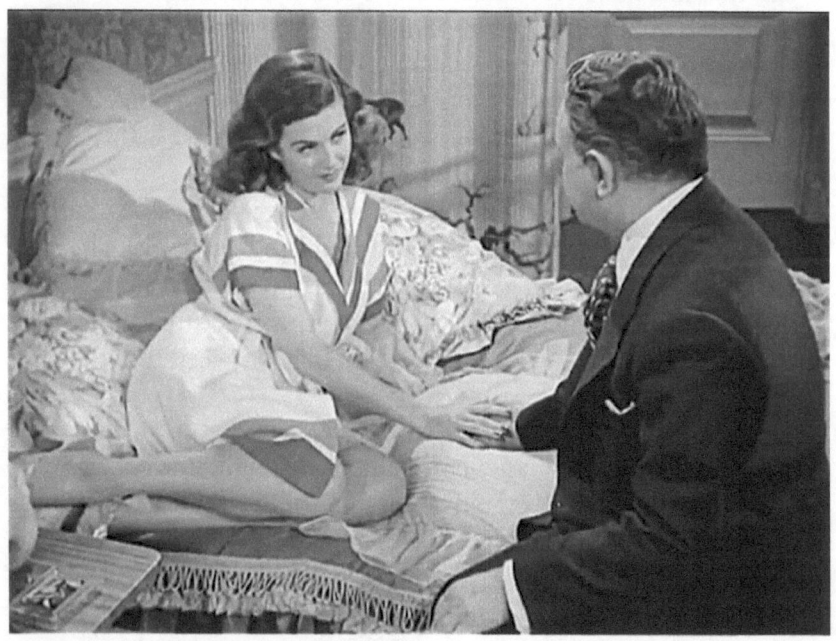

In Fritz Lang's Scarlet Street *(1945)*, Chris is an amateur artist who desires after the much younger Kitty and needs recognition for his talent. Kitty wants *money* and needs *romantic love, which Johnny is not fulfilling. The tragic ending means no-one attains their* goals.

Why two *goals*? Why not three or four *goals* so the characters are even more complex and interesting? Due to clarity. Two *goals* provide *internal conflict* and can be clearly communicated. If there is ambiguity about *goals*, the audience won't be sure what the characters *want* and won't engage in dramatic situations—having three or more *goals*, which potentially conflict, gives each *goal* less screen time and, therefore, less importance. The number of *goals* is not directly related to the complexity of a character. There have been complex psycho-killers (e.g. Hannibal Lector) who have no more than two *goals*. The *goals* relate to how the characters engage a viewer dramatically, and not how brilliant or skewed a character necessarily is. A protagonist with clear *goals* is the foundation for producing engaging experiences for a spectator.

To summarise:

• A character's *identity* can have one or two *goals*. The primary *goal*, or *want*, is set up at the beginning of a film and is actively pursued by the character. More complex characters will introduce a secondary *goal* or *need* that the audience is aware of and becomes active during the story. A *want* or *need* can be set up with a *motive*.

• *External conflict* is developed when another character or event in a scene opposes an *objective* for either type of goal. *Internal conflict* is developed when a character's *want* and *need* oppose each other and create a personal dilemma. This dilemma provides the character an opportunity for growth and change, as they **must** choose between their *need* and *want*.

Chapter Five

Schema

Screenwriting must always be done with an awareness of what a potential viewer will think and how they will react to this thinking. Character *identity* is useful for a writer because it reflects how viewers think while watching a film. Therefore, an audience's thinking is not guesswork but a cognitive process based on character actions. When film audiences are actively engaged with a drama, they ask questions about each character's intentions in a story. This chapter examines how audiences cognitively engage with fictional characters.

Inside-out is an approach to screenwriting where the story emerges from a character's desires and psychology. It applies cognitive science to explain how audiences think when watching a movie and argues how screenwriters should work. It promotes an awareness of the character and audience's thinking and that all written actions are told with this dual awareness. The definition of a character's *identity* creates a dichotomy between a character and the audience's thinking.

All people share similarities in how they think while watching a film. In social science, a schema describes common characteristics of how people think to organise knowledge. These characteristics describe how objects and events are categorised and guide people's cognitive processes. How viewers think about characters can be defined using a schema, which explains how film characters guide their attention and form expectations. A schema will help describe a screenwriter's thought process, where a viewer's thinking is driven by what characters desire (i.e. *goals*) and why they want it (i.e. *motives*). This specific schema will be referred to as a *character schema*, as all dramatic characters can be evaluated using this schema.

A schema recognises that people worldwide, even communities diverging profoundly from one another, share certain regularities in "human psychology and physical environment which all human societies face, which have given rise to common conventions and practices."[26] A *character schema* represents a global audience's cognition, allowing a cross-cultural approach to understanding a viewer's experiences. Throughout this book, I will use a *character schema* to help explain how a screenwriter can develop a wide variety of experiences for film spectators.

The *character schema* posits that as a film story unfolds, an audience tries to understand what the characters are doing and for what reasons. Actions are meaningful in a story because characters provide a context for viewers to interpret these actions. The *character schema* describes how audiences mentally represent this context for actions as fictional people onscreen.

Alignment

Every character in a film will play some kind of role in the audience's experience. These roles set up expectations for a viewer and perform a function in telling a story. Understanding how audiences identify particular roles in a film, such as the protagonist or antagonist, is crucial.

Not all characters in a film are equal. For viewers, it is usually obvious who the main character is because they feel most strongly about their plight. From a screenwriter's perspective, deciding which characters will play the key roles in a story is necessary. This decision may not always be straightforward; it may pay to focus on a character who, on first thinking, is not the obvious candidate to be the protagonist. For example, the story of *Little Red Riding Hood* implies the eponymous character is the protagonist; however, a writer may find a fascinating tale by focusing on the hungry wolf whom Little Red's father is constantly hunting. There is no right or wrong, but different kinds of experiences and the experience that works best for the screenwriter should be the one chosen.

The term *protagonist* refers to the central, active character in a story and literally means the person who initiates *agon* or struggle.[27] This definition suggests the protagonist is the main character who actively drives the story forward, which may be true for most stories but isn't always so. For example, in *A Christmas Carol*, Scrooge is the main character that the story revolves around. Still, he is reluctant and doesn't provide any active drive for the story. His old colleague, Jacob Marley, has arranged the visits from the ghosts, and these ghosts change Scrooge by showing different versions of his life. Another example is Robert Altman's *Short Cuts* (1993), which has multiple storylines and no single character providing a central through-line.

One candidate for defining the protagonist is to use a moral judgement, where the 'good-guys' are the story's heroes. Wes Andersen directed a version of Roald Dahl's *Fantastic Mr Fox* (2009) that follows the trials and tribulations of Mr Fox and his family. Why does an audience care about a carnivorous fox that out-smarts a farmer to eat chickens? In contrast, *Chicken Run* (2000) centres on chickens. Why aren't audiences barracking for the chickens in *Fantastic Mr Fox*? Moral judgment may influence a viewer's interpretation of actions, but it doesn't define the protagonist.

Instead, the protagonist could be defined in relation to the antagonist. Both *Fantastic Mr Fox* and *Chicken Run* cast farmers, who hold a position of power on the farms, as the villains, which suggests a protagonist/antagonist relationship. A protagonist only exists in relation to some kind of antagonist. An antagonist has a role in a story to oppose the protagonist and develop conflict. Alfred Hitchcock observed the "more successful the villain, the more successful the picture" and referred to a potent antagonist creating compelling drama.[28] Therefore, it is a strong choice to have the empowered farmers as the antagonists in *Chicken Run* and *Fantastic Mr Fox*, as it naturally creates dramatic situations.

Does a story even need a villain? Victorio De Sica's *Bicycle Thieves* (1948) follows a father searching for his stolen bike. Initially, it may appear that this thief is the antagonist, however, post-war poverty provides the necessary conflict for this story. This film doesn't have a villain, yet it is dramatic and highly moving. *Titanic* (1997) is another example where conflict is developed through circumstances, in this case, a sinking ship. One thing is similar to films with villains: conflict is always produced by opposing or stopping the protagonist's *goals*. Therefore, the role of the antagonist in *Bicycle Thieves* is played by the environment in which the characters find themselves.

Film director Francois Truffaut discussed a scene from *North by Northwest* (starting at 1:50:15) to illustrate how viewers align themselves with different characters:

> At the end of "North by Northwest," we shift our *affective participation* from Cary Grant, who is entering the mansion, to Martin Landau, who suddenly realises Eva Marie Saint is a spy and finally to Miss Saint. (my italics)[29]

This "affective participation" swings between characters in this scene, easily and convincingly helping to align and develop a spectator's emotions. The scene narrates several shifts for the audience and aligns them with different characters. The audience is mostly visually aligned with Roger Thornhill as he attempts to rescue Eve Kendall and watches Leonard and Vandamm interact. Thornhill is the main character in this scene, and most of the film is narrated from his perspective. However, Hitchcock moves away from Thornhill's point of view when Leonard and Vandamm start arguing. This narration aligns the viewer with the antagonists of the film as they realise Eve has tricked them with a fake gun, serving to increase suspense. Even though a scene can align viewers with individual characters through narration, this example only hints at why they care for Roger and Eve more than the villains. A view of the entire film's narration is necessary to answer this question.

The difference between the protagonist and antagonist can be understood by how the story is told. During a film, viewers *align* themselves more strongly with particular characters than with others. A viewer always enacts this process of character *alignment* through how a film narrates. This type of *alignment* occurs for the protagonist and, at times, for other characters, including the antagonist. However, the function of the protagonist for the audience is to unify the audience's experience (otherwise, a movie is a series of short stories). In terms of story, a film is about the protagonist. Therefore, not only will the story tend to be narrated from the protagonist's perspective, but, significantly, the protagonist will spend more time on-screen than any other characters.

A crucial phase in story-telling is at the beginning when the audience is looking to *align* with a character (i.e. the protagonist). Alfred Hitchcock described how he sets up the protagonist of *Psycho* (1960) by stating that the "more we go into the details of the girl's journey, the more the audience becomes absorbed in her flight."[30] The narration of Marion Crane in the first third of the film continually returns to her perspective. Hitchcock plants her as the protagonist (that is, until the famous shower scene in the movie), even though she is a thief.

Hitchcock also used an analogy of a cloak to describe a kind of *alignment* developed over multiple scenes:

> [A]s the audience sympathy for a character is built up, the audience assumes that a sort of invisible cloak to protect the wearer from harm is being fitted. Once the sympathies are fully established and the cloak is finished, it is not —in the audience's opinion, and in the opinion of many critics—fair play to violate the cloak and bring its wearer to a disastrous end.[31]

The emphasis of this passage is on the expectations of the

audience that the protagonist will ultimately survive and prevail. Expectations are crucial for screenwriters to be aware of, as they provide the basis for suspense.

Hitchcock suggested that an implied guarantee exists between a film and the audience, so their worst "fears" for the protagonist, whom they identify with, will not be realised in the film's narrative.[32] Hitchcock spoke about an error he made in the film *Sabotage* (1936), where the audience is made aware of a bomb carried by a youth: "I once committed a grave error in having a bomb for which I had extracted a great deal of suspense. I had the thing go off and kill someone, which I should never have done because they needed the relief from their suspense. Bad technique; never repeated it."[33] By killing the unsuspecting child, he breaks the audience's trust because they expect him to escape. An audience usually expects a protagonist to survive at least to the end. However, Hitchcock knowingly and successfully made an exception, which shocked audiences by killing the protagonist just forty minutes into *Psycho* (1960).

When a film follows a particular character's journey, a process naturally occurs where viewers *align* themselves with this character. It is also worth mentioning that other cinematic elements can be utilised to denote the protagonist/antagonist relationship. For example, sinister music can signal a type of character to the audience. Even though music can play a complementary role in setting up *alignment*, spending time on-screen with the central characters is always necessary.

The unification of the audience's experience, where a writer creates a sense of a single story (rather than a collection of scenes), can be done through other means than a single protagonist. For example, in *The Great Escape* (1963), there is no one protagonist but multiple inmates trapped in prison, all attempting to escape. They all have the same *goal* of escaping, which unifies the experience and the feeling of a single film rather than a variety of characters trying to do something different. In *Nashville* (1975), the experience is unified by following people from the music industry in Nashville, while in *Magnolia* (1999), the main characters search for meaning and happiness in San Fernando Valley. A unified experience is what the audience feels after they leave the cinema, and it should be one of the compelling reasons a screenplay is produced.

An audience spending time with particular characters results in the *character schema* fully developing what they want and why they want it. When viewers engage with a character over time, an *identity* is constructed based on their understanding of the character's intentions. Intentions behind a character's actions are the building blocks of the audience's thinking. For example, in *Raiders of the Lost Ark* (1981), the character of Indiana Jones wants to find the Ark of the Covenant before the Nazis do. The intention for Jones is set up at the beginning of the film, and throughout most of the story, his actions are an effort to achieve this *goal*. If this *goal* were not established at the beginning, the audience would be wondering what he is doing and why he is doing it. A viewer requires a screenwriter to give reliable access to a character's state of mind. Watching a film is an active process where audiences continually construct a character's inner journey based on each action's intention.

Identity, as defined by the *character schema*, is a cognitive representation of **what** a character is. Identification is the process of a writer or viewer constructing a character's *identity* based on the schema. In other words, identification is **how** a writer or viewer thinks about a character's *identity* while writing or watching a film. Two types of identification are based on a character's *identity*: *fiction identification* is the process of a film audience mentally constructing an *identity*, while *character identification* is the process of a screenwriter creating a character's *identity* through actions. These two processes are complementary as a screenwriter attempts to develop compelling characters, which viewers interpret through actions shown on screen.

This first way of writing enacts *character identification*. To perform this type of identification, writers must understand the characters they are writing about on a deep level. They must grasp how the protagonist thinks and feels. This thinking and feeling describe a particular psychology, which reflects the actions created for the screen. How a writer relates to psychology and develops actions for a screenplay will be the basis for a practice within the next section. The *Practice* section outlines how a screenwriter can creatively apply these concepts through a writing process.

TO SUMMARISE:

• The *character schema* describes how film audiences mentally represent the *identity* of fictional people onscreen.

• *Fiction identification* is the process of a film audience mentally constructing an *identity*.

• *Character identification* is when a screenwriter develops an in-depth relationship with a character's *identity*, allowing a process of discovery and exploration through this character's actions.

• In a dramatic film, as a character spends time on-screen, their *identity* will become apparent to a viewer. Spending time with a particular character involves a film audience and increases a viewer's *alignment* with that character.

• The most substantial *alignment* in a film dictates which character takes the role of the *protagonist*. Character(s) opposing the protagonist's *goals* play the role of an *antagonist*.

PRACTICE

There are ways to think about a character that promotes a more complex and complete inner world. The tools presented in this section help develop characters with a deeper psyche and strengthen their roles within a drama. These tools offer a dramatic way of thinking about characters and their internal worlds, which will help a writer find expression through written actions.

The first way of writing opens up possibilities for a story. Relevant practices centre on a writer developing and connecting to the story's characters and discovering how they lead to action. When applying this mindset, a screenwriter's awareness of the characters guides the writing process.

The practice of trusting your characters.

Ernest Lehman, the screenwriter for *North by Northwest*, stated that he did not know where the protagonist, Roger Thornhill, was going next as he was writing the screenplay and likened his experience to its protagonist's journey: "[I was] like my own character, always wondering, 'How can I get out of this?' And the only way I could get out of it was to 'write' my way out of it."[34] Lehman recalled that Roger Thornhill's character arc—from a smug, self-absorbed liar to a compassionate hero by the end of the film—was not a conscious effort to redeem him but happened unconsciously.[35]

This *way of writing* requires a deep and connected understanding of a story's characters. This connection is personal and, if possible, represents a writer's most profound concerns. Approaching writing in this way requires the development of characters before any fixed notion of narrative can take place, allowing the story to evolve from who the protagonist is. The more a writer feels and relates to the characters, the more the story will resonate with audiences. For this way of writing, there is no substitute for knowing the inner world of the central story characters.

There is a great temptation for screenwriters to conceive of a script by thinking it through rather than entering into each character's experience. Creating a story using pure logic will lead to cliché because it will be predictable for a viewer. The consequence of not knowing the characters means a writer will make obvious choices and result in an unoriginal work. It may be more comfortable for a writer to think only about what a protagonist is doing and why, creating a logical structure for actions; however, it will read as though the writer hasn't entered into each character's dilemmas with any conviction. Creating the illusion of a real person is difficult without a writer entering into a character's genuine experience.

Real people often do things based on emotions. A character going through a 'real' experience will act out their internal feelings, which may not be logical. When a writer knows a story's characters, they may act in surprising and unforeseen ways. Allowing characters to take on their own life supports a process that is fundamentally one of discovering who they are, what they want, and their deepest desires. This process relates to the writer. Character is a means to explore deeper themes and concerns of the writers and present these revelations in a dramatic form. This way of writing encourages a writer to find out how characters act given a situation by engaging with their experiences rather than a purely logical approach to concluding actions.

Character identification is not led by logical thoughts but is rather an emotional process for creating actions. For example, in a scene where a man who was adopted out as a child stands in front of his birth mother's house, a writer may have a plan that the man will accept that being abandoned was not his fault. Thinking logically, the man pensively knocks on the front door and confronts his mother about why she adopted him out. Acting emotionally, the man may force himself to knock, the door opens, and he just stands there, not knowing what to say. Does he start yelling, crying, running or fighting depending on the psychology and emotional state of the character at that moment? How strongly a writer identifies with a character will create more in-depth actions, which are often surprising and appear more convincing to the audience.

There are no rules for creating a character's *identity*; however, a writer must embody their inner psychology to create a story. Why a writer feels for a particular character reflects who they are and therefore provides a way to create unique stories that reflect this writer's individuality and worldview. A writer needs to search for a deep motivation (i.e. a *motive*) and a strong line of action (i.e. a *goal*) for a character. These concerns must become second nature so that the character schema is not what a writer thinks but how he or she thinks. Character *identity* provides a context for a character's emotions, thoughts and actions.

To write a character acting onscreen, a writer needs to understand what they want and their emotional state at any moment in the story. The *Inside-out* approach recognises a process of *character identification* during the development of a screenplay. *Character identification* is when a writer identifies with a character for screenwriting, which requires a 'playing' of each part in the story similar to an actor playing a role. This role-playing allows the characters to decide what to do next and what to say. Because a writer identifies with the characters, parts of the writer's psychology inevitably feed into each character's psychology, and the writer feels for and with the protagonist as the drama unfolds.

The first way of writing applies a process of *character identification* to open up possibilities for characters and discover a film story. It involves letting go of preconceived narrative ideas and finding out where the characters will take the story. *Character identification* is an intuitive way of working, where a writer needs to trust the characters to find the story. The next chapter, Creating an Identity, will examine this initial phase, where numerous practical tools are suggested for developing characters. The following chapter, How to Write Character Actions, will provide practical insights into conducting this first way of writing.

Chapter Six

Creating an Identity

Creating a film character can be approached as a process of developing a deep understanding of an individual psychology. A character's psychology directly relates to the *schema* through *motives* and *goals*. A *goal* reflects how a character **thinks** to fulfil a *motive*. How a character thinks is the reason a *goal* is manifested from a *motive*. For example, how a character deals with a situation where a man has a terminally ill brother and has no money will entirely depend on his psychology. If the character is set up as having lived a disadvantaged life, where crime is a reasonable solution to his predicament, he may choose to steal money for his brother's treatment. His *goal* is to get the necessary funds, which is his decision to solve a problem and reflects a way of thinking about this issue. An alternative decision might be to ask for help from a hospital. How a character approaches a problem reflects a thought process and is a part of psychology.

The *motive* is the psychological foundation underlying the values of a character and adds a moral dimension. A character's desires or goals build on the *motive* to create a psychological profile. This psychology is consistent throughout a story and is represented in a viewer's thinking

Creating an Identity

as the *character schema*. A *goal* is a desire which has grown out of the deeper *motive*, is abstract and becomes the reason for all of the character's *objectives*. A scene *objective* is how a character fulfils their *goals*. This psychology behind actions represents a living and breathing person who thinks, reflects, and has an underlying value system.

This chapter will focus on *motives* and *goals* contained in an *identity*, while the following chapter will examine practices for developing strategies to create character actions. The choices a writer makes about psychology for this first way of writing are led by a process of *character identification*, which can open up possibilities for a story.

The practice of creating a motive for a character

In his book *Story Sense*, Paul Lucey advised to "write simple stories and complex characters" because the story's characters engage the audience.[36] Peter Sainsbury believes a writer "must become an archaeologist on a site of primal psychology, where the strata of fear and anxiety, desire and hatred, perversity and taboo, the risks of love, pleasure and joy, and many other things that we approach with trepidation, must all be excavated in search of emotional truth. This is so whether that truth is to be represented in comic, tragic or other dramatic mode."[37] A film can be viewed as a case study of the psychology of an ensemble of characters, where the audience constructs these psychologies from actions on-screen. According to Foster-Harris, "story decisions and actions very seldom are based on reason"[38] but are rather the result of emotion or some deeper psychological need or disturbance. Foster-Harris' approach presents the character's dilemma not as a logical decision but as intuition or feeling. The character "cannot 'reason' his way out of his dilemma, he does not rationalise his problem. He does what he feels is right."³⁹ Drama does not require logical desires, but those desires are consistent and clear to an audience.

In Otto Preminger's The Man with the Golden Arm *(1955), Zosh pretends to be unable to walk to guilt her husband, Frankie (played by Frank Sinatra), into staying with her. Louie, a drug dealer, discovers she is faking her paralysis.*

From an audience perspective, a character's actions indicate a psychology. For a writer, psychology is how a character forms their actions. For example, Anthony Perkins' character in *Psycho* (1960) has a deeply disturbed psychology, which leads to his *goals*, *objectives* and actions. Perkin's *motive* is that he is a psychopath, which is all a viewer needs to know about why he acts this way. However, a writer needs to get into the heads and hearts of their characters to find out how a character will act. Working this way may result in a character evolving and changing (requiring several drafts of the story) because as a writer gets to know the character on a deeper level, the character starts dictating where the story goes.

The *motive* is fundamentally what a character represents in a story. A process of *character identification* is not a rational understanding but an emotional connection to a character. This connection manifests as the *motive* representing a primal psychology that a film audience loves, fears, hates or laughs at.

The practice of exploring villains in a story

Alfred Hitchcock created villains in his pictures who have endearing qualities and, at times, are more likeable than the 'good' police officers. Hitchcock explained, "Very often you see the murderer in movies made to be a very unattractive man. I've always contended that it's a grave mistake, because how would he get near his victim unless he had some attraction?"[40] De Rosa suggested that Hitchcock's villains "essentially fall into two categories—the charming, handsome, romantic villains, such as Cary Grant in *Suspicion*, Claude Rains in *Notorious*, and James Mason in *North by Northwest* and the clumsy, sympathetic villains such as Raymond Burr in *Rear Window* and Anthony Perkins in *Psycho*."[41] These amiable 'bad guys' offer accessible and endearing qualities that make for a more cunning and elusive adversary.

The audience will *align* with a particular antagonistic character in some scenes whose perspective dominates these scenes' narration. For example, in *Notorious* (1946), there is a scene where the villain, Alex Sebastian (played by Claude

Rains), speaks to his mother about Alicia (played by Ingrid Bergman) being a spy. This scene focuses on Claude Rains' character, which has the effect of developing more substantial conflict as he decides to take action against Alicia. When watching this scene, viewers expect Alex to do something sinister; however, they also expect his plan to ultimately fail, as he is the antagonist. Alex's relationship with his mother adds psychological depth to his character, helps to engage the audience, implements dramatic irony (discussed later) and consequently strengthens a story's conflict.

The practice of creating a multi-dimensional psychology

Character *flaws* are the reasons why characters need to change during a film. "Flaws are coping mechanisms for needs not yet understood, acknowledged or met by your character," writes Julie Gray.[42] "Think of flaws as naughty children acting out. FINE! You don't love me, I DON'T NEED LOVE ANYWAY!!" It's the psychological reason a character pursues their *want* over a *need*. For the audience, it makes sense of why a character's *want* and *need* conflict. For example, Romeo and Juliet have the *want* to be together and a *need* for family loyalty. Their *flaw* is impetuousness: they are acting on their feelings and not considering the consequences of their actions. A *flaw* doesn't necessarily have to be morally wrong, as impetuousness is often part of being young. Shakespeare's original play is timeless because it looks at human nature and is ambiguous about the right choice. From a dramatic perspective, Romeo and Juliet make the wrong choice (to follow their *wants*); therefore, the story ends in tragedy.

A film doesn't need each character's *flaw* to be explained

to the viewers — a viewer will still engage with a story with ambiguous flaws. For example, in *Tootsie* (1982), Michael Dorsey (played by Dustin Hoffman) *wants* to continue working as an actor but *needs* romantic love. His *motive* is his love of acting, and when he is set up as difficult to work with, it forces him to look for an alternative way to fulfil this *motive*. He decides to dress as a woman to get acting work. His *want* and *need* conflict because the woman he falls in love with doesn't know he is a man, and he *wants* to continue to work as an actor. His *flaw* is his chauvinistic attitude towards women. Ironically, Michael, dressed as a woman, has to contend with male chauvinism on the TV set where he works. Michael changes to become critical of male sexism and embraces a role in the media as a feminist soap opera star. His growth in moving away from his *flaw* allows him to understand Julie Nichols (played by Jessica Lange) and form a relationship with her. The climax occurs when Michael reveals that Dorothy (his female alias) is a man to the world so he can have a relationship with Julie.

A character's *flaw* adds another dimension to the *want-need* relationship by giving them a reason to change. A *flaw* that a writer has had experience with is a great starting point for creating a character and a story. When developing a character using a *flaw*, their *want* and *need* should somehow be related to this *flaw*. Most importantly, choosing a *flaw* that emotionally affects you as a writer will enable you to create complex characters.

The practice of borrowing characters from movies

One of the most fruitful sources for discovering ideas is through characters in other films. Taking a movie you love and using the main characters' *wants* and *needs* in a completely different setting allows a writer to develop similar dramatic experiences. *Character types* are defined by their *goals* (i.e. a *want* and *need*) and provide the dramatic DNA of any movie character. It is a strong starting point for writing a script and leaves creative space for the story, as the *motives* and setting can be distinctly different. By adopting another film's *character types*, a writer can borrow from and pay homage to the original and create an original story.

Alfred Hitchcock remade *The 39 Steps* (1935) twice in America as *Saboteur* (1942) and *North by Northwest* (1959). All three films share the same *character type* for the protagonist: their *wants* are 'to prove their innocence', and their *needs* are 'to find romantic love'. It was not a simple matter for the screenwriters to take *The 39 Steps*' story and transpose it into a new context (e.g. from Britain to America), as is illustrated when examining the differences in characters from *The 39 Steps*, *Saboteur* and *North by Northwest*. In *The 39 Steps*, Richard Hannay is a Canadian rancher visiting London who travels to a circled town on a map found in the murdered Annabella Smith's hand. *Saboteur* follows Barry Kane, an aircraft factory worker from California, who attempts to prove his innocence of sabotage at a factory by following the address on an envelope from the mysterious 'Fry'. Roger Thornhill in *North by Northwest* is a fast-talking advertising executive in New York who becomes mistakenly embroiled in a kidnapping and then the murder of a United Nations diplomat. To clear his name, he follows clues about the mysterious George Kaplan, leading him to Chicago and meets the double agent Eve Kendall on the train travelling there. The characters and how they deal with their situations vary; actual events are distinctly different, and even the country and places visited are not the same.

If a screenwriter enjoys a type of experience, *character types* are one way to develop characters and a story.

Creating an Identity

The practice of finding your character goals

Hitchcock indicated an approach to defining a character's journey with this following statement:

> Imagine an example of a standard plot—let us say a conflict between love and duty. This idea was the origin of my first talkie, *Blackmail*. The hazy pattern one saw beforehand was duty-love, love versus duty, and finally either duty or love, one or the other. The whole middle section was built up on the theme of love versus duty, after duty and love had been introduced separately in turn. So I had first to put on the screen an episode expressing duty. I showed the arrest of a criminal by Scotland Yard detectives, and tried to make it as concrete and detailed as I could.[43]

Hitchcock's explanation looks at the underlying experience of a character's conflicting emotions from an audience's perspective. The entire narrative was developed around the characters' emotions of love and duty—the first act introduces these two aspects to the audience, the second act explores love versus duty, and in the final act, the characters must choose between these two emotions. William Foster-Harris suggested that the protagonist's dilemma results from two conflicting emotions,[44] where the central character needs to choose between these emotions, which affects the outcome of the story. Harris' approach views fiction as a formula where two patterns exist for a story: a positive and negative outcome. The 'right' choice results in a positive outcome or 'happy ending', and the emotional conflict is resolved. The 'wrong' choice results in a negative ending, with both emotions denied. For example, the story of *Romeo and Juliet* has two principal characters, each with the inner conflict of "love versus family loyalty". They choose "love", resulting in a negative outcome, losing love and family loyalty. The two desires must be "in the same living breast, entertained simultaneously by the one character."[45] As conflict creates character, so too "conflict grows out of character," and the "intensity of the conflict will be determined by the strength of will of the three-dimensional individual who is the protagonist."[46] It is worth repeating Foster-Harris' quote: "All main characters ... must each have his or her own internal struggle else the characters never live. *Conflict creates character*" (my italics).[47]

A way for a screenwriter to find an emotional connection to a character is to start with two conflicting emotions and let the *want* and *need* develop. It is vital at some point to decide on a *want* and *need* as they reflect the character's psychology and provide clarity for the story. An emotional origin for a *goal* is a strong choice because people often make decisions this way, which is understandable for the viewers.

Does a writer need to define *wants* and *needs* before creating a story? No. Working creatively, a writer may have an idea about a character and find out through their writing what this character's *need* and *want* are. If a writer understands a character's psychology and can communicate this internal world through actions, the character's *want* and *need* will be found through the writing process.

Creating an Identity

TO SUMMARISE:

- A *motive* explains a character's deeper psychology. When writing, a *motive* can be fleshed out to form the basis for a complex psychology. Alternatively, a writer may intuitively understand a character's anxieties and desires, which can form a *motive* for a story.

- Allow antagonists to have complex psychologies to become strong adversaries for the protagonist. The stronger your villains, the stronger the drama.

- Understanding why a character needs to change is a *flaw*. None of your characters are perfect humans, and these imperfections are the source of a story. Explicitly stating a character's *flaw* clarifies *goals* and a character's journey.

- *Character types* describe a type of movie experience for a viewer. When the protagonist's *goals* borrow from other sources (e.g. a film, novel, etc.), the central dynamic of the source drama is adopted. *Character types* are a great starting point because they leave much story space for originality while paying homage to a great story experience.

- The inner turmoil of a character is emotional. Starting character development with conflicting emotions provides a compelling dramatic portrait to write with. From these emotions, *motives* and *goals* provide clarity for the characters as a writer finds a story.

Chapter Seven

How to Write Character Actions

The dramatic principles for *identity* have the effect of setting up expectations for the audience about what the character is trying to achieve. However, a screenwriter must manifest these expectations in a screenplay through character actions. A screenwriter doesn't write characters but actions in a screenplay. If you ask someone to show you the characters in a screenplay, that person would say to read the script. If you ask someone to show you a character's action, he will point to a line in the script, e.g. "He runs down the street." A screenplay is written through actions, and a character results from those actions in the audience's minds. Because the *Inside-out* approach considers a screenplay to be made up of character actions, the writer's responsibility is to develop actions that fulfil the protagonist's motivations.

Character *actions* are the dramatic building blocks of a film—the atom for a dramatist.[48] Aristotle defined drama as "an imitation of an action"[49], which forms a progression of the events, constructing scenes and sequences. From a character's perspective, the protagonist intentionally performs each *action* to achieve something. In this sense, *action* is also called an "acting beat" or "performance beat". The intentionality of *actions* is what the audience constructs to understand a character's motivations, which fundamentally affect their experience of a story.

Actions happen in the 'now'. For example, flashbacks are events of the past shown *now* on-screen. Similarly, a character talking about the past is performing an *action* relevant to their situation *now*. Theatre director Frank Hauser states, "The consequences of something someone once did always come back to haunt the characters in the NOW of the play."[50] There is a vital relationship between a character's past (which informs who they are), the present moment (what is occurring on-screen), and the intention of an action (which sets up expectations for the audience). The intentional *action* is a "dynamic between the moment and the objective" of the character and often asks questions about the consequences of that *action*.[51] Appreciating a character is the "result of conduct"—i.e. what they do[52] and, more importantly, why. From a dramaturgical perspective, intentional *actions* inform the audience about who a character is and what they want.

This book aims to show how effective screenwriters need to think when writing. An awareness of the audience's thinking is fundamental to how a writer should think. Because characters are manifested on the page as actions, a priority when writing is to be aware of how character actions affect an audience. This attitude leads to *actions* having two purposes for a writer: one is for how the action informs a character, and the other is for how the action affects the audience. For a writer, this forms the *duality of actions*, and the two perspectives (how the character is thinking and how the audience is thinking about the character) may or may not be the same (this point will be taken up in Part Two, Structuring Actions). Actions substantiate the connection between the character and the audience. The *duality of actions* is fundamental for a writer's thinking to develop an awareness of the audience. While a story comes from the character's perspective, a writer's decisions are made with the audience in mind.

The *duality of actions* within a screenwriting process is divided into two modes of writing: *character identification* is a practice requiring a writer to forget about the audience's perspective and purely focus on character, while *structuring actions* (presented in Part Two) represents a way of working focused on how viewers think about character actions. While screenwriting, a writer will naturally alternate between these two ways of thinking to encapsulate the *duality of actions*.

An *action*'s intention is why a character performs an action and adds to a viewer's expectation of this character. Importantly, this intention is how viewers mentally engage with characters. *Inside-out* posits that audiences engage with characters not because of what they do but why they do it. This approach for writing screenplays is based on the logic of how films function for audiences. Within this context, screenplays can be considered a plan for a spectator's cognitive journey. Writing for a prospective audience is done with some knowledge of how people think and feel when watching a film. Explaining how dramatic principles affect a viewer's thinking connects a writing process with a viewer's cognitive understanding of a story. *Inside-out* offers a practical approach to screenwriting by explaining how a screenwriter can write for a prospective audience's thought process.

The practice of finding scene objectives

Once a writer has set up a character with a *goal* for a story, how does this character approach this *goal*? The answer depends on the character's psychology, which will manifest itself as a *strategy* for attaining the goal. Character *strategy* is the tactic used by a character to achieve their scene *objective*. Therefore, each scene *objective* represents a strategy a character applies to their problem. A *strategy* may change from scene to scene or be consistent throughout the entire film, depending on the obstacles encountered and how the character deals with the given circumstances. A *strategy* helps define a psychology that is not necessarily rational while connecting the scene *objective* with the character's *goal*.

In *Shawshank Redemption* (1994), the protagonist, Andy, wants to escape prison while also attempting to retain his dignity in a hostile environment. In the beginning, Andy's request for a rock hammer and a poster of Rita Hayworth is secretly his *strategy* to escape. He spends the next nineteen years digging an escape tunnel out of the prison, which is kept as a surprise for the audience. Much of the film concerns Andy retaining his dignity and surviving in difficult circumstances. *The Apartment* (1960) follows Bud, who wants to climb the corporate ladder and applies a *strategy* of allowing company management to borrow his apartment for extramarital liaisons. In *Baby Driver* (2017), Baby wants to escape a life of crime, and his *strategy* is to pay off his debt to Doc by being a getaway driver for bank robberies. When he is paid off, Doc still wants him to continue to be the driver and threatens to hurt Debora and his foster father. Baby's *strategy* is to continue driving until he and Debora can escape. When he is caught attempting to escape, he agrees to continue with the heist. His *strategy* turns to sabotaging the robbery and trying again to escape with Debora. Each example of how the protagonist approaches his *goal* communicates the type of psychology and what values are important.

Goals and *objectives* are two levels of decision-making by characters with an underlying *motive*. These decisions are based on how the character thinks (or their psychology). How characters decide to act in a scene is their *strategy* for attaining a *goal*, which often changes throughout a story. A clever character will create cunning *goals* and *objectives*. A stupid character will consider basic and obvious approaches to fulfilling the underlying *motive*.

The practice of communicating clearly to an audience

While a character's *motive* does not need to be clear to a viewer, a *goal*, *strategy* and *objective* must be communicated for a viewer to engage with their plight. For a writer, *wants* and *needs* are not a substitute for knowing a character; instead, these *goals* focus a writer on providing clarity for their intentions. Without clear intentions, audience members will interpret the reasons for the character's actions differently. The central imperative for a writer is to engage and move an audience by clearly setting up their expectations. Remember that *wants* and *needs* don't exist in a film but are constructed by the audience interpreting the character's actions. Within this context, clarity is crucial for a screenwriter.

It is always good storytelling to ensure an *objective* is clear to the audience. A writer can create a character with deep psychological traits; however, if this character's *objectives* are not communicated clearly to an audience, they will become confused, not be emotionally moved, and even potentially bored. One way to add clarity is by showing the related object for the *objective* at the beginning of a scene so the objective is clear. For example, before showing a man robbing a bank, include a few shots of the tellers counting money, the safe containing diamonds, etc. As soon as you show a character putting on a balaclava outside the bank, it is obvious what the *objective* is for the character.

The character must be unambiguously narrated on the page. An unskilled screenwriter will develop a screenplay with characters that aren't clear or coherent for a viewer. *Inside-out* aims to create clear and coherent portraits of characters by narrating what each character is thinking and feeling.

The practice of finding moments for a story

Ed Hooks discusses the importance of 'adrenaline moments' in his book *Acting for Animators*. Adrenaline moments are memorable events in a film that have great emotional significance for a character. They are "something the character has, not the audience."[53] These are such significant moments in the character's life that he will still remember this event when he turns eighty. Adrenaline moments often have a strong psychological effect on a character. For example, many scenes in *The Iron Giant* (1999) are adrenaline moments: Hogarth meeting the giant, the day Dean has a squirrel run up his pants in a diner, and when the giant intercepts a bomb in space. These scenes represent significant moments in the lives of these characters.

A writer can start creatively thinking up a series of adrenaline moments for a character and let the character's psychology develop those moments into scenes. Because these scenes strongly impact the characters, how they react will say a lot about who they are.

There is no one process for developing characters, and

using adrenaline moments potentially offers a way in. With the first way of writing, don't logically think about structure, but rather let structures emerge by finding character experiences that lead to actions. A central aim for *character identification* is to create these moments, which become significant to a character's journey.

The practice of creating objectives using emotions

Decisions are often made based on emotions. A *strategy* will often have an emotional dimension reflecting a particular character's thinking and feeling. Allowing how a character feels to dictate what they are doing in a scene benefits a writer by avoiding 'thinking through' situations, which can lead to predictable outcomes. Applying *character identification* is often about feeling with a character and following a process of finding out how emotional responses lead to actions and scene objectives.

Strategies can be cold, calculated reasoning, a rash, impulsive response, or a combination of thinking and feeling. Decision-making for how a character will achieve a *goal* may be conflicted, and therefore, they may change from an impulsive reaction to deciding on a more thoughtful strategy. All of these decisions, as well as the character's *identity*, reflect a deeper psychology aimed at engaging and moving viewers.

The act of role-playing that results from a writer identifying with a protagonist enables an embodied decision-making process to be narrated. Whether an emotional or rational action is written, it is a natural outcome of enacting this first way of writing.

TO SUMMARISE:

- Having developed an *identity* for the protagonist, what *strategies* will this character apply to get their goals? *Strategies* are how a character plans to achieve a *goal* and reflect a psychology. Every *objective* in a film will result from a character applying a *strategy*.

- A screenwriter creates a character's *identity* (i.e., *motives* and *goals*) to provide clarity for a script. By explicitly defining *goals*, *strategies* and *objectives*, a screenwriter foregrounds the task of writing actions that communicate dramatically to a viewer.

- Identifying significant moments in a story can help to develop a character's journey and involve the audience in a scene. A major event for a character can be a starting point for a screenplay, and how this character reacts to this experience offers *strategies* for the following scenes.

- *Strategies* can be an emotional reaction. Understanding a character's psychology will reflect how emotional and logical their *objectives* are.

My Practice

As an example of how one can write a screenplay, I will recount the process I undertook to write the black comedy *Doreen's Dead*. The process outlined illustrates my journey of finding characters and a story.

The dramatic idea for *Doreen's Dead* came from the Stanley Kubrick film *The Killing* (1956). George Peatty, who is married to Sherry, discovers that she is having an affair with another man. Kubrick presents Sherry's bitterness towards George through domestic arguments about broken promises and his sexual ineptitude. I loved the exchanges between George and Sherry, finding these scenes both dramatic and humorous. In the film, George kills Sherry in a fit of jealousy, having found out about her affair. I considered the core dynamic between George and Sherry (whom I renamed Doreen) a great starting point for a story where George is the main character who must dispose of her body and get away with the murder. I added George's relationship with his overbearing mother (borrowing from Hitchcock), who helps George with his problems. Throughout the coming chapters, I will build on this premise and outline my process to write a complete screenplay.

I decided to 'cast' George in *Doreen's Dead* as the protagonist before I had a story. For me, George is where all the humour for the script comes from, and he was always going to be the pivotal character. Characters make a great starting point from which a dramatic idea and a story can be formed.

In *Doreen's Dead*, George is a very insecure character and part of the process for me was to 'write out' my own insecurities as his reaction to imagined situations. Similarly, Doreen and George's mother, though very different characters, are also a part of me, and I found it interesting to 'play out' scenes with these characters interacting. I found it joyful to express myself through the characters, and I hope the fun came through to the page.

For the screenplay of *Doreen's Dead*, I didn't initially decide on any *need* for George or Doreen. I simply had a scene *objective* for George, who wanted to know where Doreen had been. It became clearer after writing that first scene that George's *want* for the film was to avoid being caught for the murder of Doreen. Only after writing a five-page story outline did I realise that George's *need* was for respect. I'm always looking to develop clear through-lines for my stories, so this outline was reworked until I was happy with how the story (and characters) were told. These tasks were done before I started writing any actions (apart from the one scene mentioned, which was the catalyst for the project).

PART TWO
STRUCTURING ACTION

Chapter Eight

A Thought Machine

Famed novelist Steven King described the act of reading his books as "telepathy in action."[1] His point was that anyone engaging with his novels is reading his thoughts, which are written on the page. "We're having a meeting of minds", states King in *On Writing*.[2] An essential assertion from King's telepathy analogy is that he is aware of his readers when writing. In a similar vein to King's telepathy, cinema can be considered a thought machine. In King's novels, the author's thoughts (even if he takes the role of a character) are communicated through descriptions, while in a film, thoughts are implied through character actions on-screen. Hitchcock also showed an awareness of cinema as a thought machine when he told the screenwriter Samuel Taylor, "Let's put ourselves in the minds of our audience."[3] The director understood how crucial it is to view the ongoing story from the audience's perspective.

Cinema's thought machine occurs throughout a film and, therefore, needs to be structured to affect a spectator's moment-to-moment thinking. The structuring of thoughts produces a journey where a viewer's cognitive engagement is the product of actions shown on screen. Music is another time-based medium that creates experiences with a fixed duration. These two art forms are written as a manuscript (i.e. a screenplay and a music score), which is not a temporal medium and, therefore, can be read at any pace and represent the structure of actions and musical notes. For a screenplay reader to get a sense of the dramatic potential of a script, they need to imagine it in film form with the characters and situations unfolding from the page in their mind.

The *Inside-out* approach understands that a screenplay, written in words, represents a film written with images, expressing a thought process. The representation of thought is initially dormant within a screenplay's pages. However, it comes to life when someone cognitively engages with the moving images of the film version, and I believe this engagement is part of the magic of cinema because it can result in an emotional response. Therefore, a critical process a viewer undertakes while watching a film is the cognitive understanding of the story and events. To create a thought machine, a screenwriter must knowingly structure a viewer's thoughts. Structuring this mental process is a significant part of what a screenwriter does. For a screenwriter, the audience's thinking is always based on a character's intentions or why a character is acting.

The second way of writing focuses on the logical structure of character actions in a screenplay, which relates to how each character thinks. Because a cognitive structure is based on logic, every film viewer will construe this structure similarly. This second way of writing approaches a screenplay structure so that each character's intention is clearly communicated to the audience. Where the first way of writing was about opening up possibilities, the second way distils those possibilities to develop clarity, conciseness and intensity. The second mindset is about restructuring and defining a story's narrative. Each of the four ways of writing in this book is distinct; it is impossible to be creatively open to possibilities and logically clarify them simultaneously.

A basic premise of *Inside-out* is that plot, theme, and emotion are essentially a function of character. This second way of screenwriting also acknowledges that dramatic structure (which plot is a type of) is a function of character. MacKendrick suggested, "*Dramatic structure* is ... the craft of keeping an audience excited, of avoiding boredom in your listeners" (my emphasis).[4] A dramatic structure has two properties: unity and conflict. Without unity, only unconnected parts remain instead of the whole. Unity needs some kind of a through-line that connects the separate parts into a single structure. Unity for a film is typically supplied by central characters in the story, reflecting their journey. The second property of a dramatic structure is conflict: the audience engages with this type of structure through character conflicts. Effectively structuring a screenplay is about continually setting up and resolving conflict. Defining a dramatic structure using unity and conflict promotes the idea of a character being central to an audience's experience.

Three types of dramatic structures can exist within a screenplay. All three have the characteristics of unity and conflict and are formed in response to a story's characters. The first structure is based on character *goals* and was presented in part one of this book. Based on the *wants* and *needs* of a character, it is the foundation for logically understanding how drama functions on the audience. As a network of character *goals* represented in a film, actions play out linearly and should be carefully ordered to heighten the drama.

The second and most popular type of dramatic structure

is a narrative. Narratives, commonly called plots, are based on events rather than character intentions. The next chapter contrasts a narrative to a structure based on character intentions to understand a narrative's usefulness for a screenwriter.

The third of these structures is thematic and often relates to character *goals*. Themes can support and strengthen the dramatic experience and develop another level of meaning for a film. For example, in *The 39 Steps*, the protagonist, Richard Hannay, has a *goal* to find romantic love. Throughout the film, heterosexual relationships are the central theme, with most scenes reflecting on this topic. This theme strengthens the significance of his *goal* by showing other characters related to 'romantic love' in the story.

When two themes are developed as opposing pairs, they create a conflict of ideas independent of the character conflicts. For example, humanity versus technology is a pair of themes often explored in sci-fi films. A screenwriter will develop these opposing themes to ask relevant questions of the audience. Adding another layer of meaning to a story deepens the screenplay's experience and involves the audience through the conflicting ideas.

Dramatic themes are related to the concerns of the characters in the story. They reflect the principal characters' conflicting *wants* and *needs* and expand to develop a separate structure that runs through subplots and other scenes. For example, in *Blade Runner* (1982), Rick Deckard (played by Harrison Ford) has a job (or *want*) to terminate replicants, which are robots made to look identical to humans. The film dramatically shows Deckard versus the replicants, or thematically human versus machines. However, it is on the thematic level where the film's meaning lives, as the distinction between the replicants and humans dissolves. The replicants don't *want* to die and seek out their creators in search of immortality. These machines ask the same questions human beings may ask. Deckard's *need* is to find romantic love, and by the end of the film, he falls in love with a replicant.

When the audience interprets *Blade Runner* on a thematic level, many related questions about being human are asked. For example, are humans just a type of biological machine, or what is the nature of consciousness? In a similar way to dramatic questions, thematic questions add interest to a story. The themes that exist independently of the characters provide a type of unity, which will be examined when discussing art house films in Chapter 18.

To summarise:

• Films can be conceptualised as a thought machine, where a screenwriter's job is to structure a viewer's thinking through character intentions.

• All dramatic structures contain unity and conflict. The three types of dramatic structures are based on character intentions, events (i.e. a narrative) and themes.

• The themes relating to a character's *goals* help to unify a narrative and provide another layer of experience for the audience. The themes relating to *goals* are commonly reflected throughout the story by events or other characters.

FOUNDATIONS

Chapter Nine

Narrative

The most popular perspective for thinking about structure in a screenplay is as a narrative. Plot or narrative is ubiquitous in film analysis and relates directly to the events a viewer sees on-screen. This perspective originated with Classical dramaturgy, which is firmly grounded on the seminal work *Poetics*, written by Aristotle in 335 BC, and has influenced many screenwriting manuals.[5] Aristotle proposed three unities of drama, one of which is the unity of action. *Poetics* highlights the need for all of the actions within a narrative to work as a whole.[6] Aristotle explained the unity of action thus:

> As to that poetic imitation which is narrative in form and employs a single meter, the plot manifestly ought, as in a tragedy, to be constructed on dramatic principles. It should have for its subject a single action, whole and complete, with a beginning, a middle, and an end.[7]

Aristotle's unity of action is a recognition of a drama's narrative. *Poetics*, however, is not all-encompassing in its interpretation of narratives because it specifically approaches drama's structure as events. A limitation of *Poetics* is that it doesn't account for a spectator's construction of character *goals*. Therefore, Aristotle did not envisage unity of action concerning the protagonist:

> Unity of plot does not ... consist of the unity of the hero. For infinitely various are the incidents in one man's life which cannot be reduced to unity; and so, too, there are many actions of one man out of which we cannot make one action.[8]

Aristotle placed primary importance on the plot and subjugated character to a role involving ethical and moral values. He saw events or the "imitation of action" as the most crucial aspect of creating drama and that "dramatic action ... is *not* with a view to the representation of character."[9] Roland Barthes also argues in his introduction to the 1966 issue of *Communications* that "the notion of character is secondary, subordinated to the notion of plot"; however, he admitted that the problem of character does not go away easily.[10]

Lajos Egri's *The Art of Dramatic Writing* (1960) is regarded today as a seminal text focusing on explaining the foundations for writing dramatic works. While acknowledging Aristotle's influence on dramatic knowledge, he proposed that Aristotle made a "basic error"[11] in denying the importance of character: "Aristotle was mistaken in his time, and our scholars are mistaken today when they accept his rulings concerning character. Character was the great factor in Aristotle's time, and no fine play ever was or ever will be written without it."[12] According to Aristotle, the primary role of character is to "reveal moral purpose" of a play, and does not consist of a unity relating to the plot.[13] Aristotle's emphasis on viewing characters from a moral perspective **is** relevant to a viewer's experience and is represented in the character schema as a *motive* (more on this in Part Three); however, it doesn't give full weight to the role characters play. In summary, Aristotle's *Poetics* foregrounds events, while Egri considers the dramatic role character plays from the audience's perspective.

Egri summarised that "narrative is driven by character progression"—denoting the relationship between character and plot.[14] Events in a narrative have a cause-and-effect relationship, which develops a sense of unity. Underpinning this cause-and-effect relationship are the characters' *goals* and scene *objectives*, which, for a viewer, naturally connect each event on screen with the next one. When a screenwriter thinks in terms of *goals* and *objectives*, the progression of actions is underpinned logically. Egri also asserts character is the most interesting aspect of a story for the audience[15] as the characters are what a viewer becomes concerned about.

As a temporal medium, a film requires viewers to develop a mental 'picture' of what the characters are trying to achieve. This notion of character is not contained in a film but rather constructed by a viewer. This active construction process of interpreting film events is critical for understanding how viewers engage with cinema and why they ask particular questions.

Seymour Chatman describes the relationship between plot and character by defining events as a function of character and setting.[16] Characters intentionally perform 'actions' that manifest themselves as events in a narrative. 'Happenings' occur in a setting where a character "is the patient" of the event.[17] *Happenings* could be natural or man-made disasters—inclement weather, a meteor heading for Earth, lack of money, or a sinking ship. Significantly, settings can act as obstacles to a character's *objective* and dramatically have relevance due to interacting with characters. Alexander

MacKendrick asserts that a "dramatic character is definable only in relation to other characters or situations that involve tension."[18]

Screenwriting manuals often take a mixed approach by including event-based structures as well as character concepts. For example, Robert McKee's *Story* suggests that character and plot are equally important: "structure *is* character; character *is* structure."[19] McKee presents a three-act structure—even suggesting approximate durations for each[20]—and defines a character's primary function as believability for a viewer.[21]

A narrative perspective is popular because events relate to the literal text of films and screenplays. However, concentrating solely on the narrative bypasses the process of how audiences engage with cinema. The second way of writing will focus on the cognitive structure embodied by a screenplay, recognising this as a vehicle for structuring a viewer's thoughts. Understanding the relationship between narrative and a character's cognitive journey is crucial for effective screenwriting.

Given that this way of writing focuses on a logical approach to structuring actions and story ideas, one potential use for narrative templates (e.g. *The Hero's Journey*, *Sequencing*) is to suggest scenes for a character's journey. In contrast to the first way of writing, where scenes come directly from the characters, new scenes can come from a predefined structure. Matching your story to a plot template is a purely rational approach to screenwriting. Narrative templates offer a dramatic shape related to the protagonist's journey. This template can help reorder scenes and suggest missing parts of a character's journey. These narrative templates don't open up creative possibilities but focus on a screenplay's dramatic shape. While other types of writing can be more creative, approaching a script as a logical structure is necessary for creating a clear and concise story for the audience.

To help look at the effect of writing using a plot template, I will introduce a fictional character, Judy, who has decided to use the Sequencing approach to writing a script. Sequencing approaches writing a screenplay by dividing it up into eight parts. Each part represents a film sequence, a series of scenes usually connected by a location or time period. The eight sequences with this approach all denote parts of a character's journey and, in doing so, develop a standardised film structure.

What Judy loves about Sequencing is each predefined sequence has a clear purpose in her main character's journey. Given that a film sequence is commonly around ten minutes (though this duration can vary), she knows how much she has to write for each section.

Sequencing for Judy offers a way of developing a robust dramatic foundation for her story ideas. As she writes and finishes a sequence, she returns to what the character has to go through next. She has explicit *wants* and *needs* for her character and compelling story moments. However, when Judy thinks about what will happen next, it pushes the narrative towards predictable and uninspired results—ultimately, prescribing a narrative structure forces a writer to think logically about a character's journey rather than entering into this character's perspective.

Judy was sold on this type of plot template because several great films were analysed and shown to use this structure. A relevant question is how these films' writers came to find their narratives. It is guaranteed to involve hard work and a deep understanding of the characters instead of copying a structure from another film. Perhaps there are similarities in how these films were written, and this is how to create a great narrative, not in copying a particular film's structure.

The *Inside-out* approach to screenwriting is averse to the way Judy is writing. It proposes that the characters find the structure, not the other way around. By entering into and understanding the central characters, a story emerges, which can then be refined to strengthen how it is told. Characters are the story because a character's plight engages the audience.

As Judy writes a sequence, she thinks, 'This event will shock a viewer' based on a logical thought process. *Inside-out* proposes that if a writer wants to shock the audience, he or she should first be shocked by what the characters have done.

When restructuring a story, rational thinking promotes clarity and conciseness, which is not necessarily achieved when 'opening up' the story using characters. It also places the writer explicitly in the audience's shoes, where they ask all the same questions that a viewer would ask. This will be the topic of the next chapter.

To summarise:

• A narrative, or plot, is a structure based on events and is a perspective that analyses what is literally onscreen.

• Events onscreen can be either character *actions* or *happenings*. *Happenings* are events resulting from the setting (e.g., a ship sinking, a meteorite hitting the earth, etc).

• Plot templates help improve an already-developed plot by providing purpose for each section of a protagonist's journey and a clear overall dramatic shape for the story.

Chapter Ten

Hypotheses

For Hitchcock, the moment-to-moment development of the audience's experience was not guesswork but the art of appreciating how to involve the audience using a cinematic medium. Hitchcock gave insight into his method when he said, "[my] methods of filmmaking ... are quite straightforward. I like to keep the public guessing and never let them know what is going to happen next. I build up my interest gradually and surely and, in thrillers, bring it to a crescendo. There must be no half-measures, and I have to know where I am going every second of the time ... Then you know automatically the tempo of each succeeding scene, and it matters not whether they are shot out of proper order." [22]

The *Inside-out* approach requires writers to mentally assimilate with characters (i.e. understand their internal worlds) and, at the same time, narrate for an audience (referred to as *duality of action*; see Chapter 7 for more). The focus on the audience's mental process, where they are actively interpreting and constructing events on-screen, allows for an investigation into how their experiences form. Viewers ask questions, have expectations, and ultimately wait to be moved. Hitchcock described how the audience's thinking is essential for their engagement:

> I think that pace in a film is made entirely by keeping the mind of the spectator occupied. You don't need to have quick cutting, you don't need to have quick playing, but you do need a very full story and the changing of one situation to another. You need the changing of one incident to another, so that all the time the audience's mind is occupied. Now so long as you can sustain that and not let up, then you have pace. That is why suspense is such a valuable thing, because it keeps the mind of the audience going.[23]

According to Hitchcock, the key is predicting the audience's mind and knowing how they will interpret and construct the drama.

Viewing a film is an active process where an audience attempts to understand each character's concerns. A viewer will initially ask, 'What is the character doing?' onscreen. This question is quickly followed by 'Why are they doing it?' or, more generally 'What does the character want?' This second question is fundamental for understanding how audiences construct characters and stories. Central to a viewer's experience is asking questions: for example, will the character succeed, or how can a character overcome some adversity? When questions asked by a viewer are about a character's *goals* or intentions, they are dramatic. This chapter will examine how dramatic questions are relevant to screenwriting and the audience experience.

A spectator is asked a dramatic question when a character's *goal* meets conflict. Theatre director Frank Hauser advises writers to "identify the story's compelling question"[24], while David Mamet maintains that "it is the [goal] of the protagonist that keeps us in our seats."[25] A dramatic question is the foundation for emotional engagement and the specific scenario where *fiction identification* occurs.

When viewers *align* with a particular character (e.g. the protagonist) and certain expectations have been set up, *anticipation* for the character is developed. *Anticipation* is when a viewer becomes 'drawn in' by a dramatic question. The stronger the conflict (with coherent *alignment*), the stronger the *anticipation* and engagement. Spectators favour certain outcomes, and when that outcome is difficult, they are engrossed by the story. For Hitchcock, a spectator's anticipation was an essential ingredient for the development of suspense: "Knowing what to expect, they wait for it to happen. This conditioning of the viewer is essential to the build-up of suspense."[26] Therefore, with *anticipation* come certain expectations of the suspense's outcome.[27] Richard Allen describes suspense as an "emotional focalisation" because the audience is entirely focused on what is going to happen next in this story, and "are forced to entertain the prospect of a narrative outcome that is contrary to the one that is desired."[28]

Suspense is set up when there is clarity about a character's *role* (e.g. protagonist) and *goals*, which leads to a dramatic question and anticipation. Hitchcock explains this preparation for suspense: "In the usual form of suspense, it is indispensable that the public be made perfectly aware of all of the facts involved. Otherwise, there is no suspense."[29] A writer must constantly be aware of both his characters and the audience's experience. Warren Buckland notes the "compositional structure of any narrative film attempts to anticipate specific responses from spectators."[30] He refers to a "communicative contract" setting up the conditions that "determine the spectator's set of experiences".

In his book *Narration of Fiction Film*, David Bordwell suggests that narrative films cue spectators to generate inferences or hypotheses.[31] Bordwell draws on a theory by Meir Sternberg, who defines two types of hypothesis: curiosity and suspense. Curiosity hypotheses "pertain to past actions that the text refrains from specifying", commonly set up in films with a mystery. Viewers will develop theories to explain past events and potentially solve the mystery. A suspense hypothesis "sets up anticipations about forthcoming events"[32], which creates the potential for character conflict.

Previously, a *character schema* was introduced with *goals*, asking, 'What does a character want?' The result of a viewer inferring this question from actions is a hypothesis, which can change during a film. A third process of hypothesis building by a viewer relates to understanding a character's *goals*. This *goal hypothesis* is the process of the audience attempting to understand what each character tries to achieve in a story. When viewers develop a *goal hypothesis*, they represent a character's internal desires. As described in the *character schema*, humans are fundamentally interested in recognising each character's intentions. A *goal hypothesis* shows how intentional actions are the basis for an audience to construct a more significant intention (or *goal*), ultimately defining the character. *Goals* are built from actions and become a context for a character's future actions.

To contrast *curiosity* and *goal hypotheses*, I will give an example of a murder-mystery film. This film opens with a scene where the murdered body of Belinda is found. A mystery is set up through events, so viewers don't know who did it. Detective Bunch enters the story with the *goal* of identifying the murderer. As the detective questions suspects, the audience decides who is most likely to have killed Belinda. A *curiosity hypothesis* is about finding a *goal* (e.g. to murder someone) within a group. This *goal* is not dramatic as it happened in the past. In contrast, a *goal hypothesis* is about a character's internal desires **now** and what they want from the future. *Goal hypotheses* are the active process of constructing goals based on actions and events. *Curiosity* and *goal hypotheses* may change during a film; however, the *curiosity hypothesis* does not develop any anticipation for future events.

Goal and *suspense hypotheses* offer two different perspectives for any dramatic question. A *suspense hypothesis* takes a formalist approach by considering "the possibility of future narrative events"[33] and develops anticipation. According to Bordwell, inferences are drawn from current story events and tested with upcoming events.[34] Hypothesising over future events is the process of developing a *suspense hypothesis*. A *goal hypothesis* is an inference about what characters want, which sets up the potential for future conflict. For a screenwriter, *goal hypotheses* focus on characters, their psychology and what they want. This dramatic question is tied to who the characters are, which engages the audience. When a viewer constructs a *goal hypothesis*, they are forming the internal desires of that character.

These two types of hypotheses work together: a *goal hypothesis* captures how viewers perceive characters in their minds, which sets up a *suspense hypothesis* focused on events that create anticipation. In other words, when a writer sets up a character with an *objective* that asks a dramatic question due to conflict, the *objective* is a *goal hypothesis*, and the dramatic question offers possibilities for a *suspense hypothesis*.

A fourth type of inference is a *moral hypothesis* where a viewer judges whether a character is 'good' or 'bad' based on an ethical evaluation of their actions and *motives*. *Moral hypotheses* will receive an in-depth examination in Part Three of this book. The act of a spectator constructing all types of hypotheses is guided by principles, which I have represented as the *character schema*.

Bordwell states audience hypotheses are validated, invalidated, or left dangling.[35] For example, Eva Mary Saint's character's *want* in *North by Northwest* initially appears to be about helping Cary Grant's character on the train (a *goal hypothesis*). However, through an omniscient shot, the audience learns she is aiding the villains (invalidating this hypothesis and initiating a new one). A further twist in the story uncovers her true intentions as she is a double agent working for the CIA.

Hypotheses can also occur on two levels: macro (over the entire film) or micro (within a scene). These micro and macro levels of construction reflect how a character's *goals* and scene *objectives* are constructed by a viewer as a *goal hypothesis*. These two perspectives also apply to suspense, where a *suspense hypothesis* can occur on a global or scene level (more on this point in the next chapter).

A viewer is constantly creating hypotheses while watching a film. For every character, audiences construct *goals* based on actions. A drama unfolds through a network of interacting characters whose *goals* are disrupted and obstructed by other *goals*. Lajos Egri developed the concept of 'orchestration' to highlight the awareness a writer needs for how character interactions affect an audience. *Orchestration* refers to a writer creating "well-defined and uncompromising characters in opposition" whose actions lead to conflict.[36] With the *Inside-out* approach, *orchestration* refers to how a screenwriter structures a viewer's experience using character *goals.*

In *Witness for the Prosecution* (1957), Leonard Vole is accused of murder; however, a barrister, Sir Wilfred, believes he is innocent. Throughout the film, a viewer's *goal hypothesis* (or *want*) for Leonard is that he wishes to prove his innocence. At the film's end, Sir Wilfred realises he did commit the crime. So Leonard Vole's actual *want* is to get away with murder; however, the audience only realises this at the conclusion. Vole's *goal hypothesis* that an audience initially constructs (i.e. Leonard as innocent) is a context with which they view all his actions. When writing this type of story (with a false *want*), a writer plays with the fact that the protagonist has been set up with a misleading *goal*.

Throughout a film, this *schema* forms an 'intentional system' in a screenplay, as a writer plans each character's decision-making for the audience's minds. For example, in *North by Northwest* (1959), Roger Thornhill tries to clear his name of a murder he didn't commit. His decision-making throughout the film (e.g. he decides to track down 'George Kaplan' and travels to Chicago) develops an 'intentional system' or framework for the film, which includes all of Thornhill's decisions. Most importantly, for the audience to engage with the character's journey, they must understand why he makes those decisions (e.g. Thornhill travels to Chicago because he believes Kaplan is staying there).

A *character context* for a film is a cognitive structure comprising all characters' *goals* as a network of desires and adversities. Viewers constantly update and amend the *character context* during a film as more information is shown. Because a *character context* evolves throughout a movie, it offers a timeline of how a viewer's thinking is affected and manipulated. This type of context, as a network of character *identities*, provides the foundations for spectator experiences.

The term 'narrative context,' or 'narrative scenario,' has been used similarly to a *character context*. Carl Plantinga describes the importance of 'narrative context': the "affective response depends in large part on an understanding of [the character's] situation (given in the narrative) and on the sympathy with" this character.[37] Noël Carroll highlights the 'narrative context' as significant for a spectator during point-of-view editing in signifying a character's emotional state.[38] A 'narrative context,' however, has a different emphasis as it is based on events and not specifically from a character's perspective. Notably, a *character context* is not part of the narrative but is constructed from it and exists as its own independent cognitive structure.

TO SUMMARISE:

- The audience develops four types of hypotheses while watching a movie: *curiosity, suspense, goal and moral.*

- *Curiosity hypotheses* are possible answers to a mystery that has occurred in the past.

- A *suspense hypothesis* is a possibility for an outcome from a dramatic question and will create anticipation.

- From a viewer's perspective, a *goal* is considered a hypothesis because it can change due to the story.

- *A moral hypothesis* is when a viewer makes a moral evaluation of a character.

- All hypotheses are either proven to be correct (validated), proven to be wrong (invalidated), or left as a mystery (left dangling).

- A *character context* is a cognitive structure representing how a viewer perceives a movie. It comprises all characters' *goals* as a network of desires and adversities.

Chapter Eleven

Suspense

> The cinematic logic is to follow the rules of suspense.
> Hitchcock[39]

The audience's understanding of a character's thinking can vary depending on how a story is narrated, where viewers can have the same or different awareness of story events as a character. *Knowledge* relates to the audience's awareness of a character's thoughts. *Knowledge* of the central characters' intentions and related conflict can set up three types of suspense. A screenwriter's decision as to the kinds of suspense employed in a screenplay will significantly influence the audience's experience and the film's structure.

Hitchcock's films develop an emotional journey, where the characters' point of view is central to narrating events. Richard Allen emphasises this point by writing:

> Hitchcock's deployment of suspense ... foregrounds our sense of an orchestrated fiction by dramatising the gap between *character point of view* and *spectator point of view*, by constantly shifting the forms and modes of suspense, and perhaps most distinctively, by exploiting and amplifying the ironic edge of suspense. (my

| italics)⁴⁰

Hitchcock referred to one form of suspense as a 'chase' and described it as essential to "movie technique as a whole."⁴¹ The "chase is someone running toward a goal, often with the antiphonal motion of someone fleeing a pursuer. Probably the fox hunt would be the simplest form of the chase."⁴² Using this technique, a spectator experiences events at the same time the character does in a film. Susan Smith uses the term 'shared suspense' to denote this type of narrative technique as the character and audience share the same awareness of the 'pursuer' and potential conflict. Hitchcock elaborated that in a chase, the character can be fighting or fleeing an opponent.⁴³ When the chase involves reaching a particular point or by a specific time, it becomes a "race" for the character.⁴⁴ Hitchcock refers to *The 39 Steps* as "a close-knit chase structure" where "the police are after the hero who is after a spy ring, and at the climax, the police close in on him at the moment he is exposing the spies."⁴⁵

In *North by Northwest*'s crop-dusting scene, Hitchcock deliberately left time between plane attacks to build suspense in a classic chase sequence. He further heightened the drama by indicating—via point-of-view shots—that Thornhill has no cover close to him. Hitchcock narrates his chase scenes to complement the narrative in a way that maximises emotional responses in a spectator.

In practical terms, Hitchcock offers an audience perspective on suspense: "knowing what to expect, they wait for it to happen. This conditioning of the viewer is essential to the build-up of suspense."⁴⁶ The audience expectation becomes key to delivering suspense through cinema, creating tension and anticipation of what may be. Hitchcock spoke of the need to communicate information before the conflict: "In the usual form of suspense it is indispensable that the public be made perfectly aware of all of the facts involved. Otherwise there is no suspense."[47]

When Lajos Egri refers to "foreshadowing conflict is really tension," he summarises another condition for suspense.[48] This second type of suspense, *dramatic irony*, is best illustrated through an example. Hitchcock offers this scenario:

> A curious person goes into somebody else's room and begins to search through the drawers. Now, you show the person who lives in that room coming up the stairs. Then you go back to the person who is searching and the public feels like warning him, "Be careful, watch out." Therefore even if the snooper is not a likeable character, the audience will still feel anxiety for him.[49]

This description is an example of a situation in which a spectator feels anxiety for the "snooper", even though that character is unaware of the other person coming up the stairs.

Hitchcock affirmed, "It adds greatly to the excitement if the audience is let into a secret."[50] With *dramatic irony*, the audience is privy to information the character is unaware of, while during a 'chase' or *shared suspense*, the audience and character have the same information regarding the potential conflict. Typically, with *dramatic irony*, a secondary event or action—which the audience is aware of, but not the character—develops parallel to the character's *objective*. This type of set-up communicates this secondary event using a different character's perspective or omniscient narration, a perspective not tied to the character we are feeling for. In the movie *Rope* (1948), a missing guest at a dinner party is lying dead in a chest in the same room as the other guests. He was murdered at the beginning, setting up *dramatic irony* for the rest of the film. Hitchcock explained about the film that the "audience knows everything from the start, the [characters] know nothing. There is not a single detail to puzzle the audience. ... The fact that the audience watches actors go blithely through an atmosphere that is loaded with evil makes for real suspense."[51]

At the beginning of *Beauty and the Beast* (2017), the film lets the audience in on a secret: the 'beast' is a prince. Dramatic irony is developed for most of the film as viewers watch the protagonist, Belle, react to the 'beast' while expecting a happy ending. With *Titanic* (1997) it is common knowledge that the Titanic was a ship that sank. Anyone not knowing this fact would find the film significantly less suspenseful, at least until the boat sinks. The film's title, *Mutiny on the Bounty* (1962), is essential in developing *dramatic irony*. Without this title, when Bligh is disciplining the sailors (e.g. flogging them on the deck), a viewer would think about the harshness of these times rather than any imminent peril for Bligh. With the title comes knowledge of the story, and suspense is developed every time Bligh disciplines his sailors.

Another technique that Hitchcock uses sparingly is *surprise*. Hitchcock spoke about the relationship between surprise and the creation of suspense using dramatic irony:

> Let us suppose that there is a bomb underneath the table ... then all of a sudden, "Boom!" The public is surprised, but prior to this surprise, it has seen an absolutely ordinary scene ... Now let us take a suspense situation. The bomb is underneath the table and the public knows it. The public is aware that the bomb is going to explode at one o'clock and there is a clock in the decor. The public can see that it is a quarter to one.

> In the first case, we have given the public fifteen seconds of surprise ... in the second we have provided fifteen minutes of suspense. The conclusion is that whenever possible the public must be informed.[52]

Suspense and surprise evoke emotional responses in an audience; however, suspense is sustained, while surprise is a sudden experience. Hitchcock voiced his preference for suspense when saying there "is no terror in the bang, only in anticipation of it."[53]

Screenwriter Samuel Taylor, who worked on *Vertigo* (1958), was shocked when Hitchcock wanted to let the audience know—forty minutes before the movie's end—that Madeleine and Judy are the same woman. The Paramount Studio executives were also against this decision because they wanted a surprise ending.[54] However, Hitchcock knew it was much more powerful to let the audience in on the secret and anticipate what Scottie would do when he found out.

Just because a story uses suspense does not mean it cannot end in a surprise. *North by Northwest* offers many twists and turns, particularly surrounding Eve Kendall as a double agent. Once Thornhill has met and becomes emotionally attached to Kendall, the audience is shown that she is working for the antagonists. Roger Thornhill believes she is aligned with villains after she seems to send him to his death in the famous crop-dusting scene, and later in the film, he is surprised to find out she is a double agent working for the government. Hitchcock uses these techniques to create narratives that take an audience on an emotional journey with many highs and lows.[55] Two more examples where surprise is applied to great effect are the endings of *American Beauty* (1999) and *The Sixth Sense* (1999). Both films create a sudden dramatic shift in the story, leading to a very satisfying and unexpected ending for the audience.

A third type of suspense, *suppression suspense*, is developed through a mystery about what an antagonist wants. When an audience thinks particular characters have the potential to be the cause of conflict (e.g. one of them is a killer), then situations with these characters create suspense. Cinema can set up *suppression suspense* through narration, using shots and music to indicate to viewers that a character or situation is dangerous.

In *Murder on the Orient Express* (1974), the structure is based on a mystery where a murder occurs; a detective tries to solve the murder by collecting evidence and the resolution shows who the murderers are. *Suppression suspense* develops because the audience knows someone is a murderer, so they must enter into the prospect that each character could be the killer, which adds tension to the viewing experience. In *The Thing* (1982), a monster can take the form of people; therefore, anyone at the Antarctic base could be the 'thing'. Even Kurt Russel's character, who is the protagonist, becomes a suspect. In *The Hateful Eight* (2015), all the characters are stuck in the cabin and could be killers. The viewers aren't given any reason for them to kill; however, the potential for them to be killers is enough to create tension throughout the movie.

An example of a classic (if not cliché) use of *suppression suspense* occurs with a haunted house. The story goes something like this: an amicable family move into an old house on a hill in a small, rural town. All the locals gasp and look at each other when they hear the family has moved into 'that' house. The audience knows something is up. Then, a child from the family decides to explore the cellar (or attic), and spooky music cues the viewers for a fright. A series of shocks follow, which are all non-events at this point in the story (e.g. pigeons flutter, a floorboard breaks). The audience expects, of course, scares as they bought tickets to see a horror movie. At some point, the children realise the pipes moaning at night are not pipes but a ghost kid who wants to terrorise them. Viewers still don't know why, but the ghost kid is determined. The parents keep telling their children that ghosts don't exist and that they should get over moving to a small town from the city. *Suppression suspense* will continue until the children determine what the ghost kid *wants*, which is often in the latter half of the movie.

Three types of suspense (*shared, dramatic irony* and *suppression*) have different relationships to the character and spectator's awareness of story information. These audience relationships with the characters can be defined as types of *knowledge*: *shared* knowledge, where the characters and spectators have equivalent awareness; with *extended* knowledge, the audience has greater awareness than the characters being followed; and *suppressed* knowledge, where characters (usually antagonists) possess *goals* unknown to the audience. When screenwriters set up suspense, they play with conflict and a viewer's *knowledge* of a story.

The structure of a film will influence the audience's *knowledge* of the characters. For example, given a Western scenario where a man walks into a bar and is shot, the audience's *knowledge* dictates how the scene is narrated. For *shared* knowledge, the narration follows the man into the bar, and the audience is as surprised as the character is when he is shot. In this case, there is no *shared suspense*, only surprise, because the conflict is sudden and has no duration. With *extended* knowledge, before the man walks into the bar, the villains are being paid to shoot the man for some reason. When the man enters the bar, the narration highlights the villains, and *dramatic irony* develops. With *suppressed* knowledge, the man enters the bar, and all the other patrons take notice. One of the men may gesture towards the man to the other patrons. The viewer doesn't know why or if they will shoot the man; however, tension is developed because screen time is dedicated to showing a threat from the other men.

The most suspenseful way to tell a story depends on the type of story and the experiences a writer wants to communicate. For the *Inside-out* approach, when creating a story structure, a writer should be aware of the audience's thinking and let a structure develop for the viewer's experience.

To summarise:

- The three types of suspense are *shared*, *dramatic irony* and *suppression*.

- With *shared suspense*, the audience and character have the same knowledge as the story is narrated (i.e. *shared knowledge*).

- *Dramatic irony* requires a writer to foreshadow potential conflict that a character isn't aware of. *Extended knowledge* is when the audience has more awareness about a dramatic situation than a character.

- Mysteries often precede *suppression suspense*, which denies viewers knowledge about what a threatening character wants. This situation can be set up in numerous ways, including an unsolved murder, a violent setting, or ominous music.

PRACTICE

Chapter Twelve
Finding Dramatic Structures

The second way of writing focuses on how a spectator rationally thinks while watching a film. All of the practices in Part Two emphasise writing with an awareness of the audience's thinking and provide logical techniques for manipulating this thought process through a story's narrative. Audiences think locally about what is happening in a scene and globally as they remember the main events in a plot. The screenwriting practices in this chapter develop a viewer's global or macro-level thinking to help create a dramatic structure for a film story. The following chapter examines the practicalities of writing scenes by developing a viewer's thought process.

The practice of asking the central dramatic question

When the protagonist's *goal* meets some conflict, a crucial dramatic question is asked: will the main character get what they desire? The central dramatic question for a film is developed by the protagonist's *want*, which is influential when structuring the overall narrative. The expectation around this *want* sets up suspense and creates anticipation and tension.

Finding Dramatic Structures

The point where the central dramatic question first occurs is called a story's *inciting incident*. An inciting incident is an event that clearly sets up this active *want* and consequently associated problems for achieving this goal. The central dramatic question asked at this point will last for most of the remaining story. Before the inciting incident, the protagonist's status quo or 'normal' world is defined, as well as how the character views him or herself. Often, inner conflict may be hinted at but typically won't become relevant until at least a film's mid-point.

For example, the inciting incident in *Star Wars* (1977) is when the uncle and aunt of the protagonist, Luke Skywalker, are killed. At this point, Luke decides to become a Jedi knight and help the rebellion. The inciting incident of his uncle and aunt's death has freed Luke of any responsibility so he can follow his dreams.

The inciting incident is crucial for the audience to set up the relevant goals in their minds. This turning point in the story and the protagonist's active *goal* must be clearly defined through an unambiguous narrative. Without clarity, the audience will become confused (a cardinal sin for a screenwriter) about the central dramatic question and, therefore, won't feel emotion.

The practice of finding a structure using suspense

Typically, films are structured around suspense, which engages through asking dramatic questions of the character: either a single type of suspense (i.e. *chase*, *dramatic irony* or *suppression*) or some combination of the three is applied in developing the macro-level of the narrative. Creating an overall structure that develops suspense and anticipation provides the foundation for creating individual scenes.

If a writer has started their process by writing compelling characters and collecting story ideas, shifting to the second way of writing focuses their thinking on the overall structure. Thinking about the three types of suspense provides an engaging structure based on conflict and the character's desires.

For example, *North by Northwest* has a more complicated overall structure than most films due to the use of a double agent. The film's narrative can be viewed as an amalgamation of four overarching kinds of experience for a viewer:

- Mystery and shared suspense: Beginning with Roger Thornhill's abduction, the audience follows his involvement in a criminal world. A mystery lasts until the CIA's discussion explains who George Kaplan is.

- Dramatic irony: The audience knows that George Kaplan is a non-existent decoy. For most of the film, a spectator watches Thornhill attempt to clear his name, knowing that Kaplan is part of the CIA's plans.

- Surprise: A series of three surprises, that is, Eve being a double agent, the fake shooting and Eve staying with Vandamm.

- Shared suspense: The film's final part is told with Roger Thornhill's knowledge.

Suspense is about developing certain types of experiences, which, as the story unfolds, provide a structure for a story. When a suspenseful passage in a film is set up correctly, it can last any time, depending on what happens to the character. During the writing process, a writer does not need to guess the duration of a suspenseful section but rather simply find out how suspense affects the story and spectators.

The practice of representing a structure

While the format of a screenplay does not directly show the visuals of a film, it can offer a clear representation of the dramatic structure of a movie. An alternative format of an outline (where, for example, bullet points indicate new scenes) is an even more straightforward representation of this kind of structure than a screenplay.

An outline allows for the whole structure of a film to be written on a few pages. It gives a clearer sense of how the structure works as a whole and provides a valuable tool for mapping out characters' journeys. An outline can help to clarify the story structure and complement the writing of a screenplay. Once a writer is happy with a story's outline, it can provide clarity for each scene. Any outline is not fixed or unchanging but serves as a snapshot of the current iteration of a screenplay's structure.

Alternative forms of writing will be examined in Part Four of this book.

The practice of finding a structure

The simplest structure divides a story into a beginning, middle and end. One way to dramatically define this structure is around the protagonist's *want* and *need*: the beginning is about setting up the main character's *goals*; the middle is how the *want* and *need*, which are conflicting internally and externally, manifest themselves in the story while the ending is after the character has succeeded or failed in achieving these *goals*. The classic 'three-act structure' is a variation where the ending also includes the film's climax.[56]

This simple dramatic structure is significant for a writer

because each beginning, middle and end contains another beginning, middle and end on a different level. So, using this structure, a film can be broken down into sequences, scenes within these sequences, dramatic blocks within these scenes, and even groups of character actions.

What I like about this structure is its dramatic clarity when applied to a screenplay. No matter how a writer interprets the beginning of a film, it provides a clear structure for a story down to the character's actions. When developing an initial outline for a story, there is probably sufficient detail by stopping at each scene's beginning, middle, and end.

The practice of dramatically connecting sequences

Another valuable approach to creating an overall structure is dividing a film into sequences (usually eight to twelve) that form distinct narrative units. Typically, each sequence will show a series of scenes connected by a location or a time period. Another type of question asked throughout a film occurs at the end of a sequence. Since a narrative contains a chain of relating events, sequences likewise are connected through a cause-effect relationship. Each sequence (apart from the final one) ends with an open question about a main character, or 'hook', which leads directly onto the following sequence.

A *hook* keeps the audience interested after completing a sequence and generally indicates a high-level structure. When developing a story, if any sequence doesn't have a *hook* (i.e. a viewer asks a dramatic question on finishing), then a writer should question how the story's through-line is maintained.

The movie *Raiders of the Lost Ark* (1981) will be analysed

to show the beginning, middle and end of the film and each sequence. Also, the *hooks* for each sequence will be highlighted. *Raiders of the Lost Ark* consists of eight sequences. The first two sequences are the beginning of the film, which sets up Indiana's *want*; the following five sequences are the middle, while the end is the final sequence, providing a resolution to the story.

The first sequence introduces the character of Indiana Jones and is set in an Amazon forest in 1936. This sequence starts with Indiana entering a jungle to find a cave; the middle shows him entering the cave to retrieve an idol, and the conclusion presents him with the problem of escaping the native Indians. This first sequence has Indiana Jones as the protagonist, setting up the genre and the promise of more adventure with Indy (an expectation), which is the hook (i.e. what adventures will Indy attempt next?).

The second sequence returns to civilisation and the university where Indiana works as a professor. The beginning of the sequence shows Indy teaching; the middle is a meeting with two government officials, while the end is at Indy's house. During the meeting, several questions were opened up: where is the missing Ravenwood, where is the missing headpiece, and where is the ark? This meeting is the inciting incident that sets up Indiana's *goal* to find and return the ark. The *hook* is: can he find Ravenwood to locate the headpiece for the staff of Rah?

The third sequence is the start of the film's middle section and takes the viewers to Nepal, where he knows Ravenwood's daughter, Marian, is running a bar. The beginning shows Indy travelling by plane to Nepal; the middle is meeting and rescuing Marian; while at the end, he finds the medallion and becomes partners with Marian. The *hook* is: how will Indiana use the headpiece to find the ark?

The fourth sequence takes Jones to Egypt. In the beginning, he meets with a friend and finds out the Nazis are also looking for the ark; the middle is an extended chase scene with the Nazis trying to capture Indy and Marian; while the end is him meeting with his antithesis, the French archaeologist, Belloch. The next step is for Indy to travel to the map room and use the medallion, which is the *hook*.

The fifth sequence starts with a meeting to interpret the headpiece, moves to the map room and finally ends with meeting Marion. Since he knows where the ark is located, the *hook* is: will he get the ark? The sixth sequence begins with him digging for the ark's location, then he enters the chamber (with many snakes) and finally escapes the tomb by the end. Because the Nazis have taken the ark from him, the hook is: will he get the ark back from the Nazis? The seventh sequence is the most action-packed of the film: firstly, he destroys the plane the Nazis were going to use to transport the ark, then chases a convoy of trucks carrying the ark to Cairo. The final scene is *relief* for the audience as a boat ships the ark back to America. The *hook* is: will the Nazis give up on the ark? Of course not.

The final sequence provides the ending for the film. It starts with a submarine intercepting the boat and taking the ark; the middle shows the opening of the ark; and the final scene follows Indy back to America.

This analysis shows that dividing a story into sequences and having a clear connection between them can break a film into smaller parts, which are easier to focus on when writing. A writer may choose to initially focus on the beginning, middle and end of a story and let the sequences and scenes emerge from the overarching structure. The development of

Finding Dramatic Structures

the overall structure should be flexible and be found through a writing process rather than pre-determining a framework to hang a story on. Ultimately, it is the character's journey that decides this overall structure.

The practice of borrowing dramatic ideas from other movies

At the heart of every story is a dramatic idea, which is a situation that implies a character's *want* and some kind of conflict for this *goal*. For example, the dramatic idea of someone 'finding hidden treasure' suggests a character's *goal* of searching for the hidden treasure. Because the treasure is hidden, usually somewhere remote, it provides an obstacle to getting the treasure. It suggests other *objectives* for the beginning of a story (e.g. finding a treasure map) and what the character will do for the rest of the story (e.g. searching for the treasure). A dramatic idea can also have a secondary conflict or complication; for example, on the ship sailing for the treasure, the main character befriends a crew member who is a pirate. Now, this idea implies a journey for the character and the audience, which provides a secondary or parallel tension for the story.

Identifying particular dramatic situations implies a type of journey for the audience. For a writer, a dramatic idea can provide a foundation for a story. Adding a complication into a type of situation stops the story's conflict from being one-dimensional. For example, a *goal* to 'find someone' indicates conflict (as the 'someone' won't have their name in a telephone directory); however, if a character needs to 'find someone who can prove his innocence of a murder', a writer now has a compelling situation with a complication to create a journey around.

In *The Silence of the Lambs* (1991), Clarice Starling wants to 'find a serial killer'. This idea alone is a classic concept that inherently has strong conflict. The complication is that she enlists the help of the imprisoned Hannibal Lecter, a convicted serial killer, to help figure out who is doing the murders. This complication makes for a compelling situation and a great dramatic idea.

The beauty of a dramatic idea with a complication is that most movies can be described in these terms. So, writers can 'borrow' these ideas for their films, allowing them to develop similar experiences. This borrowing is not copying because a dramatic idea can be placed in many different settings and cultural contexts. A writer needs to adopt dramatic ideas that resonate with them personally.

What does a dramatic structure look like?

North by Northwest (1959) is an example of where the protagonist, Roger Thornhill, has a *want* to prove that he is innocent of murder and a *need* to find a romantic relationship. In this short analysis of the first three sequences, each *objective* indicating a scene is linked to the next. Also shown are the *hooks* for each sequence, illustrating how the sequences are connected within the story's structure. I recommend watching *North by Northwest* to gain some context for this analysis. This kind of breakdown of a character's *objectives* can also be applied to all characters in a story.

The film starts with the abduction of Roger in the first two minutes. After being taken to a mansion, he is interrogated, and Roger's *objective* is to convince them he is not the spy, George Kaplan. His abductor then gets Roger drunk to kill him by running a car off a cliff. Roger's *objective* during this scene is to avoid the cliff while drunk and then escape the thugs following him without crashing. The police arrest him for drunk driving and speeding.

There is no *hook* at the start of the first sequence.

- Objective 1: To go to meet his colleagues.

- Objective 2: Convince the thugs he is not George Kaplan. FAILS

- Objective 3: To avoid dying (while driving drunk in a car). SUCCEEDS

- Resolution: Roger is arrested by the police for drunk driving and speeding.

After a judge doesn't believe him, Roger and the police travel to the mansion where he was taken in the first sequence. His *objective* is to find the thugs who abducted and interrogated him. After failing to convince the police at the mansion, Roger's *objective* is to speak to Kaplan at the hotel where he was kidnapped. He meets and escapes the two thugs who initially abducted him and then decides to find Lester Townsend, a UN delegate who owns the mansion. This *objective* fails when Townsend is murdered. In an attempt to save Townsend's life, Thornhill looks guilty of the murder (this is the inciting incident that sets up his active goal).

The second sequence begins with the *hook*, can he prove he was abducted?

- Objective 1: To convince the police he was abducted. FAILS

- Objective 2: To convince the police by finding the thugs at the mansion. FAILS

- Objective 3: To find Kaplan at the hotel. FAILS

- Objective 4: To escape the thugs he meets in the hotel lifts). SUCCEEDS

- Objective 5: To find Lester Townsend, who owns the mansion. SUCCEEDS

- Resolution: Townsend is murdered, and Thornhill looks guilty of his murder.

After two sequences, Roger Thornhill's *want*, that is, to prove his innocence of a murder, has been set up. The audience knows he is innocent, which creates sympathy for Roger. His *need* has only been suggested at this point. His love interest will be introduced in the following sequence.

The third sequence starts with an intelligence agency meeting and informs the audience that George Kaplan is not a real person but rather a 'decoy'. Roger decides to catch a train to Chicago, as that is where Kaplan has reportedly moved to. The complication in this sequence is to avoid being caught by the police during this journey. Avoiding capture is initially played out at the train station in New York and then on the train itself. Roger's love interest is introduced once aboard the train, where she helps him avoid the police and train conductors.

In the third sequence, Thornhill aims to travel to Chicago to find Kaplan. The *hook* is how is he going to prove his innocence?

- Objective 1: To buy a train ticket. FAILS

- Objective 2: To catch the train. SUCCEEDS

- Objective 3: To avoid being caught by police. SUCCEEDS (with the help of his love interest, Eve Kendal)

- Resolution: He avoids being caught and travels to Chicago.

The *objectives* in each sequence highlight the dramatic nature of the story. Explicitly stating what each character *wants* for a movie and scenes helps to write compelling drama by clarifying each character's journey. The coherence of the dramatic structure provides a robust framework on which to explore the characters on a scene level.

TO SUMMARISE:

- A central *dramatic question* for a story occurs at the *inciting incident* for the protagonist and is crucial to setting the relevant *goals*.

- A narrative can be structured around one or more types of suspense.

- An outline allows for the whole structure of a film to be written on a few pages.

- The pattern of beginning, middle and end can be applied to the structure of an entire film, a sequence, a scene or even a dramatic block within a scene.

- A *hook* is a dramatic question that keeps the audience interested after completing a sequence and connects sequences, indicating a high-level structure.

- A dramatic idea with a story complication can be adopted from other movies and recast in different settings and scenarios.

- *Goals* and *objectives* provide a dramatic structure for any script. *Objectives* can also be viewed from a *sequence* perspective to offer an intermediate structure between scenes and the whole film.

Chapter Thirteen

Creating Character Journeys

Each scene within a film narrates a small journey about characters in a story, which needs to be structured to maximise a viewer's engagement. While Part One examined the first half of the duality of actions from a character's perspective, this chapter focuses on the other half (i.e. the audience's experience) to discuss how a writer can structure a viewer's moment-to-moment cognitive experience in a scene. These practices encourage a mindset for a writer that foregrounds the mental journey of a film spectator.

The practice of writing using characters

Characters can be viewed as a context for actions and their implied intentions. Audiences remember what characters have done, try to understand what they will do and apply their knowledge about characters to interpret new events in a film. This knowledge about a film character is called a *character context*.

Character contexts are a screenwriting mindset focused on what spectators know about the characters at any particular point in a screenplay. When audiences interpret actions, they do so from their existing knowledge of this character. This mindset towards characters interprets actions as intentions and is a process whereby the audience is trying to understand a character's internal world, i.e. how they think and feel.

From this mindset, it is not important what the character does, but why they do it. This 'why' engages viewers and makes a writer's screenwriting dramatic. This 'why' is the character and a central concern for an audience watching a film. The *Inside-out* approach considers actions as secondary to intentions because actions serve their intentions. A story is about characters who are presented as a chain of intentions relating directly to the same cause-and-effect logic of the plot. People remember this chain of intentions as a desire or *goal*, as has been described with the character schema.

When writers use a *character context*, they write actions in a script based on a character's intentions. These intentions come from the character's inner world (i.e. their thinking) and provide more information about who this person is to the audience. A screenwriter must always consider a viewer's possible interpretation of events when writing characters using a character context.

Character contexts constantly change during a film. These changes have two reasons: either the character is changing, or the audience is learning more about who the character is. How a writer narrates this change with a *character context* is the story. Structuring the narration using suspense with this type of mindset is the foundation for screenwriting using the *Inside-out* approach.

Writing a scene using suspense

Francis Truffaut writes about Hitchcock's approach to suspense:

> In Hitchcock's personal form of cinematic storytelling, suspense obviously plays an important role. Suspense is not what is too often considered the manipulation of violent material, but rather the dilation of a span of time, the exaggeration of a pause, the emphasis on all that makes our hearts beat a little harder, a little faster. What distinguishes Hitchcock's style … is this special manipulation of slowness and rapidity, of preparation and sudden flashes, of anticipation and ellipsis.[57]

Truffaut's quotation emphasises the timing, duration, and ordering of events on a scene level. Susan Smith recognises that Hitchcock films have "clearly definable, local suspense dramas" within the main phases of suspense, supporting the idea of local and global suspense.[58] A film is a culmination of smaller moments (often suspenseful) in each scene, which result in an overarching film experience.

The same three types of suspense can be applied for a short duration within a scene. As suspense plays with the audience's knowledge of what a character is aware of, a writer using suspense can employ *character contexts* to foreground a viewer's thinking. The most compelling way to narrate a scene is with an awareness of the viewer's knowledge of the characters. Structuring intentions and conflict within a scene necessitates the application of one of three types of suspense. The application of suspense makes structuring a scene a conscious and logical decision and opens up various ways to tell the story and engage the audience.

The first sequence of *North by Northwest* will be examined

for the role played by suspense in each scene. The first scene (after the credits, at 2 minutes 10 seconds) spends time with Roger Thornhill and his secretary. This scene is exposition and builds the Thornhill character as a busy businessman with no problem lying. By aligning the audience with Thornhill, the suspense in the film is written primarily around him.

The second scene has Thornhill visiting friends at a bar called the Oak Room. The suspense starts when two thugs mistakenly think Thornhill is someone named Kaplan. This situation is set up by a waiter calling for Kaplan when Thornhill flags the waiter for a phone call. Therefore, *dramatic irony* proceeds for the audience as they realise the thugs want Kaplan (i.e. Thornhill), while Thornhill is oblivious. When I first watched *North by Northwest*, I missed the waiter calling for Kaplan and, therefore, missed the mistaken identity. In this case, *suppression suspense* ensues when the two thugs surprisingly pull a gun on Thornhill. It was still dramatic, yet I didn't understand why were kidnapping Thornhill. In some respects, *suppression suspense* gave me a similar experience to the character Thornhill, who also had no idea why these men were abducting him.

The third scene (at 7 minutes 19 seconds) starts as the car enters the grounds of a mansion. When Thornhill asks, "Who is Townsend?" a mystery is set up that will be answered in time. The central villain, Phillip Vandamm, turns *dramatic irony* (or *suppression suspense*) into *shared suspense* as Thornhill realises they have the wrong man. When Vandamm suggests Thornhill will not "survive the evening", the stakes rise (the situation is now a matter of life and death), and the *shared suspense* is heightened. The thugs "give Mr Kaplan a drink" by forcing him to consume bourbon.

Scene four starts with a drunken Thornhill sitting in a car with the thugs, who clearly intend to drive him off a cliff. This set-up is *dramatic irony* as Thornhill is entirely oblivious of their intentions. Then occurs the moment when *dramatic irony* turns to *shared suspense* as Thornhill, in his drunken stupor, realises the car is headed for a cliff. He somehow pushes the thug next to him out of the car and, in a humorous car chase, avoids driving off the cliff and crashing into other vehicles. The scene ends with him being arrested by the police for speeding and drunk driving.

The fifth and final scene in the first sequence is at the police station. The scene plays as relief as there is no suspense and a lot of humour. The relief in this scene gives the whole sequence a dramatic shape, which peaked at scene four's attempted killing at the cliffs.

The practice of manifesting character intentions

When applying the *Inside-out* approach to this second way of writing, creating a screenplay becomes a process of structuring character intentions. Because screenplays don't directly contain intentions, a writer must manifest actions that represent those intentions. Manifesting intentions as actions, however, can be problematic when the actions are not clearly defined. Ambiguous actions lead to incorrect interpretations and even confusion for the audience. An essential part of a screenwriter's craft is finding exciting actions and unambiguously communicating the related intentions.

Enscription is the process of writing actions based on character intentions and manifests a *character context* from a writer's perspective. I am using the term *enscription* to denote character intentions as a fundamental dramatic unit from a cognitive perspective, which foregrounds a viewer's thinking.

Enscribing is the ability to narrate a character's internal world. This term encompasses two ways to communicate character intentions: actions, where a character is shown onscreen to be doing something, and montage, where the juxtaposition of images—e.g. a character's face followed by a point of view shot—indicates a character's intention (montage has an in-depth examination in Part Four).

I consider Alfred Hitchcock the master of *enscribing*, whose scenes are efficiently and unambiguously narrated. It should not be underestimated how much of an art *enscribing* is and how good Hitchcock was at it. Take, for example, the beginning of *Psycho* (1960), where Marian is stealing money from her boss. Critically watching this sequence shows how the timing and duration of shots brilliantly involve a viewer. For example, how Hitchcock has Marian justify in her mind that stealing the money from Tom Cassidy, and the paranoia she feels having committed the crime. This kind of visual storytelling is what Hitchcock is greatest at with his craft.

The practice of writing actions

Screenwriters write actions in a screenplay, not characters. Even though actions develop a unity, referred to as 'character', what's written literally in a script are the actions. The audience mentally constructs the concept of a character (as defined by the *schema*). Character doesn't exist as any one action but rather as a culmination of actions within the story. It is understood through a structure of intentions and their related actions.

The *Inside-out* approach posits that a screenplay represents a cognitive journey for the audience. However, the form of a screenplay cannot directly represent characters or their intentions. This way of writing is about representing a cognitive journey as a film.

A character's intentions are communicated to a film viewer in three ways. The first way is that an intention can be shown onscreen by a character doing something. This 'doing' is an *action* in a screenplay and is represented using prose descriptions in a script. An *action* includes dialogue where characters are actively speaking with an intention. Screenplays denote dialogue using specific conventions (i.e. the character name is capitalised followed by indented speech).

The second way is to employ montage to communicate an intention. Montage communicates an intention typically with point-of-view shots cut together with other shots to indicate a character's perspective. This technique is examined in Part Four of this book.

The third way to communicate intention is through voice-overs. While a character's dialogue appears in a scene, a voice-over is another mode of communication. A voice-over can be a character's thoughts or an omniscient narrator, which can communicate a character's intentions.

The practice of not writing dialogue

Hitchcock's attitude to dialogue is evident from the following statements: "Dialogue is something that comes out of the mouths of people who are telling a visual story" and "When we tell a story in cinema, we should resort to dialogue only when it's impossible to do otherwise."[59] Hitchcock was critical of many film directors who he felt had not utilised visual storytelling techniques but employed coverage to shoot people talking.[60] Against the argument that talking pictures have a "bigger range of subjects," Hitchcock would argue "that it also lessens the field of appeal. What appeals to the eye is universal; what appeals to the ear is local."[61]

However, dialogue communicates differently from visual storytelling. Even though spoken language is cultural, speech can be more efficient and effective than images at evoking particular responses from the audience. An interesting example from Hitchcock's *Frenzy* (1972) is the cooking scene where the visuals and dialogue are telling two different stories: the conversation is discussing a police officer's assignment of finding a murderer, while the visuals tell the story of his wife's cooking, as she experiments with new dishes on her husband.

Dialogue is something that someone does and is interpreted for its meaning and intention. An often repeated screenwriting adage is 'show, don't tell', which suggests that dialogue is replaced with visual equivalents. While cinema is a visual medium (examined at length in Part Four), because dialogue is perceived differently by a viewer from a film's pictures, it can not only complement visuals but also add another layer to the drama. Any suggestions that dialogue can't be dramatic are incorrect. A scene can be told dramatically using spoken and physical actions; however, they must work together to create the desired experience. *Pulp Fiction* (1994) is an example of dialogue and visuals working together to create compelling cinema. For example, Vincent Vega and Jules Winnfield are discussing Amsterdam and other trivial topics while we watch these two hoods arrive, get guns out of the boot of their car and wander up to an apartment.

Dialogue and physical actions can complement each

other in a film; however, dialogue should be removed when they communicate the same information. Another common mistake is when what a character speaks does not move the drama forward, therefore failing to serve the story. Creating a script that constantly engages viewers mentally through actions will develop a compelling experience.

The practice of finding interesting scenes

Part of the screenwriter's role is understanding the character's psychology and motivations and defining compelling ways to realise these motivations as actions onscreen. Finding interesting ways to narrate a scene is the act of manifesting character intentions originally and uniquely.

The Lubitsch touch is a term used to describe how film director Ernst Lubitsch would find creative and innovative ways to narrate his scenes. An example in *The Smiling Lieutenant* (1931) is set up with a queen having an affair with a lieutenant. The latter watches as the king leaves his wife in their bedroom and walks down a long set of stairs before slipping into the bedroom after the king has left. By the time the king makes it to the bottom of the stairs, he realises he has forgotten his belt. So he slowly (developing *dramatic irony*) walks back up to the bedroom and enters. A second later, he emerges with a belt and walks down the stairs, trying to put it on. The belt does not fit, as it is too small. The king stops and realises what has happened. (Billy Wilder, in a YouTube clip, wonderfully explains this clip on the American Film Institute channel.) Lubitsch's scene is amusing, original and engaging. There are many ways to tell a scene where a husband realises his wife is having an affair, but Lubitsch chooses to make comedies, adding a lighter touch to the material.

A scene, written as a simple outline, can be told in various ways. Finding the most compelling approach to telling a scene creates an engaging viewer's experience. Often, scenes can have multiple dramatic questions, providing a more dynamic engagement for a viewer. Trying to read scenes as if you don't know what will happen and finding out how you react will help you to understand how an audience will respond. An alternative is getting feedback from someone independent of the writing process and whose opinion you trust.

The practice of creating story ideas

Joseph Campbell wrote about how characters match the journey that they undertake:

> In [myths], the adventure that the hero is ready for is the one he gets. The adventure is symbolically a manifestation of his character. Even the landscape and the conditions of the environment match his readiness.[62]

A viewer expects the protagonist to go on a challenging journey and eventually succeed in what they are setting out to do. With the *Inside-out* approach, this journey comes from characters, and these characters should have some meaning for a writer. When finding scenes and a structure for a screenplay, it can be valuable to return to why a writer has chosen these characters and situations, what themes are explored, and what the writer wants to represent about the characters onscreen.

Themes are a great way to create scenes or situations. For example, if a story is about a failed marriage, contrasting the central story with other scenes commenting on marriage (e.g.

a successful marriage, singles, etc.) and how these characters respond to these situations, provides a way to strengthen and deepen a story.

TO SUMMARISE:

• *Character contexts* represent a mindset with an awareness of what spectators think about characters. When writers use a *character context*, they write actions in a script based on a character's intentions.

• Structuring a scene with conflict necessitates the application of one of three types of suspense.

• *Enscribing* is the ability to narrate a character's internal world. A screenwriter needs to develop this mindset to manifest characters for an audience.

• There are three ways to write character intentions: as actions (visually and verbally), montage (e.g. point of view editing) and through a voice-over.

• Dialogue and physical actions can complement each other in a film; however, dialogue should be removed when communicating the same information.

• Find exciting ways to narrate a scene by manifesting character intentions originally and uniquely.

• Allow themes and characters to influence how a story is structured.

My Practice

Before writing each scene in *Doreen's Dead*, I would take time to find the most compelling way to narrate it. For example, when George commits the first murder for his mother and stabs Hilda, the outline is very basic and has one level of conflict. I decided to re-introduce Doreen into the story and had her 'ghost' egging George on to do the deed. This change added more conflict (i.e. a complication) as George was hesitant to do the crime, and also made George less of a psychopath (which I thought was essential to the story). This idea of re-introducing Doreen affected not only this scene but the rest of the story; consequently, I had to re-write the outline for the film.

The title of *Doreen's Dead* was chosen to set up *dramatic irony* for the film's first act. As the audience watches Doreen, the title develops an expectation about her fate in the story. Most of the story is *shared suspense*, as viewers follow George and share his *knowledge*. There was an opportunity for *suppression suspense* with George's mother and the reason for his father's death. I decided to reveal this information as a surprise for later in the film instead of *suppression suspense*. *Dramatic irony* develops when George puts poison in his mother's tea. She is unaware of what George has done, and tension develops as the tea sits in front of her tea. Will she drink the tea? Or will there be another twist?

When writing my story outline, I found my first attempt was not homogenous — it contained many extra characters and no clear through-line for the central character, George. After getting some feedback, I completely rewrote the outline, which resulted in a journey focused more on George. In terms of narrative, it was more straightforward; in terms of exploring this character, it was more complex.

PART THREE

MAPPING EMOTIONS

Chapter Fourteen

Emotional Context

When Hitchcock stated that "art is emotion, therefore the use of film, putting it together and making it have an effect on the audience, is the main function of film"[1], he suggests that writers treat their screenwriting process as the creation of an emotional journey for the audience. The third way of writing focuses on a screenwriter structuring a viewer's emotional journey, which offers a means to order scenes and develop new story elements to satisfy this journey.

Screenplays can embody a strong dramatic shape by structuring on an emotional level. Hitchcock felt that his films needed a particular emotional shape and used music as an analogy to describe this shape: "Construction to me, it's like music. You start with your allegro, your andante, and you build up."[2] John Michael Hayes, the screenwriter for *Rear Window* (1954), would formulate "an emotional roadmap" for his scripts and would always insist on completing the first draft before giving it to a producer so that the emotional journey for the audience was explicit.[3] The term 'emotional map' suggests a way of working where a writer decides on the emotional journey for a viewer, relating directly to a character's journey. If an emotional map provides the 'feeling' for scenes, there is a requirement for a screenwriter to know how to create particular emotions.

Though the emotion elicited from a film depends on its narration, for a viewer, the story logic (i.e. the causal relationship between events) is independent of its emotional journey. This independence reflects a cognitive and emotional separation and an interplay between the two while watching a movie. For a screenwriter, recognising a script's emotional logic (i.e. the relationship between emotional experiences) can be considered equally important as the story logic, highlighting the need for a way of writing focused purely on the affect of a screenplay.

When Charles Thomas Samuels wrote, "this pattern of tension and relaxation, not the silly spy story, is what The [39] Steps is 'about'", he suggested that what's important to the audience is an experience.[4] In a similar vein, director Kent Jones explained, "When the emotional through-line [in Hitchcock's films] is working, then you do not notice" plot holes or implausibility of situations.[5] When creating his films, Hitchcock treated the audience´s emotional experiences as more important than what the story is about:

> I put first and foremost cinematic style before content. Most people, reviewers, you know, they review pictures purely in terms of content. I don't care what the film is about. I don't even know who was in that airplane attacking Cary Grant [in *North by Northwest*]. I don't care. So long as that audience goes through that emotion![6]

Hitchcock's emphasis on emotions (where a narrative is constructed to heighten emotional responses) sometimes comes at the detriment of story logic or plausibility. François Truffaut recognises that beginning with *The 39 Steps*,

Hitchcock took liberties with scenarios in his films by sacrificing the story's plausibility to develop more substantial emotional situations.[7] This movie has a variety of unlikely scenarios throughout its plot, which provide great excitement and continuously keep the protagonist active. Hitchcock insisted that realistically presenting a movie "is just as ridiculous as to demand of a representative painter that he shows objects accurately."[8] The director was fully aware that his movies' stories were "arbitrary and unjustified"[9], which allowed him the freedom to develop dramatic situations without concern for plausibility.[10] Hitchcock said a "critic who talks to me about plausibility is a dull fellow."[11]

Hitchcock prioritises emotions over plausibility, which is another way of saying that for him, emotional logic is more important in his screenplays than story logic. The *Inside-out* approach posits that the audience gains satisfaction not through plausibility or story logic but through an emotional journey. The success of a film, on some level, depends on this satisfaction.

Susan Smith observes that Hitchcock was aware of "suspense's ability to provoke both an intellectual *and* affective response."[12] The intellectual aspect derives from a spectator's narrative construction, which precedes an emotional response. This basis for writing emotions is the cognitive process outlined in Parts One and Two and is applied through the three types of suspense: *shared*, *dramatic irony* and *suppression*. A separate process, called *fiction identification*, occurs when the audience cognitively engages with characters and produces an emotional response. The next section, Foundations, introduces a process for *fiction identification* to explain how and why viewers feel emotions while watching a film.

Emotional Context

Each new emotional experience in a film is received within an *emotional context*, depending on where it takes place in the story. While a *character context* uses a character schema to cognitively map out what a character has done in a story, an *emotional context* reflects a structure of emotional experiences for the audience. A screenwriter can examine these two contexts at any point in a narrative to create a picture of what a spectator thinks and feels. The awareness of what a viewer thinks and feels is crucial for developing an engaging experience.

This way of writing has two purposes for including in a screenwriting process:

1) To perceive emotions independently of characters, allowing emotions to influence character actions. This process complements *character identification* from Part One, where the writer's emotions lead to character actions, which can lead to the audience's emotions. When a screenwriter searches for a dramatic shape that fits the character's journey, tension is created between each character's actions and a viewer's response to these actions. A screenwriter must **always** be aware of how their narrative affects the audience.

2) To fulfil expectations for a particular type of emotional journey. This purpose reflects a screenwriter's awareness of genre and how an emotional journey fits a specific genre.

This way of writing focuses on an awareness of the audience's emotion, where the affect of a screenplay is not an afterthought but one of the reasons a screenplay is produced.

Mapping emotions, as a way of writing, is distinct from the second way of writing, structuring actions. Structuring actions presented the foundations for writing focused on a viewer's cognition, while structuring emotions presents the foundations for writing as a viewer's emotions. While awareness of a viewer's cognition and emotions are linked (discussed throughout Part Three), focusing on the audience's emotional journey can be done independently of cognition and offers ideas for scenes and actions.

For example, a screenplay may be best served by including a scene that adds relief for a spectator. This type of scene often comes after a tense, climactic scene. The writer may use humour when adding this new scene and begin a process of *character identification* (the first way of writing) to create a situation in keeping with the existing characters. Once this scene is roughly written, the screenwriter critically analyses its structure (the second way of writing) to ensure it is clear and concise. This scene is then investigated as an emotional journey focused on the dramatic shape. Any issues with this scene may require the writer to return to the character or narrative perspectives to fix any shortcomings. Each time a writer switches between one of the ways of writing, they are 'changing gears' as each mindset is distinct and focuses on different aspects of the writing process.

When I talk about emotional journeys in this section, I am referring to the audience's journey (which is developed through narrative techniques), not the character's (see *character identification* in Part One for this perspective). Notably, the correlation between a character in a story and the audience's emotions is *not* directly dependent on the character's emotions being communicated. It would be a misunderstanding of this process to assume that the emotions portrayed by an actor correlate directly to the audience's emotional response; instead, the "emotional life of the actor/character comes primarily from actions that are wedded to *wants* that are contextualised by—embedded in—dynamic relationships and circumstance" (my italics).[13]

Emotion is evoked through a process and not imitation—i.e. because an actor feels an emotion, it does not mean the audience will feel the same emotion.

The following section, Foundations, connects the cognitive process in Part Two, Structuring Actions, with the emotional process of structuring a film by explaining how a viewer's cognition develops emotions. *Fiction identification* defines two processes (biological and cultural) based on the same cognitive foundations (i.e. the character schema). The Practice section proposes ways to fulfil audience expectations for particular kinds of emotional journeys. Ways to develop an emotional journey will be introduced, which satisfies genre and the audience's expectations.

FOUNDATIONS

Chapter Fifteen

Primal Emotions

Alfred Hitchcock's films have shocked, thrilled, and entertained spectators worldwide. He enjoyed knowing people from diverse cultural backgrounds could look at his movies and feel the same emotions.[14] Hitchcock did not know any other medium where "the different audiences of different nationalities can be shocked at the same moment at the same thing on that screen."[15]

How can the global appeal of Hitchcock's films be translated into a set of cognitive-emotional experiences developed by narrative techniques? To answer this question, the origin of emotions needs to be located on a primal, cross-cultural level. Hitchcock spoke about the enjoyment of fear: "...millions of people pay huge sums of money and go to great hardship merely to enjoy fears seems paradoxical. Yet it is no exaggeration."[16] With this kind of fear, spectators know they are witnessing fiction and consequently can enjoy the despair of the central character. Fear in a film is a primal, hardwired reaction for an audience felt while spectating fictional characters under adversity. Because characters do not exist, this fear for the story's hero becomes a type of game that is enjoyable, as there are no actual costs. This vicarious pleasure comes from a spectator's engagement with the film's characters, which imitate the desires and intentions of real people and ourselves.

How come audiences feel emotion even though they know it's not real? Films create a world of fantasy where incredible things can occur. Even though a movie like *The Bicycle Thieves* (1948) may use a realist style and draw from historical events, the audience still needs to enter into the fictional fantasy of the characters and their situations. Understanding a process of *fiction identification*, where audiences are aware that they are watching an illusion yet feel emotion, will be the topic of this section. Fictional notions for emotion, belief and identification will be defined, providing writers with the knowledge to develop fantasies for their screenplays that engage viewers emotionally.

There have been several efforts to understand the "paradox of fiction", where fictional characters emotionally move viewers.[17] In *The Philosophy of Horror*, Noël Carroll distinguishes between objective reality and formal reality: objective reality "of a being is the idea of the thing ... [without] a commitment to its existence. We can think of a unicorn without thinking that unicorns exist."[18] Formal reality refers to an idea of a being that exists in reality.[19] Carroll argues that characters and experiences can be imagined and gives an example of standing on a precipice and entertaining the thought of falling over the edge. He concludes, "We are not frightened by the *event* ... of falling, but by the *content* of our thought of falling—perhaps the mental image of plummeting through space."[20]

Carrol argues that a protagonist and a 'monster' are thought of differently by a viewer when defining the emotion of *art-horror*. For Carroll, "the particular object of art-horror—Dracula [or any monster], if you will—is a thought."[21] Nevertheless, Carroll still discusses how positive characters, like the protagonists, think and feel. I view all fictional characters as "objective reality", where viewers construct an idea of the non-existent person or being. *Inside-out* proposes that an audience's *act of cognitively representing*—through their imagination—a fictional character's thoughts, beliefs, and desires mentally assimilates them with the character.

Fear is a primal emotion induced by a perceived threat or danger. This type of emotional reaction for a viewer occurs when a fictional character's life is perceived to be in danger. The primal aspect of emotions relates to a desire (a character's *goals*), such as survival, sex, hunger, and revenge, which develops immediate interest for the audience. A character's desire in a story creates tension when jeopardising this goal.

How does the *character schema* result in *fiction identification*? The *character schema* represents the intentionality of characters. Intentionality is "a property of actions and mental states" directed at or towards an object.[22] Emotions typically have an intentional object—for example, one is angry with someone or afraid of something. Cognitivists have responded to claims that some emotions do not have intentional objects[23]—for example, anxiety or depression—by "placing them in some distinct class of mental states, such as moods, or attributing to them a subtle or suppressed intentionality, which then explains away their apparent objectlessness."[24] Plantinga makes the distinction between emotion and affect by stating, "emotions are intentional in the sense that they are directed toward some 'object'," while affect lacks intentionality, or "aboutness."[25] Noël Carroll also states that by definition 'affect,' or "sheer bodily states," cannot be emotions as they do not involve the cognition of some object: "You cannot be angry unless there is someone or something that serves as the object of your anger."[26] Therefore, Carroll is orientating our cognition towards some diegetic object that cues emotion.

What process takes a viewer's cognitive understanding of a story and forms an emotional response? Theorists Amy Coplan, Torben Grodal, Alex Neill, and Berys Gaut[27] maintain that **identification** is a requirement for emotional engagement to occur, arguing that it is founded on the idea that a spectator associates him- or herself with characters through each character's point of view. Other theorists—including Noël Carroll[28] and Carl Plantinga[29]—argue that audience identification rarely occurs in a film. They claim the audience's predominant experience is sympathy or antipathy. As Carroll states:

> We respond to fictional situations as outside observers, assimilating our conception of the character's mental state into our overall response as a sort of onlooker with respect to the situation in which the character finds himself.[30]

Carl Plantinga argues against identification because the audience does not have "the same thoughts and [feel] the same emotions as the character does"[31], and puts forward a similar explanation to Carroll—even using the word "assimilation."[32] I am borrowing the term *assimilation* to describe the cognitive construction of character intentions.

A film requires believability for an audience to identify with a character. From an audience perspective, this believability enables a fictional acceptance of the film's world and characters. Susan Feagin expresses identification within the context of real people and situations through the idea of second-order *beliefs*—i.e. beliefs about someone else's beliefs—where a connection "between my mental state and yours is made by way of *belief*" (my italics).[33] In empathising with another, she argues, "a belief that something may happen to him affects me emotionally as if I were him."[34] When dealing with fictional characters—which cannot have beliefs because they do not exist—Feagin states, "We do not form second-order beliefs about an individual's first-order beliefs, but rather *imagine* what these beliefs, desires, etc. might be" (my italics).[35] Imagining a character's desires describes a situation of *shared knowledge*, where viewers react directly to what they imagine a character is thinking. *Shared knowledge* leads to a type of *fiction identification* called *empathy*.

According to Neill, *empathy* with a fictional character "does not depend on whether we 'feel' the way the character feels"[36]; it "requires that I imagine the world, or the situation that she is in, *from her point of view*" (my italics).[37] The audience then becomes the "protagonist" where "I represent to myself her thoughts, beliefs, desires, feelings, and so on *as though they were my own*" (my italics).[38]

Feagin and Neill's theories of identification account for empathetic responses, where a viewer has *shared knowledge* with a character; however, their ideas don't describe situations set up as *extended* or *suppressed knowledge*. Gaut suggests when spectators identify, they imagine being in the character's situation rather than being the character. Gaut's attitude towards identifying with a character's situation has similarities to Carroll's term, 'assimilation'. Assimilation takes "an external view" of a character's situation while acknowledging "a sense of how the character assesses the situation."[39] Hence, a viewer can assimilate a character's "internal evaluation of the situation without becoming, so to speak, possessed by her."[40] This term can, therefore, describe empathy (from the character's viewpoint) and sympathy (a perspective of a character's situation, e.g. *dramatic irony*) as a single process. Carroll objects to calling his process identification because "the audience has emotions (suspense, concern, pity, etc.) that the characters do not, while protagonists have emotions and fears that the audiences lack (e.g. fear of extinction)."[41] *Fiction identification* recognises that: 1) spectators imagine a fictional character's internal world; 2) requires a level of believability in how characters are represented on-screen; and 3) comprehends characters as fictional (i.e. they don't feel emotion), thereby encompassing empathetic and sympathetic situations.

Fiction identification occurs when an obstacle to the character's objective creates *conflict*, which challenges the character's *objective* or *goal* and asks a dramatic question for an audience— whether or not the character achieves the aim. The audience's desire for a particular character to succeed against adversity is the moment of identification. *Fiction identification* describes a process whereby the audience's internal representation of the drama—as a structure based on the character's intentions (i.e. a *character context*)—results in emotion. Compelling drama is structured to maximise the emotional impact of a scene where the audience shares the ups and downs of the characters.

Fiction identification locates an audience's emotional engagement at points of character conflict (internal and external) in films. This type of identification explains how suspense elicits an emotional response from a global audience and is developed through a film's narrative, implying that its creation occurs during the screenwriting phase. While *character identification* develops actions from a writer entering into a character's thinking and feeling, *fiction identification* explains how character actions elicit emotions in a film audience. Understanding how to apply *fiction identification* provides a powerful tool for screenwriters.

In Chapter 5, the following scenario was examined:

> At the end of "North by Northwest," we shift our *affective participation* from Cary Grant, who is entering the mansion, to Martin Landau, who suddenly realises Eva Marie Saint is a spy and finally to Miss Saint. (my italics)[42]

Interpreting the "affective participation" as the result of *fiction identification*, Hitchcock aligned the narration with particular characters to maximise the conflict these characters face. The main focus of the narration is the empathy for Roger Thornhill and the sympathy for Eve Kendall, who is unaware that Vandamm knows she is an agent. The shift of *alignment* to Leonard during the scene is a director's choice to emotionally engage the audience with the moment when Leonard realises Eve is an agent. *Fiction identification* in a scene is an interplay between character *alignment*, the *knowledge* used to set up the scene, the type of suspense applied and the emotional quality due to the level of conflict for the aligned character.

There are two types of emotion derived from fiction identification. The first is *immediate emotions*, which occur during the conflict due to asking a dramatic question. For example, at the beginning of *Jaws* (1975), when the girl is swimming alone in the ocean at night, viewers immediately feel fear as soon as they realise the film has taken the shark's point of view. The second is *responsive emotions*, which we feel after the conflict resolves itself one way or the other. In the example of *Jaws*, when the shark attacks and kills the girl, viewers feel some degree of sadness and loss due to her death. This response comes as a result of the resolution of the conflict, which has the potential to be either positive or negative. A positive resolution would occur in the scene above if the girl happens to escape the shark, and then naturally, the audience would feel happier about the outcome.

By focusing on a screenplay's characters and narrative, the *Inside-out* approach examines particular kinds of emotion that Plantinga calls "fiction". *Fiction emotions* develop through a film's narrative, which builds a story using characters' actions and creates a journey for an audience that brings about responses such as suspense, fear, anger, and curiosity.[43] Carl Plantinga also suggests that a second kind of phenomenon could cause our emotional response to a film: the audience responds to the cinematic form, the image, the music, and the aesthetic qualities created by the filmmakers. This kind of emotional response, which Plantinga calls "artefact emotions", is produced by a direct engagement with the film medium. Examples include the beauty and awe of a dramatic landscape or the image of a young child crying. Though a screenwriter should think visually when writing, a screenplay can only describe images or sounds using words, and therefore, "artefact emotions" cannot be directly represented by a script. In Part Four, I will examine the process of visual writing.

TO SUMMARISE:

- *Fiction emotions* are intentional and directed at or towards an object. The *character schema* represents this intentionality for characters (i.e. *objectives, goals*).

- *Fiction identification* locates an audience's emotional engagement at points of character conflict (internal and external) in films.

- *Shared knowledge* leads to a type of *fiction identification* called *empathy*, while *extended* or *suppressed knowledge* develops *sympathy*.

- *Immediate emotions* occur during the conflict due to asking a dramatic question, and *responsive emotions* arise after the conflict resolves itself as success or failure.

Chapter Sixteen

Moral Emotions

Can cultural influences induce a process of evoking emotions? Historically, the foundations for feeling emotions are viewed as biological or cultural—or, put another way, nature or nurture. Naturalists argue for the "existence of innate, biologically grounded emotions that are more or less uniform across cultures and subcultures", while constructionists argue that emotions are culturally specific.[44] Hitchcock's global popularity confirms his films' ability to travel and affect audiences worldwide and fits into a naturalist model for emotion. More recently, it has been suggested that the naturalist and constructionist positions can be reconciled "if emotions are viewed as (a) shaped by evolutionary processes and implemented in the brain, but also (b) situated in a complex network of stimuli, behaviour, and other cognitive states."[45]

Fiction Identification explains how the *character schema* forms the foundations for eliciting emotions from a film audience. Two processes based on the *character schema* enable emotional responses in viewers: a naturalist process (discussed in the last chapter) and a constructionist process based on the cultural values of a spectator. This second process involves a moral evaluation of a character's actions and will be the topic of this chapter.

The *character schema* comprises *motives* and *goals*. *Goals* are the driving forces behind a dramatic story and are the cognitive foundation for a naturalist process. The *motive* describes the underlying character behind the actions and contains a moral or ethic for those actions. *Motive* describes the intrinsic type of person by defining their moral compass. While the *motive* is the moral essence of a character, the *goal* is how the character will fulfil this attitude towards life. When the audience morally judges a character's *motives*, they enact a constructivist process, because moral evaluation is culturally specific. Due to this process being based on the cultural values of each individual in the audience, a writer needs to be aware of a latitude of interpretations existing to evaluate a *motive*.

Associating moral judgments with identification is an approach that several scholars have applied. Jesse Prinz presents a subcategory of emotion called "moral emotions", which are responses to actions in the story and either conform or fail to conform to moral standards.[46] Vorderer and Knobloch go one step further to state that as "long as their actions can be observed and their intentions can be inferred, the audience is ready to morally evaluate the characters and to develop dispositions toward them."[47]

In Part Two, a *goal hypothesis* explained how a viewer constructs *goals* and *objectives* based on actions. As the audience creates *goal hypotheses*, another question arises: Is what the character is doing 'good' or 'bad'? The answer to this question is a *moral hypothesis* that naturally accompanies the realisation of a *goal*. A viewer's *moral hypothesis* (a particular character is doing wrong or right) can change during a film.

For example, Eve Kendall in *North by Northwest* initially helps Cary Grant's character, which is 'good' as he plays the protagonist. Then, the audience is shown a shot of her planning with the villains, having the effect of reversing the initial *moral hypothesis*. Close to the film's end, the audience realises she is a double agent, reversing their *moral hypothesis* about her character. Developing this *moral hypothesis* requires a moral evaluation of a character's actions.

How different viewers respond to a moral evaluation depends on cultural influences: upbringing, personal bias, social environment, etc. Whether a *goal* is good or bad is subjective, and people from diverse backgrounds may respond differently when morally evaluating. Moral evaluation of character actions creates an additional emotional dimension to the primary, biological affect. The same cognitive framework based on the *character schema* is utilised to understand the audience's moral and primal reactions and, therefore, are the two sides of *fiction identification*. On a scene level, the moral evaluation of *objectives* adds emotional complexity to the dramatic situations. For example, during a scene showing a bank robbery, a viewer reacts very differently if the reason for the theft is to get money for his brother's operation, compared to pure greed. Therefore, when any hero has two conflicting inner *goals* and needs to decide which *goal* to follow, the viewers make moral judgements about this character's choices. Defining *fiction identification* as possessing two distinct processes allows writers to understand why the audience feels complex emotional responses to dramas and provides a way of writing primal and moral emotions.

The two central characters in *Stagecoach* (1939), Dallas and Ringo, have *goals* that develop internal conflict and *motives*, adding complexity to these characters. Dallas' *want* is to find a new home. Her *motive* for this *goal* is due to her being kicked out of her last home because she is a prostitute. An audience member may feel she deserves to get kicked out because of her questionable profession and therefore see her as 'bad'. A particularly judgemental viewer may even want her *goal* to fail, so she suffers even more. Dallas' *need* becomes apparent after she meets the Ringo Kid (played by John Wayne): she desires romantic love. This *need* provides conflicting *goals* as her *want* implies she will continue her profession once she has a new home. The *motive* for her *need* is to escape prostitution and have a family. This *motive* is revealed near the film's end and shows her real character. The way this character's two *motives* are revealed (the *motive* for her *want* at the beginning and the *motive* for her *need* at the end) provides an emotional arch for how the audience morally views this character.

Ringo's *want* is to get the Plummer boys, which is set up as soon as he is introduced. Even though Ringo is an outlaw, when the audience learns that the want's *motive* is because the Plummer boys killed his family, they generally sympathise with his plight. Ringo's *need*, similarly to Dallas', is to find romantic love. His *motive* for this *goal* is that he doesn't have a family or anyone who cares for him. Outlaws and prostitutes are often portrayed as simple characters who immediately get tied to a particular *moral hypothesis*. *Stagecoach* reverses this initial hypothesis and, in doing so, creates complex and memorable characters.

The characters make their own moral judgements throughout a story, which a writer must also be aware of. There is tension between the character and the audience's moral viewpoint (e.g. a character may think they are doing 'good', but a writer wants the viewers to think of this character as 'bad'). Each character's choice in a story is driven by their moral views and will inevitably be judged by viewers and contrasted with their own ethical values. When developing a character, a writer should have reasons why an *objective* (e.g. robbing a bank) is morally acceptable from the character's worldview.

On the one hand, writers need to be aware of how the audience will react to certain behaviours while also understanding why characters possess particular scene *objectives* in a screenplay. There is an inner dynamic for film viewers between the moral judgement of actions and the reasons why a character is committing these actions. How these reasons are communicated to the audience will depend on the narrative and what affects a writer wants to elicit.

The Morality of the Anti-hero

Richard Allen recalled that in "his interviews with Truffaut, Hitchcock claims that suspense is not intrinsically tied to moral evaluation."[48] Allen views situations in Hitchcock's films where audiences are encouraged to sympathise with villainous characters and their predicaments as "an occasion for undercutting our conventional moral responses."[49] Thus, according to Allen, a spectator embraces a state of affairs that is "contrary to the desirable narrative outcome."[50]

Psycho (1960) is valuable to examine from a moral perspective because the main protagonists are a thief and a psychotic murderer. Hitchcock and Truffaut discussed identification within the film:

> Hitchcock: When Perkins is looking at the car sinking in the pond, even though he's burying a body, when the car stops sinking for a moment, the public is thinking, "I hope it goes all the way down!" It's a natural instinct.

> Truffaut: But in most of your films the audience reaction is more innocent because they are concerned for a man who is wrongly suspected of a crime. Whereas in *Psycho* one begins by being scared for a girl who's a thief, and later on one is scared for a killer, and, finally, when one learns that this killer has a secret, one hopes he will be caught just in order to get the full story![51]

The moral evaluation of characters doesn't dictate whether they are the protagonist. The setting up of which character is *aligned* as the protagonist is a separate process to moral evaluation. *Psycho* is an example where, though the main characters are morally reprehensible, the choice by screenwriter Joseph Stefano is dramatically strong and provides original twists to the film. Often, the protagonist is set up to be likeable and able to be viewed in a positive moral way because this is the most dramatic way to tell that particular story.

Morality of Themes

Human beings look for unity to make sense of what they are watching. We try to make meaning of a story, the whole from the parts. Unification in a dramatic film often occurs through the main characters, where the audience searches for which characters to follow and care about. This type of unification focuses on an action's intention and is what makes action into scenes and scenes into stories. Another type of unification, thematic, is a simple and concise way to connect a story's meaning, typically described by a single or pair of words (e.g. greed, pride, family values, etc.) to summarise the story's meaning.

For example, what is *The 39 Steps* about? Is it about a spy story where Richard Hannay must prove his innocence by solving the mystery of the thirty-nine steps? Or is it about the moral implications of an innocent man being accused of a murder he did not commit (a moral judgement), being isolated in his journey because the police and a spy ring are attempting to catch him, and having no one else to turn to as everyone thinks he is guilty? Or is it about how Hannay finds true love in his darkest moment (though done with plenty of humour)?

The story is thematically about marriage. Every scene in the film explores the topic of marriage: some scenes make fun of matrimony, while others show different types of marriage. Though the word 'marriage' will not appear in any synopsis of the film, it is the idea that the film explores. The spy story is a dramatic situation that isolates the protagonist and emotionally engages the audience. However, if you look at what ideas each scene explores, the central idea throughout the film is marriage.

A theme in isolation has no moral dimension. A single scene about marriage may encourage viewers to morally judge the situation; however, a theme is a unifying idea and simply relates to the topics explored in a film. *The 39 Steps* presents the 'good' and 'bad' of marriage; however, the theme of marriage in the film does not argue for or against marriage. Themes usually relate to the on-screen drama but are not inherently dramatic. The *goals* and *objectives* of each character provide emotional engagement but are constructed separately by the audience to the themes (i.e. it is a separate process). A theme may relate to a character's *goal*. For example, in *The 39 Steps*, Hannay's secondary goal is to find romantic love, which relates to the theme of marriage and allows this theme to connect to Pamela and Hannay's relationship. The relationship between themes and the *character schema* is crucial for a writer to understand.

Themes can directly relate to the character *goals* in a story and describe the topics a film is about, the story's central conflicts (not just for the protagonist) and how the dynamic between two opposing themes feeds the on-screen drama. Dramatic themes make it clear and concise what the central drama is about in a story.

Earlier the following quote from Hitchcock was examined from the perspective of a character's emotional conflict:

> Imagine an example of a standard plot—let us say a conflict between love and duty. This idea was the origin of my first talkie, *Blackmail*. The hazy pattern one saw beforehand was duty-love, love versus duty, and finally either duty or love, one or the other. The whole middle section was built up on the theme of love versus duty, after duty and love had been introduced separately in turn. So I had first to put on the screen an episode expressing duty. I showed the arrest of a criminal by Scotland Yard detectives, and tried to make it as concrete and detailed as I could.[52]

Love and duty can also be viewed as themes which relate to the central characters' goals and therefore conflict. As themes, these two topics are explored more generally within the story. Conflicting themes can ask moral questions about these topics.

Another example of love versus duty (though using family duty as opposed to police duty in *Blackmail*) is contained in the classic story of *Romeo and Juliet*. The story's two protagonists have the same *goals* (to find romantic love and to be loyal to their families), which conflict and cause inner turmoil for these characters. This tragedy ends with Romeo and Juliet taking their own lives. The moral of the story (which is not a judgement by a viewer, but the result of their internal choice and whether *goals* are fulfilled or not) is 'being loyal to your family is more important than romantic love'. Viewers may judge their young love as more important than family loyalty when morally evaluating these two goals. I personally do; however, I can understand how another person could place more importance on family duty. Both *goals* can be viewed in a positive moral light, which is why *Romeo and Juliet* is such a timeless story.

Themes can act as a writer's compass to produce explicit meaning for a screenplay. Using themes provides a creative tool for writing dramatic situations and complex characters. Writers need to identify what the story is really about for them. When a writer realises what their story is concerned with and has a solid dramatic situation, adding a relevant scene that continues the thematic exploration strengthens a drama. For a writer, themes are hugely important, and exploring themes can provide ideas for their story.

The *Inside-out* approach considers *fiction identification* to consist of biological and cultural processes, forming the overall experience. These two processes develop more complex experiences because of how they interact. Based on fear, the biological process is dominant and is supported by cultural influences. Both processes are based on the same cognitive framework, which is an application of the *character schema*.

Fiction identification elicits emotions at points of character conflict in the story, but it does not mean that a viewer's feelings are simple or generic experiences. The possibilities are varied and depend much on the situation and what each character is attempting to achieve. In *North by Northwest*, for example, a viewer may feel betrayed by Eva Marie Saint after the crop dusting scene when Cary Grant meets her again in a hotel room. Clearly, Saint's character likes Grant's, which makes the situation even more complex. Given that characters are defined by two *goals*—which may conflict internally—and that multiple characters in a scene typically obstruct each other, complex experiences can be understood using this *schema*. Stanislavski saw a series of character actions as leading to an emotion, where even "complex and difficult emotions are also broken down into a series of actions."[53] A screenwriter's job is to write actions that develop complex and engaging experiences. The screenwriter can knowingly orchestrate the two separate processes for *fiction identification*, and this knowledge is essential for writing compelling experiences.

To summarise:

- *Fiction Identification* explains how the *character schema* forms the foundations for eliciting emotions from a film audience.

- The reasons for film narratives to elicit emotions are biological and cultural.

- A viewer creates *moral hypotheses* about whether characters are doing wrong or right. These hypotheses are updated as a movie unfolds.

- *Fiction identification* possesses two distinct processes, allowing writers to understand why the audience feels complex emotions.

- The moral evaluation of characters doesn't dictate whether they are the protagonist. *Alignment* dictates the roles of characters.

- A theme in isolation has no moral dimension, while two themes in conflict tend to relate to the main character's inner turmoil (i.e. conflicting goals).

PRACTICE

Chapter Seventeen

Writing for a Market

The practice of writing an emotional map

Fiction emotion results from how the audience thinks about characters and can be knowingly developed by a screenwriter. When a writer narrates a story populated with character intentions, a viewer re-constructs it using the *character schema* while watching the movie. Therefore, a writer can develop their craft of writing emotions, which empowers an ability to structure a viewer's emotional journey knowingly. The third way of writing starts with the decisions about this emotional journey to inform scene choices and characters' actions.

An emotional map is a separate document a screenwriter creates that structures the audience's experience. It can be an overview showing each sequence's emotional impact or a detailed document, including a breakdown of every scene. For a screenwriter to utilise an emotional map, they need to understand how a screenplay can 'contain' emotions and be able to apply this knowledge within their stories actively.

In Part Two, the structure of *North by Northwest*'s narrative was examined to illustrate how a cognitive process relates to suspense in a screenplay. This structure also represents a pattern of emotions developed through *fiction identification*. An existing film's emotional patterns could serve as a template or narrative architecture to orchestrate a remake. Hitchcock discusses the importance of being aware of the emotional experience: "As the picture approaches the climax of the tension, everything should begin to move faster. The threads of the plot become tauter and I even change the style of acting, broadening it. The tension is then released into the final physical chase, which must be short and breathtaking, to avoid the error of anti-climax."[54]

An emotional map for a film can also fulfil genre expectations. The remainder of this Practice section will examine what genre is and how *fiction identification* can realise the expectations of genre.

The practice of screenwriting as genre-making

It is Friday night, and you decide to see a movie. You open the website for the local cinema and peruse what's on offer. There are comedies, kids' films, dramas and often horror films. As you study the various titles with their directors and actors, you ask yourself, 'What do I feel like watching?' Each film sells itself as offering a type of experience. Films are marketed as a particular genre. For some films, like the James Bond franchise, your expectations are even more refined: spies, action, some romance, with Bond typically saving the world from an evil villain.

Every film sets up an expectation for the audience, even before a single frame has been screened. For example, unless a movie is marketed otherwise, the audience expects the main character to succeed by the end. A film may buck these trends by offering, for example, a surprise ending where the

The poster for Alfred Hitchcock's The Birds (1963) marketed the film as a horror-thriller and set up clear expectations for the audience.

protagonist dies. However, a screenwriter uses the spectator's expectations when writing this type of ending. Expectations exist in the audience's minds and play an essential role in their cognitive process of constructing the story and developing emotions. A screenwriter needs to be aware of any expectations and should play with them to provide an engaging and original experience.

Genre offers a set of expectations for a viewer, applied throughout a movie. These expectations form a regime of *verisimilitude* dictating what is plausible and believable within the story world. If a character suddenly starts singing, the audience is likely to hypothesise that the film is a musical and anticipate that more singing is likely to produce a recognisable experience. A film may subvert these genre expectations by providing a plot that doesn't fulfil a viewer's hypotheses. This surprise needs to be applied in a way that recognises the subversion for audiences to make sense of and enjoy the new twist to an old formula.

From a screenwriter's perspective, genre is like a contract between the audience and a screenplay. This contract allows a writer to play with the genre's limits and, when subverting the genre, beyond these limits. Most significantly, screenwriting is done with the knowledge of what audiences expect from a particular genre.

Genre is a vital tool for marketing a film and offers a way of screenwriting focused on engaging viewers with particular kinds of experiences. This approach requires an ability to develop the relevant experiences in a screenplay. This Practice section offers a way of fulfilling the promise of a genre for an audience using the knowledge presented in Parts One, Two and Three.

The practice of recognising expectations

The type of movie audience that a film appeals to is the market. Audiences can be diverse and appreciate a variety of genres. For example, someone can be part of the mass, cineplex type of crowd yet still enjoy experimental film festival offerings. Film marketing uses recognisable genres, which are labels associated with a particular experience – for example, comedy, westerns, horror etc. Genre, as a set of film types, creates expectations for an audience.

Film expectations could also be influenced by a star in a movie, a sequel, or an adaptation of another work (whether a novel, play or film). A screenplay can be considered a *product* for a particular market (e.g., a Christian or a kids' movie). Different types of scripts can cater for a variety of film markets. These markets comprise the paying audience who expect a type of experience.

Viewing a screenplay as a product doesn't cheapen or decrease the quality of your writing. It means you are writing for a particular audience, which should always be the case, rather than just writing for yourself. Also, it views your work from the perspective of a producer who has to find the required money to make the film. Most importantly, a producer wants an original and surprising product, not one that is clichéd and boring. When creating your product with an awareness of the audience, being true to yourself allows a uniqueness to permeate your work while sitting within a particular market, however small it may be. To try to manufacture a 'hit' is the quickest road to banal writing.

The difficulty in defining genre

Defining the term genre for a screenwriter helps understand how people think about different experiences and how to fulfil expectations. Knowing how to create genre experiences enables writers to apply the relevant systems to their screenplays. They need to understand why genres exist and how different types come about. Given that the paying audience intuitively knows what genres are, it would seem straightforward to understand what makes this experience. Unfortunately, though genres appear self-explanatory, it is a notoriously difficult term to define.

Genre (from the French 'genre' meaning 'sort, kind') is an easily understood and natural term, while also being difficult to define. We all know comedies are funny, and Westerns have cowboys, but is there a logical system behind all genres, or is each genre category for a screenwriter learnt individually?

Even though genre can be considered cultural and shared knowledge, it is a very fluid concept, which may vary in meaning from person to person. Some stand out by the subjects or themes (e.g. Western, sci-fi), while others by emotions elicited (e.g. comedy, horror). Someone who loves sci-fi films and can recognise sub-genres may have more expectations about what will occur than someone who rarely watches this genre. Films also often combine genres, which may offer a different experience again.

Bordwell and Thompson note: "Most scholars now agree that no genre can be defined in a single hard-and-fast way."[55] Genres can use any system to define a film. To illustrate this point, if we take a short list of genres: Westerns, gangster films, musicals, social dramas, horror films, and historical epics, though they are probably familiar to you, there is not an obvious system for this list. Instead of viewing genre as a static classification, genre is a cultural process of creating new types and consolidating the existing ones.

How genres are established

How does a cultural consensus for genre get established, and what role do the film industry and film critics play? François Truffaut, French critic turned filmmaker, suggests an avenue for understanding the formation of genre:

> Though a screenwriter can use many meters to measure 'success', popularity is the most universally accepted. A critic's analysis of a film's quality, which is based upon subjective critical consensus, could completely ignore a film's social and economic impact. Given the costs of film production, a popular film legitimises a screenwriter's output due to financial returns.[56]

From a genre perspective, this type of success must gain a certain social status. Truffaut added that "when a film achieves certain success, it makes a sociological event, and the question of its quality becomes secondary."[57] Since genre is a social consensus, popularity is an obvious explanation for how new genres are established. A production company may create a marketing name or label for a genre; however, this label wouldn't exist if particular types of experiences weren't already popular.

The effect of genres emerging is a phenomenon known as cycles. Cycles occur when a popular film produces a burst of imitations. *Stagecoach* (1939) resurrected the Western genre, while *The Godfather* (1972) triggered a spate of gangster films. Similarly, *It Happened One Night* (1934) was a hit and was the start of the 'screwball comedies' genre (such as *Bringing up Baby* (1938), *His Girl Friday* (1940), etc.). Modern audiences are less likely to be aware of screwball comedies; however, it was a common term and recognised as a genre in the past. The sword and sandal epics of the 1950s and 60s disappeared until the acclaimed film *Gladiator* (2000) revived the genre, which inspired other filmmakers to take on this type of experience. A new genre springs into life when a new experience becomes culturally recognisable for the first time.

His Girl Friday (1940) is a 'screwball' comedy directed by Howard Hawks. Screwball comedies were popular during the 1930s and 40s.

When audiences interpret a film as a genre, the traits they seek are culturally defined. A screenwriter must be aware of cultural norms to understand how screenplays are marketed.

The practice of subverting genre

Because there is no formal system for what a genre should be, two or more genres are often mixed to create a more compelling yet recognisable hybrid. *An American Werewolf in London* (1981) is a comedy-horror, while *Thelma and Louise* (1991) is a feminist road movie. *Groundhog Day* (1993) is a fantasy and romantic comedy (a mix of comedy and romance).

Often, breaking expectations of an established genre offers a fresh take on an old formula. *Dances with Wolves* (1990) appears as a Western yet breaks the mould by showing the native Indians in a positive light. *Star Wars* (1977) is sci-fi but has an experience more in common with a Western. *Pocahontas* (1995) and *Avatar* (2009) tell the same story with different settings. Audiences ultimately want a recognisable experience with a twist and some level of originality.

A screenwriting solution to genre

When Cook and Bernink state, "while the existence of the major genres is in some ways a self-evident fact, the business of definition and demarcation is less clear-cut. *Description gets tangled up with evaluation*, both of which snag on the problems of *historical change*"; they describe a fundamental problem with defining the term genre.[58] To take a particular genre and analyse it for principal characteristics requires that a body of films be isolated that represent that genre. However, the principal characteristics must be known to isolate these films. As Tudor explains, "We are caught in a cycle that first requires that the films be isolated, for which purpose a criterion is necessary, but the criterion is, in turn, meant to emerge from the empirically established common characteristics of the films."[59] Altman summarises this problem: "To locate each genre in a property or properties of the text itself that's **creating the illusion** that the genre arises directly out of the film, rather than out of texts produced in reaction to the film."[60] Therefore, defining the cultural phenomenon, genre, is purely based on consensus without any homogenous underlying system.

Yet there are shared genre conventions in films, even though "genres are based on a tacit agreement among filmmakers, reviewers, and audiences."[61] Understanding how genres generally came into existence (and were formed) is a very different question to defining a specific type of genre (e.g. a comedy or Western). Therefore, a problem occurs when defining the term genre, which encompasses all kinds, using a single unified system. Subsets of genres may conform to particular systems; for example, thematically, the "wilderness versus civilisation opposition in Westerns and the human/non-human opposition in science fiction."[62]

Significantly for the approach set out in the next chapter, a subset of genres can be defined by the emotion they attempt to elicit in an audience. For example, "romance may try to elicit tears; horror, fear; thrillers, thrills; comedy, laughter."[63] Rather than attempting to define all genres, an alternative approach is to base the classification on a prior system and relate this system to the accepted genres. *Fiction identification* offers a system for explaining how particular emotions develop and create recognisable experiences. The term *archetypical film experiences* denotes a set of universally recognisable emotional experiences. In the next chapter, these experiences will be defined and related to traditional genres, and, most importantly, a writer can create these new categories using techniques outlined in this book.

To summarise:

- A writer creates an *emotional map* for a story to foreground a viewer's emotional journey.

- Genre offers a set of expectations that form a regime of *verisimilitude* dictating what is plausible and believable within the story world.

- Treating a screenplay as a product for consumption by a particular market promotes a writer's awareness of viewer expectations.

- Defining the cultural phenomenon genre is purely based on consensus without any homogenous underlying system.

- As there is no formal system for what a genre should be, two or more genres are often mixed to create a more compelling yet recognisable hybrid.

- *Fiction identification* offers a system for explaining how particular emotions develop and create recognisable experiences.

Chapter Eighteen

Archetypical Film Experiences

Fiction Identification can categorise film experiences, creating an approach for a screenwriter to develop genres. Though this classification may not define all genres existing today, it reflects the significance of emotion and the schema's influence on the genre experience.

Archetypical film experiences (AFE) apply *fiction identification* to create film experiences, identify categories related to genre, and facilitate writing marketable, recognisable emotional journeys. AFE is not a substitute for genre but rather an approach to writing films with particular emotional appeal. For example, AFE don't communicate how to write a superhero film; however, it does define the characteristics of *action* films, which could be extended to the nuances of that particular genre. How AFE relate to a specific genre is for each screenwriter to negotiate.

These *archetype film experiences* are not being defined for a writer to slavishly set out to write a comedy or drama. It is more about providing a tool for creating particular types of experiences. A screenwriter may set out to create a drama but find out the story is best told as a comedy, in which case this writer may want to strengthen the comic elements of the script. Similarly, someone writing a thriller may introduce horror elements and decide that they want the film to be identified as a horror movie.

These categories are not discrete: a screenplay can embody multiple categories simultaneously. I hope *archetypical film experiences* provide an awareness of what makes film audiences respond in a particular way and the know-how to create these experiences. The point of AFE is not to categorise films but to provide tools and a mindset for writing certain film experiences. These film experiences also offer a way of fulfilling audience expectations for a script. When a writer realises they have written a horror film, and the screenplay will be pitched to producers as such (and hopefully, once produced, to an audience), then this writer understands how to strengthen what makes it a 'horror' experience. In short, understanding these archetypical film experiences gives a writer the basic knowledge to fulfil or subvert a genre experience.

Action and Drama

A dramatic question about a man on the run from spies and the law develops an intense emotional experience for the audience because the character's situation is life-threatening. The choice of setting for a story is a strong indicator of whether an *action* or *drama* is being written. The fundamental difference between these experiences is that *action* films have a setting that promotes a life-threatening situation for the main characters, while in the *drama* category, the central conflict is domestic and not life-threatening. In *action* films, the dramatic questions about the characters are heightened by threatening their existence in some way, and therefore, the story is about how they survive in such circumstances. By

Archetypical Film Experiences 178

their nature, life-threatening situations are outer conflict, while the more domestic situations in a *drama* tend to emphasise the inner conflict through the narrative.

Life-threatening scenarios typically have a setting where the protagonist attempts to survive in some environment. Examples include sci-fi (with advanced weapons or unfeeling technology), western (set in a lawless society), disturbed psychologies (where individuals show inconsistent and murderous behaviour), supernatural (consisting of ghosts and other undead), war and crime. These can be considered survival settings that deal with external conflicts involving life-threatening situations where the ultimate failure is death. *Raiders of the Lost Ark* (1981) is set shortly before the Second World War and follows Indiana Jones attempting to find the Ark of the Covenant. Importantly he needs to attain this ark before the Nazis do (his *goal*). This *action* film predominantly uses *shared suspense* as the audience follows Jones through a series of life-threatening situations.

Drama films are set in domestic situations which don't have a life or death scenario. The emotional impact comes from the inner conflict of the main characters and can potentially use any type of suspense. Films with a domestic setting, such as courtroom drama or melodrama, do not typically have life-threatening situations and engage viewers through the internal struggles of the main characters in the story. For example, *All that Heaven Allows* (1955), is written and directed by Douglas Sirk and follows a middle-aged widow who has an affair with her much younger gardener. This film provides distinct social commentary and is set in a small American town where the main threat to the characters is what other people think and say. Films such as *First Blood* (1982) and *Blue Velvet* (1986) take domestic settings but are *action* films because they shift these settings to become a more deadly world (war and psycho-killers, respectively).

The primary emotions in *action* films tend to be based on *shared knowledge* of events with the story's protagonist. In contrast, *thrillers* and *mysteries* apply *dramatic irony* and *suppression suspense* as the central structure for a film.

Thriller and Mystery

Hitchcock contrasted a spectator's response to suspense with mystery. He considered suspense to necessarily involve emotion, while mystery is a "void of emotion."[64] While mystery is concerned with events that took place in the past and generate curiosity, "a sort of intellectual puzzle" without emotional appeal[65], suspense is concerned with the events taking place in the character's present, engaging a spectator with dramatic questions about what will happen next. For Hitchcock, "emotion is an essential ingredient of suspense," while for mystery, it is not.[66] Though a mystery only creates curiosity for audiences, it can be used to set up *suppression suspense*, as shown in Chapter 11.

A mystery in *The 39 Steps* (1935), which runs for the entire film, is 'What are the government secrets being smuggled out of the country?' This mystery hangs over the film, though it has no dramatic purpose for the narrative (i.e. it doesn't set up *suppression suspense*) and is answered in the film's final moments. The term 'MacGuffin' has become a popular Hitchcockian catch-word for describing a central object everyone in a story is after, but ultimately is unimportant to the audience. Hitchcock explained the origins of the word:

> It's called a MacGuffin because the story goes that two men are in an English train, and one says across to the

other, "Excuse me, sir, what is that strange-looking package above your head?"

The man says "Oh that? That's a MacGuffin."

"What's that for? "

"That's for trapping lions in the Scottish highlands."

So the other man says, "But there are no lions in the Scottish highlands."

"Then there's no MacGuffin."[67]

This phenomenon became apparent to Hitchcock while working on *The 39 Steps* (1935) during the early stages of story construction.[68] Hitchcock recalled to Truffaut: "Our original idea was that this MacGuffin should be something big and pictorially striking. ... Anyway, whenever we found ourselves getting terribly involved in this way, we would drop the idea for something very simple", to which Truffaut replied, "In other words, not only is there no need for the MacGuffin to be important or serious, but it's even preferable that it should turn out to be something trivial and absurd as the little tune in *The Lady Vanishes*."[69]

A MacGuffin is a secret, often contained in plans, documents, micro-film, etc., which develops a mystery; however, it doesn't serve any dramatic purpose. The character's actions and the internal struggle keep viewers in their seats, not any explanation or description. Notably, a MacGuffin is not a *goal* or *motive* but tends to explain a *motive* (e.g., uranium being smuggled in *Notorious*, 1946). In *The 39 Steps*, the smuggling of government secrets is generally considered immoral, regardless of the secret. When a viewer finds out in the film's last seconds that the secrets are plans for a silent plane, the only purpose of this information is to resolve any curiosity they have.

Hitchcock argues that his "best MacGuffin, and by that I mean the emptiest, the most nonexistent, and the most absurd, is the one in *North by Northwest*."[70] The movie's screenwriter, Ernest Lehman, admitted, "I have no idea what was on that microfilm, nor did Hitch, and that's what a MacGuffin is."[71]

Thrillers and *mysteries* are distinguishable by the type of suspense a film is structured around. While *action* films are predominantly *shared suspense*, *thrillers* apply *dramatic irony*, while *mystery* films develop emotions around a secret, which sets up *suppression suspense*. Similarly to *action*, *mysteries* and *thrillers* present the protagonist with life-threatening situations that they must combat to achieve their active outer goal.

Halloween (1978) creates a lot of suspense by using a point-of-view camera from the perspective of Michael Myers (a mental patient), allowing viewers to watch him sneak up on the unsuspecting protagonist, Laurie Strode. The film is a *thriller* structured around three sequences that create suspense through *dramatic irony* since the audience is aware of the antagonist, Myers, while the protagonist isn't.

Mystery films set up a secret for the viewers that exist for most of the film. Typically *mystery* films involve a murder, and the audience attempts to solve the question: who is the murderer? This process involves deducing the murderer by inferring a *motive* from the *goal* of killing the victim. Therefore, a writer will often create characters in mysteries where their *motives* are vague or misleading. *Suppression suspense* develops around this mystery because of the potentially life-threatening scenario.

Archetypical Film Experiences

George A. Romero's Night of the Living Dead *(1968) is an independent horror film where seven people are trapped in a farmhouse, under assault by flesh-eating ghouls.*

Bordwell and Thompson suggest that "the horror genre is most recognisable by its intended emotional effect", which "aims to shock, disgust, repel - in short, to horrify."[72] These types of experiences are typically supported by dramatic music, a dark setting and orchestrated using suspense to maximise the emotional engagement with the viewers. For example, a common scenario for a horror film is a haunted house where the audience is made aware of the sinister setting; however, the main characters remain unaware. This situation leads to sequences where the unsuspecting characters are placed in potentially life-threatening events. A horror film can be structured using *shared suspense*, *dramatic irony* or *suppression suspense*. The shock and horror tend to be derived from the visual aspect of horror films using aesthetic emotions, which are processed independently from fiction emotions. Music also plays a crucial role in horror films as it cues the audience for a shock of horror.

Art-House

When the unity for a film experience is thematic, it is categorised as an *art-house* film. The AFE of *art-house* films displays a thematic intent that takes precedence over any dramatic elements of the story. Characters may be performing actions in a scene with *objectives* yet lack overall *goals*, providing film unity. While an *art-house* film can be emotionally moving, its general intent is to narrate a story thematically, providing a film's purpose. The market for an *art-house* film may be small and include film festivals, but it still provides a clear focus and experience for a writer.

The protagonist of a film creates unity through their *goals*. Even in a movie like *The Great Escape* (1963), the multiple protagonists share a *want* (to escape), providing viewers with an apparent unity. If the main character's *goal* doesn't provide unity, that character cannot be considered a protagonist. In these cases, the theme will provide the overarching connection between scenes rather than a *goal*.

Magnolia (1999), written and directed by Paul Thomas Anderson, tells several stories set in the San Fernando Valley in the United States. The main characters in the four stories have clear *goals*, and Anderson creates compelling dramatic situations throughout. The stories are linked in several ways: the location, character relationships with the TV show 'What Do Kids Know?' and even the cross-cutting editing, which merges the stories into a continuous flow. However, the theme of abuse from parents unifies the film into a single experience. Each story examines reconciliation and the forgiveness of past actions by the parents. Even though the characters' journeys provide the emotional foundation for the film, it is the exploration of the theme which makes this a single movie.

The importance of conflicting themes is evident in *Baraka* (1992), a documentary film without characters, a narrative or even a voice-over. However, the movie develops the themes of nature versus technology. The film shows a series of disparate scenes told visually. Viewers naturally search for meaning for how these scenes are connected. Without meaning, the film would lack purpose and be just a series of scenes. *Baraka* sets up thematic conflict, which asks questions about humanity and nature.

For a screenwriter, thematic writing is when characters and situations develop from the ideas being explored. For example, an *art-house* film could be about forgiveness and hope. A theme describes a general overarching word invoking a meaning and perhaps feeling you want the audience to experience. Finding conflicting themes creates engagement for the film. Forgiveness could conflict with hate, ignorance or blame, while hope could conflict with despair, apathy or resignation. There is no right or wrong; however, the type of story can depend on the conflicting pair of themes chosen. A story about forgiveness, which conflicts with hate, has different qualities to forgiveness conflicting with ignorance. The process of defining thematic conflict can be revisited as the characters and story become more evident to the writer, which provides clarity for what the story is about and attempts to communicate.

Comedy

Hitchcock suggested that the root of a viewer's film-going

pleasure comes from a sense of humour:

> ... in producing the movies that I do, I find it would be impossible without a sense of humour. I play with people's emotions, it's true. I know how to prepare them, how to give them a laugh at the right moment, and I know how to make them react by clutching their seats with fear, almost screaming because I know that they will finally go out giggling. ... If you take the average fairground, you will find people paying money to be frightened — the haunted house, for example, where the floorboards move up and down, skeletons pop up, spiders drop down — and it's all done on a basis of humour.[73]

With any discussion of emotional patterns in Hitchcock's narratives, humour plays a vital role in the overall experience for a viewer. Hitchcock stated, "In your serious chase when you have comic relief, it's important that the hero as well as the audience be relieved."[74] He said that "suspense doesn't have any value unless it's balanced by humour."[75] Comedy relieves suspense, allowing the following sequences to build naturally to new climaxes. The director described this process: "I take a dramatic situation up and up to its peak of excitement and then, before it has time to start the downward curve, I introduce comedy to relieve the tension."[76]

Richard Allen suggests the contrast of humour with suspense offers a "broader structuring principle of an entire narrative in Hitchcock's work."[77] Comedy can work with suspense to provide a more complex and ironic experience: black comedy develops "the moment we are aware of the irony that the protagonist's fate is being toyed with, that our emotions are being orchestrated, and our anxiety being exploited."[78] As director John Schlesinger said of Hitchcock,

"I can think of no other director who has combined suspense, irony, and humour into such extraordinary results."[79]

When humour dominates a film's experience using any structure, it becomes a *comedy*. *Comedy* presents an ironic edge to the drama that provides laughter and relief. There are different kinds of humour that a writer can deploy. A classic example of telling a joke is one type, while the visual comedy of Chaplin is another. Though the roots of comedy can be viewed as cultural, there is, however, a sort of comic situation with universal appeal. This situation is a kind of comedy often employed in silent films with greats such as Charlie Chaplin, Buster Keaton and Harold Lloyd. It is a visual type of comedy based on the clown: a central character the audience empathises with yet at the same time laughs at. This type of character provides an endearing and often poignant experience for the audience.

I will introduce the concept of *status* to understand how a character is set up to be a clown and what makes their actions humorous. There are three types of status: social, psychological, and dramatic. Social status concerns where a character lies within society in a story. A king is at the top of the social status, while a beggar is at the bottom. Commonly, a clown is depicted as having a lower social status. Psychological status relates to how a character thinks of him or herself. In the comedy series *Fawlty Towers*, Basil Fawlty is an arrogant character whose psychology is one where he thinks or wants to be better than other characters in the stories. The tramp, played by Charlie Chaplin, is a humble character with a positive, unbreakable attitude towards life. Basil Fawlty and the tramp have conflicting psychological statuses and are examples of clowns whose actions develop humour.

Dramatic status is what a character does rather than what they are. This type of status creates situations that lead to a kind of humour. Throughout a scene, the central character in a conflict will try to obtain a higher *status* than the opposing character(s). Generally, during the 'battle', there is an oscillation between the characters for who obtains the higher status. In this sense, the term *status* is borrowed from Keith Johnstone's definition, which focuses on doing, not a character's state. "Status is a confusing term unless it's understood as something one does. You may be low in social status, but play high, and visa versa."[80] Therefore, status describes the kinds of actions being played by a character and represents who is winning the conflict at a particular point in a sequence.

The changing of a *dramatic status* through actions can develop humour. A king in a story with a high social status generally also has a higher *dramatic status* but could have this status lowered by someone throwing a pie in his face. This lowering of status develops humour. The clown is a character whose actions lower their status or that of others around them, creating comedy. Where the clown is the protagonist, it is desirable to make this character likeable and endearing. Even though Basil Fawlty comes across as a prat (in my opinion), he is still an endearing character, and one may enjoy his antics as we don't dislike him as a character. He always tries to play a high status but ends up as the lowest-status character. Even though the *dramatic status* of a character is not part of the *character schema*, a writer with an awareness of *status* can add another dimension to the unfolding drama on-screen. *Comedy* also may change the effect of the story's villain as our fear for the protagonist is dissipated. A writer needs to understand the type of experiences that they want to create and apply status appropriately.

Archetypical Film Experiences

Charles Chaplin directed, wrote, produced and starred in The Gold Rush *(1925). The Little Tramp acts as a low-status character who leads other characters (like Big Jim McKay shown here) down to his status.*

In Billy Wilder's *Some Like It Hot* (1959), the lead characters dress as women to escape some criminals. This situation develops many ironic comic situations because the audience is always in on the joke (they are men) while the other characters are unaware. The Pink Panther movies follow Detective Clouseau, who acts with high psychological status, yet the reality is his actions are incompetent and constantly have a low *dramatic status*. In the movie *Toy Story*, Buzz Lightyear thinks he is a real space ranger (high social status), but the other toys and the audience know he is just a toy.

A comedy can be set in domestic or life-threatening situations and develop any type of suspense. For example, *Lady Eve* (1941) is a comedy that uses dramatic irony; Jacky

Chan's films are action comedies; while *Young Frankenstein* (1974) and *Abbott and Costello Meet Frankenstein* (1948) are a comedy/horror genre.

Subgenres

The *archetypical film experiences* describe six types of films: action, drama, mystery, thriller, comedy and art-house. These types of experiences can be broken down further into sub-categories by the *character types* (see Chapter 6) narrated in a film. An overall emotional journey is generated by the orchestration of *character types* (e.g. James Bond), manifesting as a network of characters interacting to produce a recognisable experience. *Character types* create an aspect of an experience independent of *archetypical film experiences*. For example, the *character types* represented by the *goal* to prove their innocence identify traits in *The 39 Steps*, *Saboteur* and *North by Northwest*, distinguishing these films from many other of Hitchcock's. The *goal* of 'proving his innocence of a murder' also resonates with other emotional qualities, such as isolation and loneliness due to the double pursuit (i.e. the police and spies) and even a feeling of guilt due to a spectator's association with the protagonist being wrongly accused. The choice of *goals* used with narrative techniques (such as suspense) is a significant determiner of the emotional qualities produced. The fact that *character types* are defined using a schema allows a cognitive approach to understanding an audience's thought process.

Archetypical film experiences provide a pragmatic approach to fulfilling expectations that relate to recognisable genres. It highlights the structure of the overarching experience (i.e. a macro perspective) by focusing on how viewers engage with suspense, setting and status to develop specific emotional affects. A screenwriter needs to be not only aware of a

Archetypical Film Experiences

character's journey but how that journey creates a type of film experience that fulfils an audience's expectations.

Which one comes first: the genre or the story? The answer depends on how a screenwriter wishes to work. Using one of the AFEs to structure a story is a valid process for finding the type of film. There is no right or wrong process, but rather the application of techniques to create the effects you want viewers to experience.

TO SUMMARISE:

- *Archetypical film experiences* describe six categories of films (action, drama, mystery, thriller, comedy and art-house) related to genres.

- *Action* films are told using *shared suspense* and contain life-threatening scenarios where the conflict is external to the protagonist.

- *Dramas* are predominantly inner conflict and tend to be set in domestic settings.

- *Thrillers* apply *dramatic irony* to tell life-and-death tales.

- A secret that develops *suppression suspense* is at the heart of a *mystery* film. A classic example is a 'who dun it' where a murderer needs to be found before he or she strikes again.

- *Comedies* can apply any type of suspense to an ironic comic situation. Of the three types of status (social, psychological, and dramatic), a character lowering their *dramatic status* can create s.

- *Character types* set up a kind of experience that complements *archetypical film experiences*.

My Practice

For the writing of *Doreen's Dead*, I didn't explicitly create an emotional map, though I needed to understand the emotional impact of each scene. This decision was not a purely cognitive process: I needed to feel emotion from each scene when I formulated the character journeys as an outline. I would change it if there wasn't an emotional dimension to one of the scenes (which I could feel).

Generally, the screenplay was formed by asking myself, "Would this be funny if..." which reflects the comic nature of the film I was writing. The initial scene I wrote for *Doreen's Dead* was created this way, and many scenes were included as long as I thought they were funny and engaging. Because I wrote an outline first (after the first scene), I filtered out ideas I thought were not serving the story. By the time I had finished this outline, I felt I knew the characters well enough to start writing individual scenes.

The overall structure of *Doreen's Dead* was determined primarily by the emotional journey I wanted for the audience. At the film's end, I knew I needed a climax that would provide high tension and an exciting ending. At the start of the film, I wanted more humour before the sudden shock of the inciting incident when the audience sees George kill his wife. It was also important that after the inciting incident, the mood became a lot lighter through comedy.

One of the pleasures of writing a black comedy is the interaction and contrast of the comedy and a dark topic (i.e. the tension between relief and drama). The structuring of emotional experiences within the story, I hope, provides a satisfying journey for the audience. It was an emotional compass that helped find an order for the scenes and created a congruent journey for a viewer. In other words, I aimed for the structure to make sense emotionally.

PART FOUR
VISUAL WRITING

Chapter Nineteen

Roles and Responsibilities

"For whom, primarily, do we make films? Whom is it most important to please?"[1] This question was posed to Hitchcock at a Film Society party not long after the opening of *The Lodger* (1927). This kind of searching question about cinema was often asked at the society's regular meetings, which Adrian Brunel organised at his small London flat. These were referred to, jokingly by members, as "Hate Parties" because all of the cinephiles present would "descant on everything [they] didn't like – or even did – in cinema."[2] They were often held after the screening of films, which became the target of their criticism. Regulars included Iris Barry, the film critic of the *Spectator*; Walter Mycroft, an editor and critic of the *Evening Standard* (who would later terrorise Hitchcock as an executive); the up-and-coming filmmaker Ivor Montagu; actor Hugh Miller; sculptor Frank Dobson; and Sidney Bernstein, owner of a chain of cinemas.[3] Even Noel Coward and George Bernard Shaw offered their names for promotional purposes.[4]

There were several possible answers to the question posed above. Ivor Montagu, who was present at this social event, recalled that "the public" would be considered too obvious for the small group waiting on Hitchcock's reply. He also avoided another unsatisfying answer, "the boss", or head of the studio.[5] At that time, everyone in the room was fully aware of the traumas that C. M. Wolf had caused Hitchcock during the making of *The Lodger* (1927), and someone present suggested that "unless the distributor liked and would push the picture, the public might never have a chance to give it a fair box-office reaction, even if you had your own boss's support."[6] Hitchcock sat quietly and shook his head at this suggestion. "Hitch's deeper answer," wrote Montagu, "was that you must make pictures for the press. This, he explained quite frankly, was the reason for 'the Hitchcock touches' – novel shots that the critics would pick out and comment upon."[7] One of these touches was Hitchcock's trademark cameo appearances, a wink to the critics who knew and socialised with Hitchcock in Britain.[8] Hitchcock's answer was initially met with chagrin from some of those present at the 'Hate Party'. He explained: "If you made yourself publicly known as a director – and this you could only do by getting a mention in the press in connection with your directing – this would be the only way you became free to do what you wanted."[9] It was the creative freedom that was most important to Hitchcock. Montagu agreed:

> We all knew this was right. We all knew him well enough to know that while the fame and money of success might be to him a pleasant side-effect, it was not, could not be his primary motive, he lived to make pictures. To make them better was his use for freedom. But we also knew he would never have admitted this, and so he spoke after his manner, drily, sarcastically, cynically, teasingly, and we did not mind. He was the only one of us who might succeed in reaching his objective. We might envy him but we respected him and wished him well.[10]

Hitchcock's answer that night would, in hindsight, appear prophetic; however, his self-promotion and the eventuating 'Hitchcock cult of the personality' wouldn't come to fruition until he set sail for America.[11] In Britain, the Gainsborough publicity department was notoriously ineffectual, and the stars received most of its attention, as with Ivor Novello and *The Lodger* (1927). The publicity director for Gainsborough, Cedric Belfrage, recalled that Hitchcock at the time was "unconcerned when my efforts brought more newspaper space for Novello than for him. The director felt no need for artificial publicity."[12] Hitchcock's appearances in his films numbered only six during his British period, where he only appeared in two successively (*Young and Innocent*, 1937; *The Lady Vanishes*, 1938). Though Hitchcock realised the importance of marketing himself to the public, it was not until Hollywood, where he received valuable publicity lessons from working with David O. Selznick, that he felt a need to publicise himself.[13] In America, Hitchcock found a need to develop public relations to empower himself within the Hollywood studio system. His cameo roles in his films, advertising campaigns, and TV programs in the US (e.g. 'Hitchcock presents' from 1955 to 1962) provided the necessary media to launch himself as a public figure.[14]

In promoting himself in America as the 'master of suspense', he developed a public persona that was centred not only on the kinds of experiences (e.g. thrillers, suspense) and themes (e.g. murder) that his films would explore but also on the 'making of' his films. Over his entire career, he was very willing to share his way of working, as can be seen in Gottlieb's collection of interviews and public speeches, *Hitchcock on Hitchcock*.[15] His reflections on his process were both a generous sharing of the director's methods (invaluable for a book such as this) as well as a kind of proof that Hitchcock was indeed the central creative force behind his films, an idea which harks back to an ideal, the 'one-man picture', he first mentioned in 1927 in Britain.[16]

It was in America, however, that the publicity departments saw the benefits of promoting Hitchcock as the star by showing behind-the-scenes of his films. As early as *Saboteur* in 1942, publicity photos were used that showed not only the images from the film itself but also behind-the-scene shots of Hitchcock and his crew working, as well as photos of sketches used within the production.[17] This kind of material satisfied the public's interest in how Hitchcock was able to create the suspense and thrills experienced in his films and allowed them to marvel at how he *knowingly* produced these effects.

The promotion of Hitchcock as the primary creator of his films is ultimately a myth to promote himself as marketable, which gave him production freedom. An article on 'la politique des auteurs' was published in France in 1957, which would support the Hitchcock myth that the director was the sole creator of a film.[18] The French critics from the film journal Cahiers du Cinema pioneered a school of thought that became known as *auteur* theory, which held that the director of a film is the true author, in an effort to bring motion pictures into the pantheon of the arts.[19] Through the likes of Andrew Sarris,[20] these ideas around film authorship took hold in America. Hitchcock found it easy to embrace this notion of the director as the author. As self-serving as it may appear for Hitchcock, it was an ideal of the director having ultimate control over all creative decisions, which appealed to him. This idea harks back to his term 'one-man picture' and an article on 16 November 1927, which argued: "Film directors live with their pictures while they are being made … just as much as an author's novel."[21]

Auteur theory certainly doesn't offer a balanced view of all the work undertaken on film production, as Philip Dunne attests: "I have no wish to begrudge any director the credit he deserves; I only deplore the fact that the Auteur theory enriches him in prestige while it robs the writer of the credit he has earned."[22] The idea of laying all credit for a film at the feet of the director is misleading. The downplaying of the contribution of the screenwriter was supported by not only the growing acceptance of auteur theory but also the politics of the studio system at the time.[23]

Screenwriter as Author

Author, as a literary term, doesn't apply simply to film production. In theatre, the playwright is considered the author, not the director, because it is regarded as literary material on which the theatre spectacle is based. Film is visual, and the author of the screenplay needs to invent using the visual language of cinema. Auteur theory offers a bold assumption of a film director's role, which ultimately proves to be a half-truth. A film director does have sole creative control during a film production, but in my opinion, can't be considered the sole author.

Not all directors agreed with auteur theory. John Ford likened the role of the director to a pre-planner or structurer: "You don't compose a film on the set. You put a pre-designed composition on film. It is wrong to liken a director to an author. He is more like an architect if he is creative. An architect conceives his plans from given premises — the purpose of the building, its size, its terrain. If he is clever, he can do something within these limitations."[24] Ford sees the actual execution as the point where a film is written. However, a significant amount of 'writing' and execution occurs within the planning stage of a movie for a director to accurately visualise his composition. In later years, Hitchcock became more balanced in his appraisal of Cahiers du Cinema's ideas: "A lot of people embrace the auteur theory. But it's difficult to know what someone means by it. I suppose they mean that the responsibility for the film rests solely on the shoulders of the director. But very often the director is no better than his script."[25]

The idea of the auteur, where a director takes 'ownership' of a film, should be offensive, not only to screenwriters but all creative collaborators. Corliss observed that film directors were essentially "interpretive artists" unless the director also wrote the screenplay.[26] One approach to this problem is to consider the film director and collaborators as serving the screenwriter's vision of the story, and the manifestation of the screenplay by the actors, director, production designer, cinematographer, etc, is an act of interpretation. A central problem for crediting the screenwriter with authorship is that they create a script comprising prose and dialogue. A writer, of course, uses techniques to engage an audience and develop emotions. While a film's engagement occurs through a visual medium, a screenplay's reader generally has to interpret 'between the lines' the tropes and idiosyncrasies of cinema.

When defining the boundaries of authorship, a screenwriter and director's *responsibilities* can be defined as follows: a screenwriter writes a film, while a director provides the interpretation for a movie. In determining writer and director in these terms of responsibility, one needs to be aware of two further issues:

1) The screen credit for the screenwriter and director, etc., for a particular film (usually shown at the end) may not correctly reflect the roles and responsibilities of who actually did the writing and directing. The issue of how a film is

credited does not necessarily reflect who shaped the narrative of a movie.

2) It defines the writer as the author, though there may be other collaborators who deserve credit as co-writers.

Though the responsibility of a screenwriter is linked to the writing process, is it an exaggeration to describe the screenwriter as the sole author of a film, given the jump required from the literary screenplay to the produced film?

The film director Krzysztof Kieślowski's screenwriting partner, Krzysztof Piesiewicz, eloquently described the difficulties of screenwriting when he wrote: "It takes great skill to describe in words the pictures that exemplify pain, joy, despair, hopelessness and love."[27] Because a screenplay makes you laugh, does it follow that when manifested as a film, it will have the same effect on you? Not necessarily, as a movie functions differently from prose literature. Some produced films are overly talk-based, most likely due to the author creating a convincing piece of literature that hasn't been translated visually into a film. It is not simply that characters talking in a film necessarily cause this problem, as dialogue is a vital part of cinema. There is a difference between the experiences of reading a screenplay and watching a movie. An audience's fundamental engagement with each medium is significantly different.

When a writer writes a novel, words elicit emotions, while a screenwriter needs to use words to represent moving images, which then develops emotions. Underlying screenwriting are the principles of cinema and the visual nature of the film form, which provides the challenges (using words) of writing a film that emotionally engages audiences.

In comparing an original screenplay with the transcript

from the completed film, there are potential differences in the structure, how scenes are communicated, and even the characters. If we consider these changes part of the 'screen writing' process, the roles of the director, editor, cast and even cinematographer influence the final version of a screenplay. This attitude allows roles other than a screenwriter to also effect the screenplay and defines a screenplay as a continually evolving document that represents a film through pre-production, production and post-production.

If the responsibility of a screenwriter is to represent a film, then a writer should be aware (to some degree) of the visual direction, sound and editing contained within a screenplay. I will foreground the roles of writer and director to emphasise the cross-over of these roles as they are not distinct and share many concerns about the structure and telling of the story. When a screenwriter takes on the responsibility of directing during the screenwriting of a story, they open up the visual potential of the characters and develop a visual structure as opposed to a literary structure. A process of screenwriting will emerge that I will refer to as a 'writer-director approach,' which differs from what are standard practices for screenwriters. Hitchcock stated he allows his screenwriters to become "more than a writer; he becomes part maker of the picture" because "I ... get him involved in the direction of the picture."[28] Hitchcock was more than just a director, as he also co-wrote and developed material other writers drew inspiration from for their work. He was a writer, in an extended sense, when he created sketches, situations and story outlines, as well as providing unity and vision for the whole film. A *writer-director approach* to screenwriting will demystify Hitchcock's role in screenplay development and illuminate the collaborations that informed his films' scripts.

Steven Maras suggested an alternative way of thinking

about the responsibility of screenwriting. He defines "scripting" as writing in an extended sense: "screen writing can refer to writing not for the screen, but with or on the screen", where writing is linked to other media, not just the page.[29] Examples include art director Oscar Werndorff (who worked on *The 39 Steps*) referring to "writing with light"[30], as well as F. W. Murnau (whom Hitchcock observed working in Germany) referring to the camera as "the director's sketching pencil."[31] As a method, *scripting* highlights how different media can support the process of documenting, planning and creating a film experience.

Part Four presents a fourth way of writing, not restricted to the screenplay format. A screenwriter works visually to represent a film by using different notations to arrive at a visual structure within the literary format of a screenplay. With the fourth way of writing, the process of writing a film, not a script, is enacted. A screenplay doesn't show images; however, a screenwriter can still work with pictures and think visually. This way of working requires a re-thinking of the role and responsibility of a screenwriter. It foregrounds using other media (such as photographs, drawings, designs, plans, etc.) to create a screenplay. This way of writing means it is a screenwriter's responsibility to tell the story visually. *Inside-out* understands a screenplay, written in words, is a representation of a film, written with images that viewers understand through a thought process (which potentially elicits emotions).

A screenwriting process will be examined throughout the Foundation section, which explains the mindset of a writer, and the Practice section, which gives pragmatic techniques for visually manifesting characters. The *Inside-out* approach recognises character as the impetus for the narrative, style, design and music. It is the internal journey that becomes manifested through the story's design. In short, Part Four explains how characters can be visually manifested in a screenplay.

FOUNDATIONS

Chapter Twenty

A Writer-Director Approach

Lewis Herman suggests a screenwriter can write more than the "bare bones" of a film:

> There is nothing to prevent the screenplay writer from "directing and cutting in the script". To yield more and more to producing only the bare bones of a picture, with a master-scene screen-play, is tantamount, for the screen-play writer, to relinquishing his inalienable aesthetic rights. If he is to fulfil all the potentialities of his creativity, he must add the sinews and flesh and surface patinas, so that the finished product is his as he originally created it.[32]

Given that a script communicates to a reader in a fundamentally different way from how a film communicates to a viewer, for a screenplay to represent a film, it must 'contain' a visual structure. However, by its nature, a screenplay promotes the creation of literary structures despite delineating scenes and dialogue from prose descriptions. It is the screenwriter's role to ensure that a story is written in a visual manner, which allows the manifested film to engage, ask relevant questions and move the audience.

The fourth way of writing involves the mindset of a film director, where a screenplay not only represents a film but also embodies the cinematic form. This mindset opens up a screenwriting process to other forms of writing due to the limitations of the screenplay format. The terms 'script' and 'writing' will be redefined to encompass a *writer-director approach*, which uses non-standard notations while developing screenplays. Rather than examining only the prose narratives of his scripts, this Foundation section examines how Hitchcock and his writers planned the visual narrative for his films during the screenwriting phase. It was Evan Hunter (co-writer of *The Birds*, 1963) who first defined Hitchcock as "the writer", "not only as the film's initiator and guide but also as a brilliant 'editor' who would listen to the writer's ideas, add his own, and get the writer to think of narrative, character, dialogue, and point-of-view in visual terms."[33] Screenwriting techniques involving a collaborative process using a variety of notations will be established in this chapter, which can be applied during any screenwriting practice.

Pre-planning

Hugh Stewart recalled how on the first day of filming *The Man Who Knew Too Much* (1934) in June 1934, Hitchcock appeared on-set and made a show of slapping his shooting script down on a desk and announcing to everyone present, "Another picture in the bag!"[34] This statement was the first time he voiced his public credo that all the work was done before the shooting began.[35] In 1937, he explained, "I plan out a script very carefully, hoping to follow it exactly, all the way through, when shooting starts. In fact, this working on the script is the real making of the film, for me. When I've done it, the film is finished already in my mind."[36]

Hitchcock's tendency to make exaggerated claims as a film director has led him to voice questionable statements that became more exaggerated over time. He once said, "I wish I didn't have to shoot the picture. When I've gone through the script and created the picture on paper, for me the creative job is done and the rest is just a bore."[37] Hitchcock even went so far as to sell himself as a master filmmaker by boasting that he never opens the script when shooting, "I never look at the script when I'm shooting. I know it by heart."[38] There is undoubtedly a sense of fun in these statements. Hitchcock was a natural storyteller and known for the anecdotes that he shared at social gatherings and parties. So, it seems this was also the case regarding his reflection on his methods.

Did Hitchcock pre-plan everything before production, as he claimed? From a promotional perspective, the pre-planning of his films was an explanation to support the Hitchcock myth, proof that he made his films before production. In his book *Hitchcock at Work*, Bill Krohn disputed that the director could pre-plan his movies and even went so far as to suggest he lacked a clear filmmaking method.[39] However, Krohn's argument against Hitchcock pre-planning his films is based on exceptions rather than what the majority of evidence suggests. For example, he points to improvisation that occurred during the production of *The Birds*.[40] Bob Burks, Hitchcock's cinematographer on twelve pictures—from *Strangers on a Train* (1951) through to *Marnie* (1964)—recalled that on *The Birds*, Hitchcock was emotional and uneasy because he used improvisation for the first time to determine how the story would be told—i.e. he ventured from his beloved script.[41] Krohn also referred to the fake storyboards that were drawn for the famous crop-dusting sequence in *North by Northwest*.[42]

A Writer-Director Approach

The origins of Hitchcock's screenwriting process can be traced to his silent period when he first started working collaboratively and visually during the writing phase.[43] Hitchcock was a member of the London Film Society, which Adrian Brunel organised. According to Daniel Gritten, Brunel and another member—Andrew Buchanan—upheld the values of silent cinema with the advent of "talkies". This minority of filmmakers, of whom Hitchcock was one, "attempted to forge a specific medium of storytelling based on the primacy of visual movement."[44] Hitchcock's process of *designing* his films moves beyond mapping out events for the plot to include visual aspects of how these events are told.

Screenwriter of *Rear Window* (1954), John Michael Hayes, recalled how Hitchcock thought through every shot in detail: "When we were in the office working on the script, Hitch visualised being on the stage and faced with the problem of blocking every scene. He thought about every shot in advance, so he wouldn't have to sit on the stage and waste everybody's time thinking about what to do."[45] This pre-planning was *the* creative phase in Hitchcock's film productions. For Hitchcock, this also included pre-editing or "cutting" of a film. Being a strong advocate of the montage approach of filmmaking meant that the pre-planning of the relationship between two images, the timing of the "cut" and the overall effect developed through a visual narrative was a primary reason for preplanning a script. Hitchcock made this point during his 1948 lecture to the British Kinematography Society: "… our picture is going to need editing and cutting – and the time for this work is before shooting. The cuts should be made in the script itself before a camera turns and not in the film after the cameras have stopped turning."[46] Art director and long-time collaborator Bob Boyle said that for Hitchcock, "the exciting part was thinking about it. Sitting behind a desk and thinking about a sequence."[47]

On most of his films, Hitchcock did pre-plan in detail down to the individual shots. Gil Taylor, the director of photography on *Frenzy* (1972), said, "Hitch was a 100% real director and the only one we've ever had.... He never looked through my camera, not once. He would arrive on the set and give me a list of 12 shots for the day. Then, as soon as I said I was ready, he would bring all the actors to the set."[48] Using a shot list is not unusual in film production; however, Hitchcock's preparation was exceptionally meticulous, and the planning of every detail before production is central to understanding his philosophy towards screenwriting. Hume Cronyn, an actor who appeared in *Shadow of a Doubt* (1943) and *Lifeboat* (1944), worked with Hitchcock on several screenplays. He recalled, "It was true; I'd seen Hitch suffer tantrums before. He never had them on-set; by the time we got there, the whole film was already shot in his head, down to every cut and camera angle.... But during the film's preparation, he could become very mercurial; his emotional thermometer would soar to over a hundred degrees in enthusiasm, only to plunge below freezing in despair."[49] Cronyn's recollections highlight an intense process the director entered into during the visualisation of his films.

Nevertheless, Hitchcock knew that pre-planning every detail is impossible because there will always be a gap between any scripting method where shots are imagined and the reality of standing on set with the actors. Hitchcock admitted that he pre-plans "ninety per cent" and leaves room for adjustment on a set.[50] However, he did add, "Everything should be ... not just guessed at, not done without reason. It's just like music—it's like composing."[51]

In this discussion, there is a prevailing idea that pre-planning a film is preferable to making on-set decisions. In the US, Hitchcock used this idea of pre-planning to publicise himself as the *author* to take ownership of his movies. "Alfred Hitchcock" and "the master of suspense" were and are marketable entities because the public expects a particular kind of experience and quality from his films. One clear advantage of pre-planning is that it affords the writer, director, and production crew *time* to think and develop compelling ideas and ways of telling a story for an audience. The writing/pre-production phase provides a personal, more intimate space to create and play with ideas. Hitchcock involved all the production heads in this 'writing' phase. Hence, during production, every element—i.e. cinematography, sound, music, acting—came together smoothly to render their combined vision of a film. Due to the expense of film production, this kind of space is typically not available during the shooting of a movie. John Michael Hayes likewise saw the consequences of visualising the film during the "writing" stage when he said, "He didn't shoot coverage the way other directors did."[52]

Raubicheck and Srebnick concluded that Hitchcock used many different kinds of notations to represent what he wanted to shoot on set. Examining *Psycho* they concluded that his:

> ... process was actually a combination of various approaches to the "decoupage" (the shot-by-shot progression of the film): some scenes were broken down shot-by-shot in the final script (usually ones with little dialogue), some were storyboarded in conjunction with the cinematographer—and some were devised during the shooting process, though the director may have already had many of these "new" shots more or less clear in his mind before the filming began.[53]

Preplanning shots is standard procedure during the

preproduction phase of filmmaking, which occurs after a screenplay is finalised. However, Hitchcock's visualisation during screenwriting influenced the structure and narration of the storytelling.

A *writer-director approach* to screenwriting represents a scripting process where the division between the actual screenwriting and pre-production visualisation is blurred. As will become apparent, Hitchcock encouraged a phase of development where the creation of a film's narrative occurred in parallel with specific visual decisions.

Hitchcock's screenwriting practices challenge basic assumptions in today's film industry, raising fundamental questions about what a screenwriter does. For example, do screenwriters have to use words in developing a story, or are other media just as valid for telling or creating a film story? Are screenwriting and pre-production separate production phases? Is a treatment "primarily a selling document to market yourself and your product"?[54] How and why Hitchcock worked in a particular way can be understood by his method of collaboration.

> To summarise:
>
> • Because a screenwriter's role is writing a film, not a script, a screenplay should encompass all aspects of a film's production.
>
> • A *writer-director approach* to screenwriting encourages writers to visualise and 'cut' in their screenplays.

Chapter Twenty-one

Collective Vision

Writing a film in the form of a screenplay (i.e. prose text and dialogue) provides a problematic terrain to navigate for a screenwriter because it functions differently for a reader when compared to a film viewer's experience. Even if the same narrative exists in different media, they will not necessarily work the same for an audience – think of the difference in experience between reading a novel and watching a film. How different media function in divergent ways for an audience is relevant to understanding the difficulty in defining a narrative in prose for a visual medium such as film. Understanding how this issue of diverging media when developing a film's narrative influences a creative screenwriting process is crucial for 'opening up' a story to a cinematic form.

Steven Maras highlights an "object problem" by suggesting that either a screenplay or a film can be viewed as the object or goal of screenwriting.[55] The experience of reading a screenplay (which can, for example, be easily 'paused' at any moment for reflection) is very different from viewing a film, which has been manifested with actors, production design, etc. This difference sets up a complex context to describe how to write a screenplay that is required to function visually like a film. A screenwriter develops a representation of a film using prose and dialogue, which potentially can emotionally move audiences when rendered in a cinematic form.

Because Maras suggests the object of screenwriting can be viewed as either the page or the screen, he questions whether a script is "the final product of the screenwriting process or just one aspect of the filmmaking process?"[56] The 'object problem' creates a "separation of conception and execution in film production, forcing particular approaches to practice and creativity."[57] This separation of conception and execution leads to the screenwriters and production crew working separately as two distinct phases in film production, which is "institutionalised by dividing production into stages (pre-production, shooting, post-production)."[58]

Hitchcock was aware of this separation in film production and visually pre-planned his films during the conception phase, which combined writing and pre-production as a single process. Hence, *scripting*, in Hitchcock's case, was writing with images, sketching, notes, production design, etc., to develop his screenplays to represent a visual narrative.

Hitchcock's use of different forms offers a creative alternative for understanding the problem of separation between concept and execution. Storyboarding requires execution by an artist, as does production design and other forms of *scripting*. Production also becomes an interplay of conception and execution as plans change due to the reality of locations and production situations. The separation of conception and execution, as a screenplay and film, now seems inadequate to describe the actual process occurring during film-making. There is a constant exchange between the acts of conception and execution in the writing process, leading to *separation* being the space between different notations—e.g. storyboard and script. Separation becomes the point of creation where problems are solved, and new ideas emerge as concepts are manifested in new forms.

A medium is 'the material or form used by an artist, composer, or writer'.[59] The act of screenwriting necessitates the transformation from one medium to another. When the art maker is in the act of creation, the 'in-between' state isn't rendered within either media. Therefore, writers are dealing with a *liminal* state between media, where retelling of the source text takes place; the story gets reformed, retold, and re-rendered; and other possible versions of this story can result.

The word 'liminal' is derived from "the Latin limen or 'threshold', occupying a position on or on both sides of a boundary."[60] There are three possible states between media during a writing process: pre-liminal, liminal, and post-liminal. Utilising the three states of liminality focuses on the importance of the 'in-between' or creative space in the process of developing a screenplay:

- Pre-liminal: interpreting the story through a particular source medium.

- Liminal: developing, editing, and re-creating the story with an awareness of conventions in the source and destination media.

- Post-liminal: rendering the newly imagined story into a different destination medium.

The challenges of screenwriting lie between the media

within this liminal state where a creative and inspired process melds with knowledge of how source and destination media function. Liminal states can represent the macro processes of developing a novel into a screenplay or a screenplay into a film. Many types of media can exist as a small part of a creative process (e.g. notes, outlines, photographs, etc.) and play a significant role in a process of screenwriting. Therefore, liminal states can also be viewed as micro processes, allowing for representations within a screenwriter's development process, where all the supporting media used to create a screenplay interact, promoting many different types of creative, liminal spaces to occur.

Curtis emphasised the importance of word and image within Hitchcock's working process, notably how their interaction provided a means to represent the qualities of the story within a cinematic context. The constant movement—between word and image, written script and storyboard—enabled a creative process restricted by neither word nor image, allowing a more expansive and open practice. The written word highlights the essential specifics of a visual telling, where "the ambiguous image sometimes requires words to stabilise its meaning."[61] Even though storyboards are often not definitive, "words cannot compete with the efficiency of the image in conveying information quickly and precisely."[62] The interplay between word and image leads to a creative conversation that generates the final representation of a film.

This *writer-director approach* to screenwriting combined the writing with words and the 'writing' with images to form a single process that encouraged visually-oriented film narratives. Hitchcock was thinking beyond the confines of the screenplay format to a more visual, material conception in planning a film. Designing sets, liaising with the production team, pre-casting and storyboarding were developed while writing the screenplay, indicating a looser division between the script and production than a traditional approach would use. Hitchcock was interested in seeing how the written material would be manifested—thus, in developing a strong visual sense of what the picture would look like. His process of writing his screenplays offers insight into a practice aware of the constraints and limitations of different media and formats used in development.

Two important points come out of this discussion on Hitchcock's working process: firstly, the process of developing a visual representation for a script was necessary for Hitchcock to create an actual written screenplay that represents the cinematic form; secondly, Hitchcock used a multimodal approach, based on how media could represent different aspects of a film, all connected through his visual thinking. Hitchcock's collaborations aim to support a shared experience, ultimately communicated to an audience. This creative exchange leads to an agreed interpretation of the story and a level of certainty in his visual designs before moving into production.

Creative collaborations

When Hitchcock crossed the Atlantic to the US, he was confronted with a system that privileged the screenplay format during the development phase of film-making. Due to the "worldwide imitation of Hollywood's successful mode of production"[63], the screenplay format has achieved a special status in film-making, both as a creative form to design a film on paper and as a document for production. Hitchcock was highly adaptive and changed his working practices in the US to integrate the screenplay format into an earlier phase of his screenwriting practices. Hitchcock can be seen as an anomaly within the Hollywood system because he incorporated the screenplay format to fit into the US film industry's way of working; however, he applied a collaborative, multi-method/multi-modal approach to screenwriting to visualise his films. Hitchcock did not see the writing process as a lone endeavour in which the writer finished the script and handed it to the director to render for the screen. Throughout development, Hitchcock was very inclusive and collaborative in his approach to creating his screen material and often included the production crew in the early stages of writing.

A process of collaboration centres on communication. Talking, writing, and drawing about a film's idea creates a space for possibilities to occur. Hitchcock enjoyed working with very talented collaborators who specialised in communicating through particular forms—such as costume, lighting, music, dialogue, the body, voice, visual art, locations, and set design. All of these media can communicate a feeling, and for Hitchcock, it served the overall purpose of the drama. While Curtis focused on Hitchcock's use of words and images, a 'writing' process can be extended to include all departments and their relevant forms used for communicating.

Hitchcock's collaborations aim to support a shared experience and meaning, ultimately communicated to an audience. This creative exchange leads to an agreed interpretation of the story and a level of certainty in his visual designs before moving into production. Clarity of intention for his visual narratives played a crucial role in the effectiveness of the rendered images in the completed film. Hitchcock's filmmaking is notably efficient in storytelling, reflecting clarity gained through developing the story using multiple collaborators. This clarity of intention within his films provides the foundation for his movies to emotionally move audiences across cultures.

Hitchcock employed a collaborative process with each of the project's designated writers: "I do not let the writer go off on his own and just write a script that I will interpret. I stay involved with him and get him involved in the direction of the picture. So he becomes more than a writer; he becomes part maker of the picture."[64] The time spent meeting with Hitchcock discussing the story and the months of writing and rewriting indicates the influence the director and screenwriter had in shaping the screenplays for Hitchcock's films. These screenwriters, as collaborators, were crucial determinants of the films' artistic quality.[65] They usually wrote all of the dialogue for each draft. They often developed the characterisations and scenes that Hitchcock would pass judgment on and decide what would be in the final film.[66]

Art directors, cinematographers, composers, and costume designers also played a significant part in the development of Hitchcock's screenplays. John Michael Hayes recalled that when he started writing the opening sequences for *The Man Who Knew Too Much* (1956), Hitchcock met with the arts, costume, and music departments, all working on their contributions to the film.[67] Hayes's recollections show how Hitchcock formed his vision for a movie: he juxtaposed different elements so that their interaction influenced each other. This process is a form of synthesis, where a narrative forms with all the other elements—visual, music, design, actors, etc.—crucial to a film's ability to communicate effectively to an audience.

Sharing the concept of a film with designers, cameramen, and other technical people provided valuable feedback to Hitchcock; thus, he could refine his thinking about the best way to tell a story cinematically. Hitchcock's method of working "established the much-discussed pattern of creating a film in his mind before the script was written, and his imaginative conception of the film was itself the product of this kind of collaboration."[68] His process fostered an environment where constructive criticism from his colleagues and himself lent depth and richness to the development of his stories. This feedback was crucial, as Hitchcock indicated when he said the "most valuable thing in creating a film is criticism at the time."[69] Collaboration promotes a group consensus and clarity of intention for an art form meant for a worldwide audience.[70] David Sterritt summed up Hitchcock's relationship with his writers and production team when he wrote, "As much as any filmmaker ever has, he channelled the talent of his collaborators and the temper of his times into coherent narrative/aesthetic patterns dictated by his own deepest instincts."[71]

Collective vision

According to Hitchcock, the reason for these different types of writing was to help visualise a story, in which his screenplays needed to be "conceived and brought to birth directly in visual terms."[72] Hitchcock was "more workman than shaman, and with the consistent collaboration of his department heads, he is visualising and re-visualising his films, synthesising disparate thoughts, and incorporating suggestions into the project's original idea."[73] Joseph Stephano recollected how Hitchcock would work when visualising: "I would try out scenes [that I thought up] on him, and he would react. But he was visualising the movie, making it in his head ... and if he could see how you could cut from this sequence to that sequence or scene, he would be happy."[74]

The term "collective vision" describes Hitchcock's process

Collective Vision

of developing his screenplays.[75] "Collective" refers to Hitchcock's openness to collaborate with his colleagues and share the responsibility for the vision of each film. Hitchcock's form of collaboration not only ensured that his vision for a movie was fulfilled but also that his production team used their skills and talent to improve on his ideas. "Vision" refers to *seeing* a film in the planning stage, usually through visual representation. On the film set, the production team executed the collective vision they built during the planning phase.[76]

The collaboration of *seeing* describes a particular open relationship Hitchcock shared with his production team and actors. With collective vision, seeing "could not take place without collaboration."[77] Schmenner also described seeing as "the task of showing rather than telling the audience", connecting Hitchcock's process of visualising with a central tenet of drama.[78] This way of working dispenses with the great Hitchcock myth that placed the director as the sole author and creator of his films.

Scott Curtis' chapter in the book *Casting a Shadow* discussed the forms Hitchcock used to visualise his movies. He identified six ways that Hitchcock represented his films during their development stage.[79] They include wardrobe sketches, production and set design drawings, architectural plans, camera placement sketches, storyboards, and sketches by the director. Significantly, these visual forms fed back into the story writing process, finding an equivalency in words when represented in the screenplay.

Curtis does not mention the ability of text-based formats to describe visual details for a shot. Hitchcock used treatments, outlines, and scene breakdowns to develop stories, capturing moods and expressing important graphic detail. While making *The Man Who Knew Too Much* (1956), Hitchcock also adjusted his script based on photographs of locations that Coleman and Ericsson had surveyed during pre-production.[80] These kinds of pictures helped Hitchcock to make creative decisions about where to shoot his film and provided crucial visual information for building a story world.

Walter Wanger, the producer of *Foreign Correspondent* (1940)—Hitchcock's second film in the US—talked about the script Hitchcock used during production: "dialogue corrections on one side; sketches showing the composition scenes, medium shots and close-ups on the other ... In addition to having art directors prepare many sketches showing lights, shades and suggested composition. Hitchcock will make as many as three hundred quick pencil sketches of his own to show the crew just how he wants scenes to look."[81] Wanger also emphasised Hitchcock's reliance on his script during shooting, noting that it was "dog-eared from many references before the first week's shooting is finished."[82]

Hitchcock's ultimate aim as a filmmaker was to develop emotional experiences for an audience. Rather than using Maras' material conception of an object as the product of the screenwriting process (i.e. either page or screen), I am considering the aim and purpose of the screenwriting process. Therefore, Hitchcock aims to create an emotional experience, not a screenplay or film. Issues surrounding the representation of a movie still provide challenges for a filmmaker because intermediate forms (e.g. screenplay, film) only allude to an audience's experience. In addition, locating the writer's goal as an interpreted experience for both the script and film asks more questions about the reading of these different media. This perspective situates the completed film as part of a process for an audience rather than the ultimate goal of a movie. This process implies a second kind of separation between the media—both script and film—and their respective audiences. The separation between media and audience is reflected in the cognitive approach used in Parts One, Two and Three. However, there are advantages to a perspective focusing on the audience's experience with different media. A filmmaker can allow various media and forms in the writing process to function differently, knowing how this representation can help inform the film. For example, a storyboard image may elicit a feeling central to a film's purpose and influence art direction, framing, and other elements within the completed film. The aim of this storyboard is not only tied to a film's narrative but the potential effect of this image on its audience.

Does an awareness of the separation between conception and execution, as suggested by Steven Maras, provide an answer to the issue of authorship for a film? If the boundaries between screenwriting, pre-production, production and post-production are removed, and writing is applied in an extended sense (e.g. where a cinematographer is 'writing' with light), then all creative personnel in a film's production can claim some level of authorship. This interpretation of the author does not distinguish between the acts of creating and interpreting. The *Inside-out* approach has championed a cognitive perspective of character, which is the primary indicator for the audience's experience, and I believe is the ultimate responsibility of a film's author. Therefore, a film's author is not tied to any medium (e.g. a screenplay) but has a role to get viewers to think in particular ways. The creative talents working on a film support a predefined experience set out by the author. This definition of film authorship does open up the possibility of the director (who may modify the narrative), actor (who can improvise dialogue and action) and editor (who may re-order scenes during post-production) being given part authorship of a film. Defining the authors for a particular movie requires carefully considering who has input into the ultimate cognitive journey of the audience. This definition of author, however, does place the screenwriter as the central force behind any film and suggests their responsibility goes beyond the written word and requires the visualisation of character actions. In short, a screenwriter writes a movie, not a screenplay.

To summarise:

• The creative act is liminal and takes place between media. A writer can use different media to facilitate finding, exploring and structuring a film story.

• Collaborating with other creative people on a screenplay centres on communication and allows for a richer and clearer story experience.

• Using various types of media facilitates different aspects of cinema to be realised. Because a screenwriter is responsible for writing a film, he or she must find ways to visualise the story.

• The ultimate aim of screenwriting is to create a cognitive and emotional experience for a viewer.

Chapter Twenty-two

Subjective Treatment

Screenwriter and theorist Jean-Claude Carrière emphasises the importance of montage when he writes, "Only by playing with the montage and the succession of the frames, we're able to penetrate the mentality and the secret of the character."[83] Eisenstein wrote that each image or shot in a film should communicate a clear idea: "Do not concern yourself with complex stylistic questions; do not struggle with graphic problems of the shots. Set up shots so that the meaning of the inner-shot action is clear. A shot should be like a line in a poem: self-contained, with its idea crystal clear."[84] Playwright and filmmaker David Mamet summarises the Russian formalists' theory of montage as follows: "understanding of the technique of juxtaposition of uninflected images to create in the mind of the viewer the progression of the story."[85] Mamet uses the term "unaffected image" to describe the clarity of intention that Eisenstein is referring to.[86] Hitchcock expressed the primary principle behind montage when he said that an "individual piece is nothing. But a combination of them creates an idea,"[87] This effect is a synergy between shots that creates a visual structure where the interaction of images combines to produce a total effect greater than the sum of the individual shots.[88]

Hitchcock used visual means to create situations that arouse the audience's emotion, and "that emotion arises from the way in which the story unfolds, from the way in which sequences are juxtaposed."[89] An interviewer suggested that with *Psycho* (1960), Hitchcock directed the audience more than the actors. Hitchcock's response: "Yes. It's using pure cinema to cause the audience to emote. It was done by visual means designed in every possible way for an audience."[90] Often, in interviews, Hitchcock talked about the importance of emotion through visual means. For example, he said, "Cinema is essentially emotion. It is pieces of film joined together that create an idea, which in turn creates an emotion in the mind of the audience. Not through spoken words, but through the visuals. It's a visual medium. And montage is the main thing. All moviemaking is pure montage."[91]

Montage, the French word for "assembly", was theorised by the three pioneering Russian film directors in the 1920s: Vsevolod Pudovkin, Sergei Eisenstein and Dziga Vertov. Pudovkin believed that shots were like bricks to be joined together to build a sequence, while Eisenstein suggested that an optimal effect is gained when shots do not fit together, creating a jolt for the viewer. Vertov disagreed with both theorists, "favouring a cinema-eye approach to recording and shaping documentary reality."[92] Hitchcock reiterated Eisenstein's ideas when he said, "You can do anything you want with montage. Cinema is simply pieces of film put together in a manner that creates ideas and emotions."[93]

The fourth way of writing requires a mindset of visualising a character's intentions in a film. Therefore, the images onscreen must directly represent intentions and add to a viewer's cognitive and emotional journey. This representation can go beyond simply showing actions by applying a form of montage called *subjective treatment* to

Subjective Treatment

communicate character intentions to the viewers' minds.

Subjective treatment is a term coined by Hitchcock to describe a particular technique of editing images together to communicate a character's intention simply and effectively. It utilises a character's view through a subjective camera and, according to Hitchcock, "is the way that you get a mental process going by use of the visual."[94] With his films, he invites the audience into the character's internal world and never permits a purely omniscient narration of action like a documentary.[95] He saw subjective treatment as a way of using the cinematic form effectively and was opposed to telling stories objectively: "Subjective treatment. As against the objective. You see, the objective is the stage. Is the theatre. We are the audience looking at the people on the stage. We aren't with them, we aren't getting any viewpoint you see."[96]

Hitchcock also referred to this technique as "negative acting" because it "enabled him to create emotion by intercutting close-ups with shots of what the character sees" rather than relying on the actor's performance.[97] This technique is often called the 'Kuleshov effect' because Russian director Lev Kuleshov first realised it. Hitchcock explained the experiment that Kuleshov conducted:

> You see a close-up of Russian actor Ivan Mosjoukine. This is immediately followed by a shot of a dead baby. Back to Mosjoukine again and you read compassion on his face. Then you take away the dead baby and you show a plate of soup, and now when you go back to Mosjoukine, he looks hungry. Yet in both cases, they used the same shot of the actor; his face was exactly the same.[98]

Hitchcock referred to a basic rhythm in the design of these shots that are a "structured series of triads—one, the subject; two, what the subject sees; and three, the subject's reaction."[99] He explained the potential of cinema using this technique: "You see, you can make him look at one thing, look at another—without his speaking, you can show his mind at work, comparing things—any way you run there's complete freedom. It's limitless, I would say, the power of cutting and the assembly of the images."[100]

The Kuleshov effect represents the triad of a close-up of a character's face, a POV (point-of-view) shot, and a reaction close-up (an objective shot of an emotional expression on the character's face). A POV shot refers to a camera shot showing what the character is seeing. This effect visually indicates a character's intention by associating the character with an intentional object through their gaze, as a person's eye line is a clear indicator of points of interest. A character's scene *objective* has an internal origin and represents some desire for this intentional object. This object may be what is wanted or alternatively obstructs the character's *objective*, developing conflict.

According to Hitchcock, the reaction shot within subjective treatment is focused on the actor's face, allowing the "visual image to register [a] thought."[101] In his films, Hitchcock wanted actors with a "mobility of the face" specifically for using this technique.[102] The actor's expression should communicate to an audience what the character thinks of the object in the internally focalised (POV) shot, which shows an 'unaffected image'. Hitchcock emphasised this point when recounting a conversation with Kim Novak on the set of *Vertigo* (1958):

> You have got a lot of expression on your face. [I] don't want any of it. I only want on your face what we want to tell to the audience—what you are thinking.... If

> you put a lot of redundant expressions on your face, it's like taking a piece of paper and scribbling all over it—full of scribble, the whole piece of paper. You want to write a sentence for somebody to read. They can't read it—too much scribble on the face. Much easier to read if the piece of paper is blank. That's what your face ought to be when we need the expression.[103]

The purpose of the reaction shot in subjective treatment is not to necessarily affect the audience (i.e. an *aesthetic emotion*) but to communicate the character's thinking about the visually shown object in the POV (internally focalised) shot. The character's response in the third part of the triad offers an emotional indicator of the situation.

A significant point Noël Carroll makes about point-of-view editing is that it appeals to a global audience because it is "keyed to biologically rooted and transcultural distributed features of perception."[104] The universality of an image is central to understanding how a film appeals across cultures.

Understanding Subjective Treatment

To help examine the role of subjective treatment in the narration of characters, the concept of *focalisation* will be introduced to distinguish the various types of shots in a film. Gerard Genette first coined *focalisation*, while Edward Branigan applied this concept to film narration.[105] From Branigan's theory of agents and levels of narration, Elsaesser and Buckland constructed a typology of four types of shots:

- objective shots, which are not focused around the consciousness of any character within the film's narrative world and are therefore omniscient;

- externally focalised shots are shots focused or focalised around a character's awareness of diegetic events, such as over-the-shoulder shots and therefore represent their awareness;

- internally focalised shots (surface) represent a character's visual experience of seeing events, as in point-of-view shots (that is, optical POV shots; when I call a shot a POV shot in the following analysis, I mean an internally focalised shot, surface);

- internally focalised shots (depth) represent a character's internal events, such as dreams and hallucinations.[106]

Edward Branigan described the basic structure of point-of-view editing involving the juxtaposition of two shots: a "point/glance" shot of a character looking and a "point/object" of what this character sees.[107] Therefore, he simplifies the triad structure by removing the reaction shot in the Kuleshov effect. Even though this new structure can be narrated using several variations, importantly, the point/object shot indicates to a spectator an 'intentional object' for a character's intention. Fundamentally, a character's eye line serves as a strong indicator of points of interest for a viewer. Carroll states that a character's face (in the "point/glance" shot) may help in "determining a character's emotional state" but will generally provide "redundant, reinforcing information" about what this person is feeling.[108] Any emotion shown on a face in a point/glance shot is *aesthetic emotion*, while the character's intentional state—indicated by its context within the story—results in *fiction emotion* (i.e. the effect of *fiction identification*).

Noël Carroll makes a crucial point when he writes, "The point-of-view structure is a *representation*. We do not take it to be the automatisation of an act of seeing with one's own eyes, but rather, we recognise it as a representation of perception" (my italics).[109] Since a fictional character does not exist, this "representation" using a POV structure is a way to narrate a character's thinking in a particular situation. Carroll argues that a connection exists between an "intentional object" in the point/object shot and the cause of emotion.[110] An intentional object can have one of two relationships with a character's scene *objective*: either it could be his aim (e.g. hero's love interest, gold) or oppose this *objective* by creating an obstacle (e.g. a terrifying monster). By acknowledging that an audience is aware of the character's scene *objective* in relation to an intentional object, their emotional response takes on a specificity not explained by individual actions or events shown.

Importantly, for a screenwriter, the correlation between a character in a story and the audience's emotions is *not* communicated through showing the character's emotions. It would be a misunderstanding of *fiction identification* to assume that the emotions portrayed by an actor correlate directly to the audience's emotional response; instead, the "emotional life of the actor/character comes primarily from actions that are wedded to *wants* that are contextualised by—embedded in—dynamic relationships and circumstance" (my italics).[111] Emotion is evoked through a process and not imitation—i.e. because an actor feels an emotion, it does not mean the audience will feel the same.

Practically, subjective treatment takes on other forms in films beyond Kuleshov's and Branigan's definitions. These alternatives communicate a character's intention towards an object necessary in developing *fiction emotions*. This alternative pattern for subjective treatment is composed of two elements: an object of intention and an associated character reaction, which indicates to a viewer a positive or negative relationship between the character's scene *objective* and the intentional object. A character's *objective* is always a 'doable' activity focused on achieving something, typically through the associated object. This object is an external entity from the character, either a person or a thing, e.g. money, villain, etc.

The first alternative is when a single shot of the intentional object is an externally focalised shot, which approximates to a character's gaze. The first or third parts of Kuleshov's triad will be redundant if a film shows an image as an externally focalised shot with the character in-frame. The externally focalised shot, in this case, is often from beside or over the character's shoulder and shows a character looking at the intentional object. For example in *Harry Potter and the Chamber of Secrets* (2002), Hagrid tells Harry and Ron to "follow the spiders" (1 hour 37 minutes). A minute later is a single shot of Harry seeing small spiders on the wall which very simply indicates the intentional object (the spiders) and Harry noticing them.

Another alternative comes through the juxtaposition of image and sound. Sound can communicate a particular emotion (a reaction) from a subject (e.g. screaming). When the image shown is an internally focalised (or POV) shot with emotional sound, a character's intention is communicated. An example in the first sequence of *The 39 Steps* has the sound of the music hall's audience laughing while showing their point-of-view of Mr. Memory on stage. Another example in the same scene is when an audience member heckles the master of ceremony introducing Mr Memory. The intentional objects are the men onstage, with the emotional response being the audience laughing at them. The subjective treatment of this example occurs in a single shot, with the laughter representing the crowd's reaction.

Examples of Subjective Treatment

Charade (1963) is a romantic comedy mystery film starring Cary Grant and Audrey Hepburn. Two examples of how director Stanley Donen used subjective treatment to narrate the story and build suspense will be examined.

Cary Grant's character changes *identity* five times during the film providing several plot twists. Later in the film (1 hour 39 minutes), Audrey Hepburn's character, Reggie, believes Grant is the villain Carlson Dyle and is being chased through a subway. Grant's character corners Reggie on a train.

This first shot shows Grant looking straight at the camera, setting up a "point/glance" shot. It also puts the viewer in the position of Reggie being 'looked at' and even suggests this shot could be Reggie's own POV looking back.

The next shot is from Grant's POV, clearly indicating his intentional object, Reggie. She is also looking straight back at Grant and the camera (putting the viewer in his position).

Reggie's POV shot is the next 'cut' in the film. This is clearly a POV because the previous shot showed Reggie looking at Grant's character. Again Grant is looking straight at the camera creating a visual sense of being in Reggie's

Subjective Treatment

position. Having characters look at the camera creates a sense of visually identifying with the character being looked at. This type of identification is a different process from *fiction identification* outlined in this book.

The tighter framing of the next image indicates its a "point/glance" shot from Reggie's perspective. The tension between the characters has been narrated using subjective treatment which represents the characters conflicting intentions.

The final image is an over-the-shoulder shot of Reggie in

the distance and Grant's character looking. It breaks the narrating of character's looking at the camera and is a single-image example of subjective treatment, as the glance and object are shown in the same shot.

The second example from *Charade* takes place at the end of the film (1 hour 48 minutes). It shows how subjective treatment can narrate a decision making process of a character.

Grant's character is trying to stop the real Carlson Dyle from shooting Reggie. Reggie runs into an empty theatre and hides in a prompt box. This first image shows Grant under the theatre's stage looking up and represents a glance shot.

Subjective Treatment

The next shot indicates that he is looking at the underside of the stage revealing a series of trap doors. Each trap door is clearly marked with a letter and a number.

Then the scene cuts to Grant's character looking down with interest.

He is looking at handles which activate the trapdoors. The next couple of shots repeat Grant's association of the handles and the trapdoors. He then walks over to the handles.

While standing next to the handles which activate the trapdoors, Grant's attention is clearly upward to the stage. Sound plays an important role in this sequence as Dyle's footsteps are even louder than the accompanying music.

Dyle realises Reggie is in the prompt box and slowly walks over to her. The majority of this shot focuses on Dyle's feet and the outline of the trapdoors are clearly marked. The exaggeration of sound of his footsteps during this shot relates directly to Grant's character. This is what he is focusing on under the stage.

Another shot of the trapdoors from Grant's perspective with the continuing sound of footsteps clearly indicate what he is thinking.

All types of subjective treatment communicate an intention to a spectator for one or more characters within a scene. It helps narrate the internal world of the protagonist through cinematic means and develops a relationship between the story's characters and the audience. For a screenwriter, subjective treatment offers a dramatic approach to telling stories as images and sounds can be written as prose descriptions. Therefore the cinematic narration of a screen story should be initiated by a screenwriter, which provides a structure primarily based on visual actions and sounds.

TO SUMMARISE:

• Montage is an essential technique for developing emotions through the juxtaposition of shots. Screenwriters can imply montage using prose descriptions, thereby creating visual narration.

• The Kuleshov effect illustrates that montage can show a character's internal response without using *aesthetic emotions* (i.e. images alone do not need to create feeling).

• Subjective treatment is the application of the Kuleshov effect using a variety of patterns and can include sound.

PRACTICE

Chapter Twenty-three

Writing a Hitchcock Film

Hitchcock conceived his screenplays in highly visual terms.[112] He described his collaboration process for visualising his films as follows:

> We went into a hustle and slowly from discussions, arguments, random suggestions, casual, desultory talk, and furious intellectual quarrels as to what such and such a character in such and such a situation would or would not do, the scenario began to take shape. The difficulty of writing a motion picture story is to make things not only logical but visual. You had got to be able to see why someone does this, see why someone goes there. It is no use telling people: they have got to SEE.[113]

The director's films present a "wide variety of cinematic devices ... [including] subjective treatment, camera, mise-en-scène, montage, sound, and transitional devices."[114] Though the screenplay format is intermedial (as it only alludes to the form it represents), Sainsbury argued that film has the potential to become autonomous of the screenplay and liberate itself from meaning predominantly determined by dialogue.¹¹⁵ Pier Paolo Pasolini highlighted the "technique" of the screenplay without which a script would represent a traditional piece of literature.¹¹⁶ How was Hitchcock able to liberate the literary screenplay to represent cinema? This chapter establishes Hitchcock's core practices used during the screenwriting phase of his films.

When searching for detailed accounts of Hitchcock describing his screenwriting process, one speech stands out as the clearest and most complete explanation. At a talk delivered at Columbia University on 30 March 1939, having newly arrived in the US, Hitchcock summarised the practice he had developed during his British period, which would become the basis for his work in the US film industry. This description of his process is divided into four developmental stages.

Stage 1

> When I am given a subject, probably a book, play, or an original, I like to see it on one sheet of foolscap. That is to say, have the story, in its barest bones, just laid out on a sheet of foolscap paper.... Now you do not have to write down very much, maybe just that a man meets a woman at a certain place, and something else happens. In the briefest possible way, this thing should be laid out on a piece of paper.¹¹⁷

This early writing period is vital for setting the foundations for a project and communicating to the screenwriter what Hitchcock wanted the audience to experience. Hitchcock insisted that his films be "unified by 'one idea' that is developed through a series of climactic scenes, each one surpassing its predecessor in its capacity to stir the audience's emotions."¹¹⁸ This story idea became his guide for developing a film version. Hitchcock would take the basic idea from this guiding material and create a plot line that would function as cinema.[119] Hitchcock once described what he wanted the spectators to take away from a film: "A member of the audience sees [a] film, and … after seeing it goes home and tells his wife about it. She wants to know what it was like, so he tells her that it was about a man who met a girl—and whatever he tells his wife is what you should have had on that piece of paper in the very beginning. That is the complete cycle that I like to aim for, as far as possible, and that is the process one works on in designing a motion picture script."[120] A one-page synopsis may be a similar type of document used in today's film industry, though notably, Hitchcock is referring to a writing process as opposed to a format that appeals to producers or even funding bodies.

Stage 2

Hitchcock's second stage emphasised a visual approach to telling his stories:

> From that, of course, we start to build the treatment of that story—the characterisations, the narrative, and even the detail, until we have probably a hundred pages of complete narrative without dialogue. But I do not mean narrative in the abstract, the practical side of what is going to appear on the screen. I always try to avoid having in the treatment anything that is not really visual. In dialogue, we indicate it by saying, for instance, that the man goes to the sideboard, pours himself out a drink, and tells the woman that something or other is going to happen to him. We indicate it in the treatment, and this is very full and practically the complete film on paper, in terms of

> action and movement. The particular reason why I prefer to do that is because I don't like to kid myself. I do not like to let myself think that there is more in it than there really is, because I believe that one should build up. That is why I prefer to start with the broad narrative, and then from that, develop into this full treatment—but purely cinematic treatment. You must not go into anything like a short story, or anything descriptive, like "with half-strangled cries" and that sort of thing. You just want the actual movement or action, and then indicate the dialogue.[121]

Through this second stage, Hitchcock focused on a "complete narrative without dialogue"—showing "what is going to appear on the screen", which typically took the form of a prose treatment.[122] Hitchcock discussed his use of a treatment as a working document: "To me, a picture must be planned on paper.... My method is very simple. I work out a treatment with my screenwriter. In order to do this, you've got to have a visual sense."[123] This statement suggests the director's preference for a prose treatment had advantages over other notations—e.g. a screenplay—for visualising a film.

According to Azlant, by the 1910s, the term "scenario" was being used to refer to a highly detailed synopsis, like the modern treatment.[124] Hitchcock worked for the British branch of the Famous Players-Lasky Corporation in the early 1920s, which commonly used synopses and treatments to develop its silent films.[125] Hitchcock's suggestion to use a treatment format in creating a film's story was standard practice at the time. Today, a treatment is "primarily a selling document to market yourself and your product."[126] Significantly, the *Inside-out* approach views notations—such as a treatment or synopsis—from a creative screenwriting perspective by emphasising practices rather than any production requirements.

Stage 3

The third stage in Hitchcock's speech is when the actual dialogue is written from the treatment:

> Dialogue is the next phase, and that depends on how much time one has. Once the story line is decided upon and one has a dialogue writer in, one usually deals with it sequence by sequence. After the first sequence, we call the dialogue writer in and hand it to him. While he has the first sequence, we start the first sequence in treatment, and build up as we go along.[127]

Hitchcock's third stage emphasises the separation of visuals from dialogue. He views the dialogue as supporting visual storytelling and, therefore, treats it as a discrete stage in his screenwriting process. This separation was a usual filmmaking practice during Hitchcock's British years. Sydney Howard and Jesse L. Lasky (both in 1937) described the procedure for the development of a 'screen play'.[128] Howard says the treatment moves to drafts of the "picture script", where dialogue is added. Lasky similarly states that after a treatment, as "many as two or three writers may now be put on the screenplay, one an expert in construction, one a specialist in the particular type of dialogue required, and perhaps a continuity writer or one qualified in camera shots and camera transitions."[129]

Stage 4

> Finally we have a whole pile of material which is

> treatment, and a whole pile of material which is dialogue. From that stage we go into the shooting script, by assembling the dialogue and the treatment. We keep building it even further, and adding to it. We do not do this in a mechanical way, but put up as many ideas as we possibly can. Finally we have a shooting script of the whole thing. Then we cast it, shoot it, and finally it is shown.[130]

This final stage is preparation for shooting and, therefore, requires careful consideration of the production's requirements. Screenwriter Ben Hecht, who worked with Hitchcock to write *Notorious*, noted how he synchronised the dialogue to camera angles and camera positions that the director planned for the film's crucial dramatic moments.[131] A screenplay is finally constructed as a production document (i.e. a shooting script). Though shooting scripts have a standard format in film production, Hitchcock suggests not using a screenplay format for the actual development process of a script. Therefore, Hitchcock's screenwriting is divorced from the screenplay format, and the shooting script only exists for the production phase of filmmaking.

To summarise:

- Using different media during screenwriting can support visual storytelling. Media can also separate aspects of a film, such as images and dialogue, clarifying how these elements affect the story.

- Starting with a one-page guide for a story helps encapsulate the overall experience a screenwriter is attempting to create.

- Working with a treatment where dialogue is only indicated is an example of using a medium to support visual storytelling.

- Production documents are derived from a screenwriting process, and not vice versa.

Chapter Twenty-four

Case Study of *Meet John Doe*

The last chapter approached screenwriting from a macro-level view, while this chapter examines a micro-level perspective of a Frank Capra film by analysing individual character intentions. This chapter aims to show how montage can influence a screenwriter's thinking when narrating a scene. An analysis connects the *character schema* and montage with a practical example and illustrates how character actions—verbal and physical—and subjective treatment relate to each character's intentions.

Meet John Doe (1941) was directed and produced by Frank Capra, written by Robert Riskin and based on the story by Robert Presnell. Riskin and Capra made eight films together, including classics like *Mr. Deeds Goes to Town* (1936) and *It Happened One Night* (1934), which the director won an Oscar for. During their working relationship, tension grew between them as Riskin felt Capra was taking partial credit for his stories. One account reported that Riskin brandished 120 blank pages and told Capra to "put the famous Capra touch on that!"[132] Riskin's screenplay for *Meet John Doe* includes shot directions such as close up, medium shot and full shot, which illustrates how this writer thought visually about the story.

The collaboration between Riskin and Capra shows a mastery of the medium in how they constructed the final scene in the film. I suggest that you see the entire movie before reading this analysis to get an appreciation for the film as well as clearly understand the context of this scene. The relationship between the *character schema* and shots is presented in the analysis to move beyond the actual narration in *Meet John Doe* to illustrate how the character intentions, or *enscription*, provide foundations for identification and can inform a screenwriting practice. The development of actions and montage that communicate *enscription* relates to a viewer's mental representation of the characters and, consequently, a viewer's emotions. It also provides an approach to a practice of screenwriting that emphasises a writer's mindset.

The film's protagonist, John Willoughby (aka John Doe), has two conflicting goals: his active *want* is to find his life's purpose, while his passive *need* is to find romantic love. At the beginning of this scene, John's *strategy* is to revive the John Doe movement by sacrificing his own life and thereby providing a purpose by keeping this ideal alive. This scene's *objective* is to jump off a building and asks a dramatic question: will John kill himself? Ann enters this scene to stop John from jumping and expresses her love for him. Her active *goal* in the film is to succeed in her job as a reporter while her passive *goal* is to find romantic love. The villain is D. B. Norton, who throughout the film is searching for power. It is only near the end where he appears to have a conscious, and attempts to stop John from killing himself. Capra and Riskin celebrate common decency and even the most corrupt characters in the story have redeeming qualities.

Case Study of Meet John Doe

This analysis will show how a scene from *Meet John Doe* communicates character intentions to an audience by investigating the composition of shots. It breaks the film into units of character intention to describe what a character is trying to achieve at every moment in the scene. These intentions form a structure of meaning parallel to the character's actions and montage shown onscreen. A highlight of the film's narration is the clarity with which the director has told the story, leading to an unambiguous depiction of character intentions.

The process of identification requires that a film *aligns* viewers with a particular character. This scene illustrates how a spectator's *alignment* with the characters can be primarily done visually through shots. The alternating of *alignment* in the scene causes a dramatic shift in the storytelling and develops a clear structure. Even though a screenwriter cannot visually represent *alignment* in a traditional screenplay format, a script should indicate it via the description. Central to a writer's decision-making is asking from which character's perspective should a scene be told.

The tables below list each shot and character intention from the scene. The columns of the table indicate the shot number starting from when John enters the scene; the character whose intention is portrayed; how the intention is communicated (either 'show', 'tell', or 'subjective treatment'); the focalisation of the shot; the intentional object; and the intention as a verb (e.g. 'to avoid').

Near the end of the movie, D. B. Norton and his cronies have preemptively gone to the rooftop of a high-rise building in an attempt to stop John from killing himself. When they arrive no-one is there and are just about to leave when John enters the scene. The first section of this scene distances spectators from John's perspective and therefore *aligns* with Norton. The analysis starts as John walks onto the terrace at 2 hours, 2 minutes and 53 seconds.

Aligning with D. B. Norton

The first shot shows John Willoughby walking towards a railing on the terrace of a high-rise building. John has been pretending to be John Doe, who represents an ideal, for most of the film. It has been set up through other characters that John wants to take his own life for the John Doe movement.

Shot No.	Portray	Narrate	Focal Type	Intent. Object	Intention
1	John	Show	Obj. Shot	Edge of building	To walk

Case Study of Meet John Doe

The camera angle moves from the high-angle view in shot 1 to a view that characters in the scene might experience and connects with the next shot of Norton looking on.

Shot No.	Portray	Narrate	Focal Type	Intent. Object	Intention
2	Norton	Subj. treatmt	External focal.	John	To observe

Norton is watching John. Viewers are initially *aligned* with Norton, as this section is visually told from his perspective. The effect of narrating Norton's character intentions engages viewers because they conflict with John's intentions.

Shot No.	Portray	Narrate	Focal Type	Intent. Object	Intention
3	Norton	Subj. treatmt	Obj. Shot	John	To observe

A single shot can communicate intentions for multiple characters. Shot 4 has been set up from Norton's perspective, but also represent two intentions from John. The first part of the shot shows John looking over the railing creating anticipation, while the second part reveals a letter.

Shot No.	Portray	Narrate	Focal Type	Intent. Object	Intention
4	Norton	Subj. treatmt	External focal.	John	To observe
4a	John	Show	Obj. Shot	Street below	To look

Aligning with John

The role of John's letter is to tell the world why he is jumping off the building. His *motive* is altruistic. He wants to reinstate the John Doe movement for the sake of other people. This *motive* is crucial for the audience's experience when engaging with him attempting suicide.

Shot No.	Portray	Narrate	Focal Type	Intent. Object	Intention
4b	John	Subj. treatmt	Obj. Shot	Letter	To consider

Shot 5 is the letter from John's POV making shot 4b a setup for subjective treatment.

Shot No.	Portray	Narrate	Focal Type	Intent. Object	Intention
5	John	Subj. treatmt	Internal focal.	Letter	To consider

John puts the letter away in his pocket and returns to the main *objective* of the scene, to kill himself. In the background, Norton and his crew are watching on.

Shot No.	Portray	Narrate	Focal Type	Intent. Object	Intention
6	John	Show	Obj. Shot	Street below	To prepare

Shot 7 is a medium close-up of John (a tighter shot to show his reactions). He looks upwards to the heavens.

Shot No.	Portray	Narrate	Focal Type	Intent. Object	Intention
7	John	Show	Obj. Shot	Up (to heaven)	To prepare

Aligning with D. B. Norton

The next shot returns to Norton who is watching what John is doing. The *alignment* is temporarily now with Norton.

Shot No.	Portray	Narrate	Focal Type	Intent. Object	Intention
8	Norton	Subj. treatmt	Obj. Shot	John	To observe

Shot 9 shows John continuing to ready himself to jump.

Shot No.	Portray	Narrate	Focal Type	Intent. Object	Intention
9	Norton	Subj. treatmt	External focal.	John	To observe

Shot 10 shifts to an internalised POV shot from Norton. Norton speaks to John for the first time in the scene, making John aware he is not alone. This visual choice of using an internalised POV shot supports Norton's decision to take action against John jumping.

Shot No.	Portray	Narrate	Focal Type	Intent. Object	Intention
10a	Norton	Subj. treatmt	Internal focal.	John	To speak

John turns towards the speaker, to see who is there. This sets up a glance shot for John.

Shot No.	Portray	Narrate	Focal Type	Intent. Object	Intention
10b	John	Subj. treatmt	Obj. Shot	Norton	To react

Shot 11 serves to visually communicate intentions for both John and Norton. For John, he is looking to see who was speaking. For Norton, it shows his clear intention to stop John. Shots where both characters are looking at each other can often indicate points of conflicting intentions and therefore are engaging for viewers.

Shot No.	Portray	Narrate	Focal Type	Intent. Object	Intention
11	John	Subj. treatmt	Internal focal.	Norton	To look
11	Norton	Subj. treatmt	Obj. Shot	John	To reveal himself

A wider POV shot of John standing near the railing emphasises the fear Norton has of John jumping. This shot being wider is significant as it focuses viewer of Norton's perspective.

Shot No.	Portray	Narrate	Focal Type	Intent. Object	Intention
12 14	Norton	Subj. treatmt	Internal focal.	John	To look

Shots 13 and 15 show Norton moving slowly towards John as he tries to convince him not to jump.

Shot No.	Portray	Narrate	Focal Type	Intent. Object	Intention
13 15	Norton	Subj. treatmt	Obj. Shot	John	To convince

Aligning with John

A medium close-up of John shifts the viewer's attention back to John's perspective. Viewers are now *aligning* with John.

Shot No.	Portray	Narrate	Focal Type	Intent. Object	Intention
16	John	Subj. treatmt	Obj. Shot	Norton	To consider

John's silence leads Norton to look at his colleague. He is wondering what John is thinking.

Shot No.	Portray	Narrate	Focal Type	Intent. Object	Intention
17	John	Subj. treatmt	External focal.	Norton	To consider

The silence is broken when John explains that he has mailed a letter about his motive for jumping.

Shot No.	Portray	Narrate	Focal Type	Intent. Object	Intention
18	John	Subj. treatmt	Obj. Shot	Norton	To explain

Norton moves even closer to John, as he tells him to "forget this foolishness."

Shot No.	Portray	Narrate	Focal Type	Intent. Object	Intention
19	John	Subj. treatmt	External focal.	Norton	To convince

John tells Norton to stop approaching or he will "go overboard with me".

Shot No.	Portray	Narrate	Focal Type	Intent. Object	Intention
20	John	Subj. treatmt	Obj. Shot	Norton	To threaten

Norton is shocked and steps back.

Shot No.	Portray	Narrate	Focal Type	Intent. Object	Intention
21	John	Subj. treatmt	External focal.	Norton	To watch

John explain that the John Does movement will be reborn.

Shot No.	Portray	Narrate	Focal Type	Intent. Object	Intention
22	John	Subj. treatmt	Obj. Shot	Norton	To explain

Case Study of Meet John Doe   268

Norton just watches on as John is getting ready to jump.

Shot No.	Portray	Narrate	Focal Type	Intent. Object	Intention
23	John	Subj. treatmt	External focal.	Norton	To watch

John begins to turn towards the railing and tells Norton to "take a good look."

Shot No.	Portray	Narrate	Focal Type	Intent. Object	Intention
24	John	Subj. treatmt	Obj. Shot	Norton	To prepare

Norton and his crew move forwards towards John in anticipation.

Shot No.	Portray	Narrate	Focal Type	Intent. Object	Intention
25a	John	Subj. treatmt	External focal.	Norton	To watch

Case Study of Meet John Doe   270

Norton hears another person at the entrance.

Shot No.	Portray	Narrate	Focal Type	Intent. Object	Intention
25b	Norton	Show	Obj. Shot	Unknown	To look

Suddenly, Ann screams "John" and enters the scene.

Shot No.	Portray	Narrate	Focal Type	Intent. Object	Intention
26	John	Subj. treatmt	External focal.	Ann	To notice

A screenwriter should develop a visual structure in their scripts with a clear focus on character *alignment*. Writing with a mindset of visualising each character's intentions, either through actions or subjective treatment, creates a cinematic experience for an audience. The use of dialogue should add another dimension to a visual telling. Dialogue can be more efficient as a character can explain in several sentences what would take multiple scenes to show. Ultimately this decision is an artistic choice as there are many ways to narrate a scene.

To summarise:

• A screenwriter using prose descriptions can narrate actions and subjective treatment, creating a cinematic experience (as opposed to a literary experience).

Chapter Twenty-five

Finding Images

This chapter closes my discussion on visual writing by offering some practical techniques for how to utilise different media as well as the importance of a visual setting when narrating a film.

The practice of visually telling a story

It is necessary to differentiate between the process of developing a screenplay, a screenplay's form as a production document and the completed film as a manifestation of a script. Because a screenplay represents a film doesn't mean all aspects of a produced film can necessarily be written 'in' a screenplay. The characteristics of any medium can encourage or hinder the process of transforming a story between forms. The shared traits of a screenplay with a film – such as narrative, dialogue and character journeys – support a cinematic representation. However, it is aspects of cinema and script that are not shared that create problems when writing using a screenplay format. These exclusive traits can have a significant effect on how a script functions as a film for an audience.

There are many types of media that a writer can use to enable the visualising of a screenplay. Which medium is used depends on how a screenwriter wishes to work. For example, someone with a graphic design background may prefer to draw relevant images, while someone else with a theatre background may prefer to 'stage' a scene by blocking out character and camera movements using a floor plan of the setting where the action takes place.

Importantly, when the development process is complete, translate the story into a standard screenplay format. Industry standards for a screenplay are not flexible: any screenplay passed on to a producer or funding body must be in a Master-Scene screenplay format. Any other format generally will not be accepted or considered. This point is a global reality of the screen industry, and therefore, as a final step, the visualisation of a story needs to be transcribed to the standard format. The extra work in visualising the story, however, will remain in the transcription to a screenplay, which will suggest the narration of the characters. Any further iterations of the script or other changes will require moving between the different formats to capture the visual representation needed.

The practice of writing a dramatic setting

Developing a visual setting can heighten a character's journey for the audience. Scenes of Monument Valley from John Ford's Westerns create a sense of isolating the protagonist in a desert environment and, when framed as a wide shot, show how insignificant the characters are in contrast to nature. A visual setting makes real the world of conflict, whether that is a film noir set in the back streets of Chicago or a futuristic setting ominously showing the dangers of technology. Baz Luhrmann in *Strictly Ballroom* (1992) shows the glitzy world of competitive ballroom dancing. This superficial setting elevates the drama by reinforcing the dream world that the central characters hold dear.

A visual setting re-enforces the genre of a film and, therefore, the expectations that viewers have. While showing a protagonist wielding a gun offers the potential for conflict, setting the protagonist in a desperate land where only the strongest survive raises the expectations and engages the audience. Visual settings also help to develop the central themes and conflict in a story; for example, *Bicycle Thieves* (1948) visually shows a city where many are poor and struggling financially. This situation is exemplified in the scene where Antonio wants to sell his linen to feed his son; however, at the pawnbroker, there are mountains of sheets that other people have sold.

The practice of developing a visual setting

Robert Mitchum understood the importance of cinema in developing a visual world when he contrasted it to theatre:

> Everything [in film] is real … except me, my character. That's fake. So you have to use the audience's belief in the setting and the props to make the character real. Onstage [in theatre], it's just the reverse. The setting and props are fake.[133]

The visual setting for a screenplay is often made up of visual references from different sources, including other films. These specific references are called iconography, where images have an inherent meaning. For example, a ten-gallon hat is synonymous with the Western genre and implies an association with this type of experience. However, Westerns aren't popular because actors wear ten-gallon hats but because they are set in an exciting, lawless land where wild outlaws and the native Indians play the antagonists to 'civilisation'.

Even though iconography doesn't directly relate to *fiction identification*, it provides a great tool to develop layers of meaning within a screenplay. A great example is shown in *Doctor Zhivago* (1965) when Lara and Zhivago separate after working together at a makeshift hospital (1 hour 23 minutes). A dejected Zhivago slowly walks through an empty room. A vase of sunflowers that are losing their leaves is highlighted by the lighting, which serves as a metaphor for Lara and Zhivago's relationship. This potent image was either written by Robert Bolt in the screenplay or added by David Lean during pre-production. A prose description of images has the advantage of highlighting what aspects of an image are essential for telling a story. Working visually while writing a script enables a screenwriter to find innovative approaches to developing ideas in the audience's minds.

Visualising the setting is fundamental for creating a cinematic experience. In-depth research of a particular period and watching as many relevant films as possible can provide great inspiration for visualising a setting. The ideas contained in a location will deepen the themes and meaning of the entire movie.

A checklist for the practice of visual writing

Research how relevant genre films are visually told.

What tropes are recognisable in each relevant genre? Can any of these tropes be subverted? Are there inspiring images from genre films that can be indirectly referenced? How does the genre use images to create different moods?

Finding Images

Decide on a specific setting and research this setting.

Build a story world by being specific about its setting. These details develops believability, depth and help visualise locations. The types and quality of images described in a screenplay can be crucial in strengthening the drama and themes explored. Researching how a real-world environment (e.g. the Chicago criminal underworld of the 1920s) came into being can suggest characterisations during the writing process. Understanding a setting is about appreciating the culture within an environment, which feeds directly into each character's behaviour and expectations. A real-world, historical setting can inspire a fantasy film by borrowing tropes and cultural norms.

Find relevant pictures for characters.

Viewers will judge a character's appearance. Finding visual attributes to a character is an effective and efficient means of giving them depth. Again, be specific, as it can become significant later in the story-making process. For example, if a character always carries a lighter for his cigars, it allows this object to become important later in the story when he sets something alight.

Visualise using alternative media.

Use a variety of forms of notations when creating a story world. Even a calendar of events can be better than writing events down in order, as it visually shows the time in between significant scenes. Human beings are visual, and writing using different media enriches any writing process.

To summarise:

- For production purposes, a script using a Master-Scene screenplay format needs to be created.

- The setting for a story contains a lot of visual information, which can strengthen character journeys and the themes explored.

- What characters look like, how they dress, and the make-up and hair add another dimension to who they are.

- Researching film genres or historical periods is an excellent source of inspiration for visual details and character ideas.

My practice of applying Hitchcock's screenwriting process

With another of my screenwriting projects, I set out to write a film remake of *The 39 Steps* using Hitchcock's stages as outlined in his Columbia University speech (see Chapter 23). Integral to the DNA of an innocent man-on-the-run genre is a foreign conspiracy, where forces from abroad attempt to undermine national security. I chose the British nuclear testing programme as the conspiracy for my story, which occurred in Australia between 1952 and 1963 because the British lied to the Australian public about the safety of the tests. This film will not preach against the government's clear lack of safety for radiation contamination but rather let the story show the gravity of what occurred in central Australia.

An audience should enjoy an emotional journey but with powerful questions about how the British and Australian governments conducted these nuclear tests.

Due to limited resources, my screenwriting project did not have access to colleagues to draw prototype images, designs etc.; therefore, Hitchcock's emphasis on collaboration was not supported. Nevertheless, I would still follow the director's process as much as possible, focusing on developing a potential viewer's cognitive understanding of the character through a visual narrative.

My screenwriting applied the four stages of Hitchcock's practices to develop my remake of *The 39 Steps*. My first stage established the schemas, themes, and historical background as the foundations for the story. This stage is equivalent to Hitchcock's first stage in his Columbia speech when he said, "When I am given a subject, probably a book, play, or an original, I like to see it on one sheet of foolscap."[134] Because the historical background was the subject on which my screenplay was based, it was necessary to research historical accounts.

At the time, Britain felt the need to develop nuclear weapons due to the perceived communist threat from the Soviet Union (USSR). Nuclear weapons were seen as providing security against the USSR and its allies. This attitude led to the proliferation of atomic weapons, and at the height of the Cold War in 1958, a total of 116 nuclear bombs were exploded around the world. The reason for Britain conducting its nuclear programme was partly due to the US not trusting Britain with any atomic knowledge because British scientists and intelligence officers had a history of being Soviet agents. The Australian Secret Service, ASIO, also had its fair share of Soviet infiltrators who leaked vital information from the 1950s through to the 1970s.

Real historical people inspired characters and their motivations and provided a solid starting point for the creative practice. These individuals will be divided into two groups, antagonists and aids, to differentiate their roles within the story (see Appendix 2 for detailed descriptions of the characters).

Like Hitchcock's approach in *North by Northwest*, three dramatic situations provided a starting point for this story. In my case, I used real historical situations from the British nuclear testing, from which I constructed a narrative. Three key events were:

- The protagonist meets Jack Tunny, the prospector who discovered radioactive rain while mining in outback Australia.

- The hero finds the Aboriginal community that was decimated by the "black cloud", which was the result of testing from Maralinga.

- Servicemen were required to fly into the mushroom cloud of a nuclear explosion to monitor levels of radiation. The protagonist will board one of these planes just before it takes off. This situation suggests that the protagonist will travel to Maralinga and witness a bomb explosion.

It was clear early on that the general shape of the narrative would be based on locations and see the protagonist start at Sydney, move to the outback, then Adelaide and on to Maralinga.

Hitchcock described his screenwriters as story

constructionists because they would take his suggestions for particular scenes and fashion an entire film narrative. For the construction of this story, I used a prose treatment form to emphasise the visual elements, as Hitchcock suggested: "I always try to avoid having in the treatment anything that is not really visual. You just want the actual movement or action, and then indicate the dialogue."[135] This stage was about finding the story by linking historical events and a plot created using individual character behaviour related to their schemas. The complete treatment I wrote can be seen in Appendix 2.

Hitchcock's explanation of stage three highlights how the dialogue was developed independently from the narrative. In a similar vein to Hitchcock's approach, a separate phase focused on creating dialogue after a treatment was completed. Developing dialogue deepened the story's characterisation and resulted in the final script.

Chapter Twenty-six

Conclusion

Due to the popularity of the auteur theory in the late 1950s and early 60s and their consequent reassessment of the director's work, it was argued that Hitchcock started to believe his own press, that he alone was the reason for his film's success, both commercially and critically. Screenwriting legend William Goldman said that "Hitchcock had become encased in praise and had himself become the man who knew too much."[1] Whether this was the reason for Hitchcock's slow decline as a film director (after *Psycho*, 1960), as Devanshu Mehta suggests[2], Hitchcock started experimenting for the first time with improvisation in *The Birds* (1963). He confessed to Truffaut that:

> "I began to improvise. For instance, the scene of the outside attack on the house by birds was done spontaneously, right on the set. I'd almost never done anything like that before, but I made up my mind and quickly designed the movements of the people inside the room."[3]

Hitchcock's improvising with the actors represents a fifth way of screenwriting, where parts of the story are developed

Conclusion

in collaboration with the actors. Filmmaker Mike Leigh has become renowned for 'writing' with his actors to create a story for films such as *Secrets & Lies* (1996) and *Naked* (1993).

There are other ways of screenwriting that have not been mentioned in this book. However, the four modes of writing offer the necessary tools for any screenwriter. Crucially, all four ways must be applied to create a screenplay that is original, emotionally engaging and visually represented. Neglecting any of these aspects will result in a screen idea not fulfilling its potential as a film.

Often, screenwriting manuals advocate a particular formula or structure for creating an engaging screenplay. This approach presents a blueprint for a writer to apply to projects and, therefore, presents a prescriptive strategy for writing. A step-by-step guide attempting to capture a process also offers a very prescribed way to write. My point is not to say that prescriptive approaches can't be valuable for influencing writing decisions. However, any guiding strategy for constructing a new work must be applied with knowledge of the underlying principles governing the art form. Screenwriting is an organic process where a writer understands film principles and uses techniques to find clarity for their story in a visual medium. Finding your method is essential, as an appropriate process relating to an established methods inevitably will emerge through the practice of screenwriting. A screenwriter needs to discover their process of working through experience, reading different types of literature (including prescriptive guides), and critically watching films that will challenge and influence their writing process.

The four ways of screenwriting is not a prescriptive

approach to developing a script. Many methods can be applied using these four ways of writing. Any screenwriting method is prescriptive and outlines a systematic procedure for creating a screenplay. Each way of writing has discussed principles (outlined in the foundation chapters) and techniques for applying these principles (presented in the practice chapters). While a technique focuses on a specific task, a method details a more general approach to screenwriting. Methods are generally based on rules (i.e. "You must do it this way.") which are typically ordered to accomplish an outcome. Business theorist and engineer Harrington Emerson stated:

> "As to methods there may be a million and then some, but principles are few. The man who grasps principles can successfully select his own methods. The man who tries methods, ignoring principles, is sure to have trouble."[4]

If the four ways of writing are a framework for thinking about and performing screenwriting, then the *Inside-out* approach is a strategy for developing screenplays. *Inside-out* focuses on understanding a story's characters' inner worlds and letting this knowledge manifest itself as a narrative. It does not dictate any specific methods or procedures but rather emphasises how characters and their inner journeys can find expression in all aspects of a film. It is a way of working where the foundations of a screenplay are the characterisations and situations that show the audience the psychological depth of those characters.

The process of *becoming* a screenwriter is one of working out how to write. As every person is unique, so is their screenwriting process. While principles are universal, methods are personal, and there is no one correct way to write. Everyone must find their process, which is an approach to working that produces the best representation of *their* experiences. The act of screenwriting is to communicate experiences using film. Screenwriting is a process of representing this experience.

A screenwriter is someone who writes at least half an hour every day. Writing in the mornings, when I am mentally fresh, is my most productive time. Setting up a daily routine is an effective way to keep engaged with a project and, when applied over months, provides the time to fully contemplate and complete your screenplays.

Finding strong ideas takes work. Screenwriters need to be constantly searching for screen characters and situations because if you are not looking, you won't find them. The best ideas tend to connect to something deep inside the writer and create an immediate emotional response. An idea goes beyond the cognitive and says something essential about who you are. You don't need to understand why; you just need to react to the characters and situations. Borrowing from other films and literature can be a great stimulus and supply constant inspiration for any screenwriter. Importantly, answer how you are going to make it original, what you are going to do differently, and how your screen ideas reflect your uniqueness as a person.

When embarking on a journey to become a successful screenwriter, some responsibilities are vitally important. Firstly, treating screenwriting as a lifestyle. This attitude reflects a dedication towards your craft and provides the time necessary to create quality screenplays. Don't be lazy. Writing is hard work, and thinking the first draft is the final draft is simply misplaced. If you don't have a passion and drive to create depth in your writing, then it's doubtful you will produce anything of worth.

Secondly, be passionate about your work and cinema in general. Knowing a lot about films is valuable. When a writer has a deep appreciation for this art form, it can even add a level of meaning to their life. Great art is inspiring, a central ingredient for creating original work. There is a lot to know about screenwriting, and there are fundamental skills that are required. Screenwriting, as an art, also has a craft. Without a relevant skill set, knowing how to structure and tell a story cinematically is like building a house without knowing carpentry. It won't end well. Skills are a learnt ability. However, not all skills are equal. For example, learning to analyse a film won't necessarily make you a better writer because it's the wrong type of skill.

Thirdly, stay grounded. Be humbled by the people who have made great cinema. The more you appreciate films, the greater your awe of the filmmakers who created them. You have a responsibility to be disciplined and create your best work at this point in time. However, writing with a deep knowledge of cinema history grounds your attitude and inspires you to work harder to reach your full potential. And be honest with yourself. Talent is another word for originality or honesty (a cutting-to-the-bone, disarming kind of honesty). As Erica Jong wrote, "Everyone has talent. What is rare is the courage to follow the talent to the dark place where it leads."[5]

Two criteria for judging a screenplay are value and quality. The market value depends on how the audience perceives a film. A sequel to a popular movie will have a high value, as a market exists for this kind of experience. Quality is something a screenwriter has complete control over while other people decide value. A writer may guess what has value, and hopefully, a producer will agree with these sentiments; however, the real value is only realised when a film enters the marketplace.

Write films with the highest quality you can create by applying the four ways of screenwriting, and your screenplays will inherently have an experience that will engage an audience. And if this experience is universal and becomes popular, then your value as a screenwriter will be recognised.

Notes

INTRODUCTION

[1] McKee, 1999 Story, p. 9.

[2] Vogler, 1992.

[3] Gulino, 2004.

[4] MacKendrick, 2004, p. 51.

[5] MacKendrick, 2004, p. 51.

[6] MacKendrick, 2004, p. 51.

[7] Raubicheck & Srebnick, 2011, p. 10

PART ONE

[1] Truffaut, 1979.

[2] Truffaut, 1979, para. 9.

[3] Moral, 2013.

[4] Hatcher 1996, p. 23.

[5] Branigan, 1992, p. 102.

[6] Zillman, 1980.

[7] Cardullo, 2009, p. 1.

[8] Cattrysse, 2010, p. 85.

[9] Seger, 1994, p. 150.

[10] Mamet, 1991, p. 12.

[11] Benedetti, 2004, p. 92.

[12] Hauser & Reich, 2003, p. 4–5.

[13] Hauser & Reich, 2003, p. 35.

[14] MacKendrick, 2004, p. 13.

[15] Blacker, 1996, chapter 2; Smiley 2005, p. 31; Egri 1960, p. 75.

[16] see also McKee, 1999; Mamet, 1991.

[17] Thompson 1999, p. 13.

[18] Chatman, 1978, p. 126.

[19] Smith, 1995, p. 82.

[20] Foster-Harris, 2012, p. 12.

[21] Egri, 1960, p. 133.

[22] DeRosa, 2011, p. 69.

[23] as cited in Moral, 2013.

[24] DeRosa, 2011, p. 264.

[25] Egri, 1960, p. 75.

[26] Smith, 1995, p. 22.

[27] MacKendrick, 2004, p. 11.

[28] Moral, 2013, p. 106/218.

[29] Truffaut, 1979, para. 11.

[30] Truffaut, 1984, p. 269.

[31] Gottlieb, 1995, p. 120.

[32] Gottlieb, 1995, p. 120.

[33] Gottlieb, 2003, p. 70.

[34] Lehman, 2000, p. 48.

[35] Lehman, 2000, p. 48.

[36] Lucey, 1996, p. 5.

[37] Sainsbury, 2002, p. 5.

[38] Foster-Harris, 2012, pp. 10–11.

[39] Foster-Harris, 2012, p. 10.

[40] Moral, 2013, p. 106/218.

[41] De Rosa, 2011, p. 70.

[42] Gray, 2013, p.61.

[43] Gottlieb, 1995, p. 253.

[44] Foster-Harris, 2012, p. 6.

[45] Foster-Harris, 2012, p. 11.

[46] Egri, 1960, p. 133.

[47] Foster-Harris, 2012, p. 12.

[48] Proferes, 2005, p. 19; McKee, 1999, p. 37; Egri, 1960, pp.125–126.

[49] Hatcher, 1996, p. 7.

[50] Hauser & Reich, 2003, p. 4.

[51] Mamet, 1991, p. 40.

[52] Hauser & Reich, 2003, p. 4.

[53] Hooks, 2003, p. 38.

Part Two

[1] King, 2000, p 78.

[2] King, 2000, p. 79.

[3] Bogdanovich, 1963, para. 136.

[4] MacKendrick, 2004, p. 77.

[5] Seger, 1994; McKee, 1999; Vogler, 1999; Moritz, 2001; Field, 2003.

[6] Aristotle, 2008.

[7] Aristotle, 2008.

[8] Aristotle, 2008.

[9] Aristotle, 2008.

[10] cited in Chatman, 1978, p. 114.

[11] Egri, 1960, p. xiv, p. 90.

[12] Egri, 1960, p. 96.

[13] Aristotle, 2008.

[14] Egri, 1960, p. 17.

[15] Egri, 1960, p. 90.

[16] Chatman, 1978, p. 26, p. 32.

[17] Chatman, 1978, p. 32.

[18] MacKendrick, 2004, p. 13.

[19] McKee, 1999, p. 100.

[20] McKee, 1999, p. 218–224.

[21] McKee, 1999, p. 106.

[22] Gottlieb, 1995, pp. 247–248.

[23] Gottlieb, 1995, p. 270.

[24] Hauser & Reich, 2003, p. 3.

[25] Mamet, 1991, p. 12.

[26] Truffaut, 1984, P. 92.

[27] Gottlieb, 1995, pp. 119–120.

[28] Allen, 2007, p. 38.

[29] Truffaut, 1984, p. 73.

[30] Buckland, 2006, p. 182.

[31] Bordwell, 1985, p. 31.

[32] Bordwell, 1985, p 37.

[33] Bordwell, 1985, p. 37.

[34] Bordwell, 1985, p 39.

[35] Bordwell, 1985, p. 38.

[36] Egri, 1960, p. 115.

[37] Plantinga, 2009a, p. 145.

[38] Carroll, 1993, p. 133.

[39] Truffaut, 1984, p. 199.

[40] Allen, 2007, p. 39.

[41] Gottlieb, 1995, p. 125.

[42] Gottlieb, 1995, p. 125.

[43] Gottlieb, 1995, p. 126.

[44] Gottlieb, 1995, p. 125.

[45] Gottlieb, 1995, p. 129.

[46] Truffaut, 1984, p. 92.

[47] Truffaut, 1984, p. 73.

[48] Egri, 1960, p. 126.

[49] Truffaut, 1984, p. 73.

[50] Gottlieb, 1995, p. 264.

[51] Gottlieb, 1995, p. 114.

[52] Truffaut, 1984, p.73.

[53] as cited in Moral, 2013.

[54] Moral, 2013.

[55] Gottlieb, 1995, p. 150.

[56] Field, 1979, p 90.

[57] Truffaut, 1979, para. 15.

[58] Smith, 2000, p. 27.

[59] Moral, 2013, p. 41/218, 45/218.

[60] Truffaut, 1979.

[61] Gottlieb, 1995, p. 247.

[62] Campbell, 1991, p. 158.

PART THREE

[1] Moral, 2013, p. 154/218.

[2] Gottlieb, 1995, p. 298.

[3] DeRosa, 2011, p. xiii.

[4] cited in Dickstein, 1981, p. 68.

[5] Jones, 2016, 15:00.

[6] Gottlieb, 1995, p. 292.

[7] Truffaut, 1984, p. 99.

[8] Truffaut, 1984, p. 102.

[9] Truffaut, 1984, p. 199.

[10] Truffaut, 1984, p. 99.

[11] Glancy, 2003, p. 93.

[12] Smith, 2000, p. 17.

[13] Proferes, 2005, p. 19.

[14] Chandler, 2005, p. 19.

[15] Gottlieb, 1995, p. 292.

[16] Gottlieb, 1995 p. 117.

[17] Carroll, 1990, p. 87.

[18] Carroll, 1990, p. 29.

[19] Carroll, 1990, p. 30.

[20] Carroll, 1990, p. 80.

[21] Carroll, 1990, p. 29.

[22] Deigh, 1994, p. 826.

[23] Alston, 1967, p. 486.

[24] Deigh, 1994, p. 846; see also Green, 1992, pp. 33–34; and Kenny, 1963, pp. 60–62.

[25] Plantinga, 2009a, p. 87.

[26] Carroll, 1999, p. 25.

[27] Coplan, 2004; Grodal, 1997; Neill, 1996; and Gaut, 1999, 2010.

[28] Carroll, 1998, chapters 4 & 5; 2007; 2008, chapter 6.

[29] Plantinga, 1999; 2009a, pp. 97–106.

[30] Carroll, 1998, p. 350.

[31] Plantinga, 2009a, p. 103.

[32] Plantinga, 2009a, pp. 103–104.

[33] Feagin, 1988, pp. 489–490.

[34] Feagin, 1988, pp. 489–490.

[35] Feagin, 1988, pp. 489–490.

[36] Neill, 1996, p. 183.

[37] Neill, 1996, p. 185.

[38] Neill, 1996, p. 185.

[39] Carroll, 1990, p. 95.

[40] Carroll, 1990, p. 95.

[41] Carroll, 1990, p. 92.

[42] Truffaut, 1979, para. 11.

[43] Plantinga, 2009, p. 74.

[44] Herman, 2013; also see Hogan 2003.

[45] Herman, 2013; also see Adolphs 2005.

[46] Prinz, 2007, p. 118.

[47] Vorderer & Knobloch, 2000, p. 56; see also Zillman, 1996.

[48] Allen, 2007, p. 53.

[49] Allen, 2007, p. 53.

[50] Allen, 2007, p. 53.

[51] Truffaut, 1984, p. 272.

[52] Gottlieb, 1995, p. 253.

[53] Benedetti, 2005, p. 92.

[54] Gottlieb, 1995 p. 128.

[55] Bordwell & Thompson, 2008, p. 319.

[56] Truffaut, 1977.

[57] Truffaut, 1977.

[58] Cook & Bernink, 1999 p. 138.

[59] Tudor, 1974, pp. 135-137.

[60] Altman, 1999, p. 88.

[61] Bordwell & Thompson, 2008, p. 320.

[62] Lacey, 2005, p53.

[63] Lacey, 2005, p53.

[64] Truffaut, 1984, p. 73.

[65] Truffaut, 1984, p. 73.

[66] Truffaut, 1984 , p. 73.

[67] DeRosa, 2011, p. 69.

[68] DeRosa, 2011, p. 69.

[69] Truffaut, 1984, p. 138.

[70] Truffaut, 1984, p. 139.

[71] Warner Brothers Entertainment, 2012, p. 67.

[72] Bordwell & Thompson, 2008, p. 329.

[73] Gottlieb, 1995, p. 150.

[74] Gottlieb, 1995, p.130.

[75] Moral, 2013, p. 49.

[76] Gottlieb, 1995, p. 248.

[77] Allen, 2007, p. 60.

[78] Allen, 2007, p. 61.

[79] Moral, 2013, pp. 46-47.

[80] Johnstone, 2007, p. 36.

Part Four

[1] Montagu, 1980, p.190.

[2] Montagu, 1980, p.190.

[3] McGilligan, 2003, p. 76.

[4] McGilligan, 2003, p. 76.

[5] McGilligan, 2003, p. 76.

[6] Montagu, 1980, p.190.

[7] Montagu, 1980, p.190.

[8] McGilligan, 2003, p. 85.

[9] McGilligan, 2003, p. 85.

[10] Montagu, 1980, p.190.

[11] McGilliagan, 2003, p. 85.

[12] McGilligan, 2003, p. 86.

[13] McGilligan, 2003, p. 85.

[14] Barr, 1999, p. 11.

[15] Gottlieb, 1995.

[16] Schemmer & Granof, 2007, p. 7.

[17] Schemmer & Granof, 2007, p. 19.

[18] Schemmer & Granof, 2007, p. 7.

[19] Schemmer & Granof, 2007, p. 7.

[20] Sarris, 1962.

[21] Schmenner & Granof, 2007, p. ix.

[22] Dunne, 1980, p.47.

[23] De Rosa, 2011, p. x.

[24] as cited in Maras, 2009, p. 121.

[25] De Rosa, 2011, p. x.

[26] Boozer, 2008, p. 16.

[27] Krzysztof Piesiewicz, cited in MacGrath & MacDermott, 2003, p. 131.

[28] Hitchcock, 1937, p. 38.

[29] Maras, 2009, p. 2.

[30] Glancy, 2003, p. 30.

[31] Maras, 2009, p. 2.

[32] Herman, 1952, p. 193.

[33] Raubicheck & Srebnick, 2011, p. 117.

[34] McGilligan, 2003, p. 164.

[35] McGilligan, 2003, p. 164.

[36] Raubicheck & Srebnick, 2011, p. 1

[37] Schmenner & Granof, 2007, p. 15.

[38] Truffaut, 1984, p. 289.

[39] Krohn, 2000, p. 16.

[40] Krohn, 2000, p. 240.

[41] Krohn, 2000, p. 240.

[42] Krohn, 2000, p. 209.

[43] Raubicheck & Srebnick, 2011, p. 5.

[44] Gritten, 2008, p. 277.

[45] DeRosa, 2011, p. 135.

[46] Hitchcock, 1948.

[47] *Destination Hitchcock: The Making of North by Northwest* 2000, 7:00 min.

[48] Moral, 2013, p. 121/218.

[49] Auiler, 1999, p. 210.

[50] Krohn, 2000, p. 12.

[51] Krohn, 2000, p. 12.

[52] DeRosa, 2011, p. 135.

[53] Raubicheck & Srebnick, 2011, p. 60.

[54] Costello, 2002, p. 71.

[55] Maras, 2009, p. 11.

[56] Maras, 2009, p. 11.

[57] Maras, 2009, p. 21.

[58] Maras, 2009, p. 22.

[59] Oxford Dictionary, n.d.

[60] Moore, 1999, p. 779.

[61] Curtis, 2007, p. 23.

[62] Curtis, 2007, p. 23.

[63] Bordwell et al., 1985, p. 624.

[64] Hitchcock, 1937, p. 38.

[65] Raubicheck & Srebnick, 2011, p. xii.

[66] Raubicheck & Srebnick, 2011, p. xii.

[67] DeRosa, 2011, p. 184.

[68] Raubicheck & Srebnick, 2011, p. 5.

[69] Schmenner, 2007, p. 9.

[70] Schmenner, 2007, p. 13.

[71] cited in Barr, 1999, p. 11.

[72] Galenson, 2006, p. 156.

[73] Schmenner, 2007, p. 9.

[74] cited in Raubicheck & Srebnick, 2011, p. 16.

[75] Schmenner, 2007, p. 9.

[76] Schmenner, 2007, p. 11.

[77] Schmenner, 2007, p. 9.

[78] Schmenner, 2007, p. 9.

[79] Curtis, 2007, pp. 19–21.

[80] DeRosa, 2011, p. 180.

[81] cited in Krohn, 2000, p. 32.

[82] cited in Krohn, 2000, p. 32.

[83] Carrière, 2013, p. 121.

[84] cited in Proferes, 2005, p. 50.

[85] Mamet, 1991, p. 5.

[86] Mamet, 1991, p. 2.

[87] Moral, 2013.

[88] Millard, 2013, p. 124.

[89] Truffaut, 1984, p. 335.

[90] Bogdanovich, 1963, para. 206.

[91] Gottlieb, 2003, p. 181.

[92] Bordwell & Thompson, 2008, p. 455.

[93] Gottlieb, 2003, p. 130.

[94] Moral, 2013, p. 122/218.

[95] Truffaut, 1979.

96 Gottlieb, 1995, p. 291.

97 Krohn, 2000, p. 9.

98 Truffaut, 1984, pp. 214–216.

99 DeRosa, 2011, p. 240.

100 Bogdanovich, 1963, para. 6.

101 Gottlieb, 1995, p. 296.

102 Gottlieb, 1995, p. 289.

103 Bogdanovich, 1963, para. 8.

104 Carroll, 1993, p. 138.

105 Branigan, 1992, p. 101.

106 Elsaesser & Buckland, 2002, p. 190.

107 Branigan, 1984, p. 103.

108 Carroll, 1993, p. 133.

109 Carroll, 1993, p. 129.

110 Carroll, 1993, p. 134.

111 Proferes, 2005, p. 19.

112 Galenson, 2006, p. 156.

113 Schmenner & Granof, 2007, p. 9.

114 DeRosa, 2011, p. 240.

115 Sainsbury, 2002, p. 7.

116 Maras, 2009, p. 50.

117 Gottlieb, 1995, p. 267.

118 Raubicheck & Srebnick, 2011, p. 3–4.

119 Truffaut, 1984, p. 71.

120 Gottlieb, 1995, p. 268.

121 Gottlieb, 1995, p. 267–268.

122 Gottlieb, 1995, pp. 267-268.

123 Curtis, 2007, p. 15.

124 cited in Maras, 2009, p. 92.

125 Maras, 2009, p. 84.

126 Costello, 2002, p. 71.

127 Gottlieb, 1995, p. 268.

[128] cited in Maras, 2009, pp. 93–95.

[129] Lasky, 1937, cited in Maras, 2009, p. 95.

[130] Gottlieb, 1995, p. 268.

[131] McGilligan, 2003, pp. 331–396.

[132] Currier, 2019.

[133] Robert Mitchum, cited in Perez, 2001.

[134] Gottlieb, 1995, p. 267.

[135] Gottlieb, 1995, p. 268.

CONCLUSION

[1] Mehta, 2006.

[2] Mehta, 2006.

[3] Truffaut, 1984, p. 290.

[4] Emerson, 1911, p. 86.

[5] Jong, 1973.

Bibliography

Adolphs, R. 2005, "Could a Robot Have Emotions? Theoretical Perspective from Social Cognitive Neuroscience", in M. Arbib & J.-M. Fellous (eds.), *Who Needs Emotions? The Brain Meets the Robot*, Oxford University Press, Oxford pp. 9–28.

Allen, R. 2007, *Hitchcock's Romantic Irony*, Columbia University Press, New York.

Alston, W. P. 1967, "Emotion and Feeling", in P. Edwards (ed.), *The Encyclopedia of Philosophy*, Vol. 2, Macmillan, New York.

Altman, R. (1999), *Film/Genre*, British Film Institute, London.

Aristotle (2008). *Poetics*, trans. S. H. Butcher, viewed 14 February 2013, <https://www.gutenberg.org/files/1974/1974-h/1974-h.htm >.

Auiler, D. 1999, *Hitchcock's Notebooks: An Authorized and Illustrated Look Inside the Creative Mind of Alfred Hitchcock*. Avon Books, Inc. New York.

Barr, C. 1999, *English Hitchcock*, Cameron and Hollis, Moffat Scotland.

Benedetti, J. 2004. *Stanislavski: An Introduction*, Routledge, New York.

Blacker, I. R. (1996). *The Elements of Screenwriting : A Guide for Film and Television Writers.* New York : Macmillan.

Bogdanovich, P. 1963, "Peter Bogdanovich Interviews Alfred Hitchcock", viewed 20 January 2014, <http://zakka.dk/euroscreenwriters/interviews/alfred_hitchcock.htm>.

Boozer, J. 2008, *Authorship in Film Adaptation*, University of Texas Press, Austin.

Bordwell, D. & Thompson, K. 2008, *Film Art: An Introduction* 8th edn., McGraw-Hill, New York.

Bordwell, D. 1985, *Narration in the Fiction Film*, The University of Wisconsin Press, Madison, WI.

Bordwell, D., Staiger, J. & Thompson, K. (1985) *The Classical Hollywood Cinema: Film Style & Mode of Production to 1960*, Columbia University Press, New York.

Branigan, E. 1984, *Point of View in the Cinema: A Theory of Narration and Subjectivity in Classical Film*, Mouton Publishers, New York.

Branigan, E. 1992, *Narrative Comprehension and Film*, Routledge, New York.

Buckland, W. 2006, *Directed by Steven Spielberg: Poetics of the Contemporary Hollywood Blockbuster*, The Continuum International Publishing Group Inc., New York.

Campbell, J. 1991, *The Power of Myth*, Anchor Books, New York.

Cardullo, B. 2009, *What is Dramaturgy?* Peter Lang Publishing, New York.

Carrière, J.-C. 2013, "SRC Bruxelles, September 2011", *Journal of Screenwriting*, vol. 4, no. 2, pp. 117–122.

Carroll, N. 1990, *A Philosophy of Horror: Or, Paradoxes of the Heart*, Routledge, New York.

Carroll, N. 1993, "Toward a Theory of Point-of-View Editing: Communication, Emotion, and the Movies", *Poetics Today*, vol. 14, no. 1, pp. 123–141.

Carroll, N. 1998, *A Philosophy of Mass Art*, Claredon Press, Oxford.

Carroll, N. 1999, "Film, Emotion, and Genre," in C. Plantinga & G.M. Smith (eds.), *Passionate Views: Film, Cognition, and Emotion*, Johns Hopkins University Press, Baltimore, MD, 25.

Carroll, N. 2007, "On the Ties that Bind: Characters, the Emotions, and Popular Fiction", in W. Irwin and J.J.E. Gracia (eds.), *Philosophy and the Interpretation of Pop Culture*, Rowman and Littlefield Lanham, MD, pp. 89–116.

Carroll, N. 2008, *The Philosophy of Motion Pictures*, Blackwell, Malden, MA.Cattrysse, P. 2010, "The Protagonist's Dramatic Goals, Wants and Needs", *Journal of Screenwriting*, vol. 1, no. 1, pp. 83–97.

Cattrysse, P. (2010), *The protagonist's dramatic goals, wants and needs*, Journal of Screenwriting 1: 1, pp. 83–97, doi: 10.1386/josc.1.1.83/1

Chandler, C. 2005, *It's Only a Movie: Alfred Hitchcock, A Personal Biography*, Simon & Schuster, London.

Chatman, S. 1978, *Story and Discourse: Narrative Structure in Fiction and Film*, Cornell University Press, Ithaca, NY.

Cook, P. & Bernink, M. 1999, *The Cinema Book* 2nd edn., British Film Institute, London.

Coplan, A. 2004, "Empathetic Engagement with Narrative Fictions", *Journal of Aesthetics and Art Criticism*, vol 62, pp. 141–152.

Costello, J. 2002, *Writing a Screenplay*, Pocket Essentials, Harpenden, UK.

Currier, G. 2019, "Fay Wray and Robert Riskin: A Hollywood Memoir", Martha's Vineyard Arts & Ideas, viewed 20 Oct 2024, <https://www.mvartsandideas.com/2019/06/fay-wray-and-robert-riskin-a-hollywood-memoir>

Curtis, S. 2007, "The Last Word: Images in Hitchcock's Working Method", in W. Schmenner & C. Granof (eds.), *Casting a Shadow: Creating the Alfred Hitchcock Film*, Mary and Leigh Block Museum of Art and Northwestern University Press, Evanston Illinois, pp. 15–28.

Deigh, J. 1994, "Cognitivism in the Theory of Emotions", *Ethics*, vol. 104, no. 4 (July 1994), pp. 824–854.

DeRosa, S. 2011, *Writing with Hitchcock: The Collaboration of Alfred Hitchcock and John Michael Hayes*, Faber and Faber, Inc., New York.

Destination Hitchcock: The Making of North by Northwest 2000, documentary, Turner Entertainment Co, USA.

Dickstein, M. 1981, "Beyond Good and Evil: The Morality of THRILLERS", *American Film* (Archive: 1975-1992), vol. 6, issue 9, pp. 49–52, 67–69.

Dunne, P. 1980, *Take Two: A Life in Movies and Politics*, McGraw-Hill, New York.

Egri, L. 1960, *The Art of Dramatic Writing*, Simon & Schuster, Inc., New York.

Egri, L. 1960, *The Art of Dramatic Writing*, Simon & Schuster, Inc., New York.

Elsaesser, T. & Buckland, W. 2002, "Cognitive Theories of Narration (Lost Highway)", in *Studying Contemporary American Film: A Guide to Movie Analysis*, Arnold Publishers, London.

Emerson, H. (1911, July). Fifteenth Annual Convention of the National Association of Clothiers. *The Clothier and Furnisher,* 78(6), George N. Lowrey Company, New York.

Feagin, S. L. 1988, "Imagining Emotions and Appreciating Fiction", *Canadian Journal of Philosophy* vol 18, pp. 485–500.

Field, S (2003), *The Definitive Guide to Screen Writing by Field*, Random House, London.

Field, S (2003), *The Definitive Guide to Screen Writing by Field*, Random House, London.

Foster-Harris, W. 2012, *The Basic Formulas of Fiction*, University of Oklahoma Press, Norman, OK.

Galenson, D. 2006, *Old Masters and Young Geniuses: The Two Life Cycles of Artistic Creativity*, Princeton University Press, Princeton, NJ.

Gaut, B. 1999, "Identification and Emotion in Narrative Film", in C. Plantinga and G. E. Smith (eds.), *Passionate Views: Film, Cognition and Emotions*: The Johns Hopkins University Press, Baltimore, MD, pp. 200–216.

Glancy, M. 2003, *The 39 Steps: A British Film Guide*, I.B. Tauris, London.

Gottlieb, S. (ed.) 1995, *Hitchcock on Hitchcock: Selected Writings and Interviews*. University of California Press, Berkeley and Los Angeles.

Gottlieb, S. (ed.) 2003, *Alfred Hitchcock: Interviews*, University Press of Mississippi, Jackson, MS.

Gray, J. 2013, *Just Effing Entertain Me: A Screenwriter's Atlas*, Lulu.

Green, O. H. 1992, *The Emotions: A Philosophical Theory*, Kluwer Academic Publishers, Dordrecht, the Netherlands.

Gritten, D. 2008, "'The Technique of the Talkie': Screenwriting Manuals and the Coming of Sound to British Cinema", *Journal of British Cinema and Television*, vol. 5, no. 2, pp. 262–279 (doi: http://dx.doi.org/10.3366/e1743452108000368).

Grodal, T. 1997, *Moving Pictures: A New Theory of Film Genres, Feelings and Cognitions*, Claredon Press, Oxford.

Gulino, P. J. (2004), *Screenwriting: The Sequence Approach*, Random House, London.

Hatcher, J. 1996), *Art and Craft of Playwriting*, F + W Media, New York.

Hauser, F. & Reich, R. 2003, *Notes on Directing*, RCR Creative Press, New York.

Herman, D. 2013, "Cognitive Narratology", viewed 11 June 14, <http://wikis.sub.uni-hamburg.de/lhn/index.php/Cognitive_Narratology>.

Herman, L. 1952, *A Practical Manual of Screen Playwriting for Theater and Television Films*, The World Publishing Company, New York.

Hitchcock, A. 1937, "Direction", in *Focus on Hitchcock* A. J. LaValley (ed.), Prentice-Hill, Englewood Cliffs, NJ [1972].

Hitchcock, A. 1948, "Film Production Techniques", Lecture by Hitchcock in 1948, viewed 27 May 2014, <http://networkninenews.com/2012/11/27/film-production-technique-from-a-talk-given-by-alfred-hitchcock-in-1948/>.

Hogan, P.C. 2003, *The Mind and Its Stories: Narrative Universals and Human Emotion*, Cambridge University Press, Cambridge.

Hooks, E. 2011, *Acting for Animators* 3rd edn., Routledge, New York.

Johnstone, K. (2007), *Impro: Improvisation and the Theatre*, Methuen Drama, London.

Jones, K. 2016, *Hitchcock/Truffaut—interview with director Kent Jones*, audio podcast, The Final Cut Radio National, ABC Radio, Sydney, 5 August, viewed 7 August 2016, <http://www.abc.net.au/radionational/programs/finalcut/hitchcock-truffaut---interview-with-director-kent-jones/7690408>.

Jong, E. (1973). The Artist as Housewife. In F. Kragbrun (Ed), *The First Ms. Reader: How women are changing their lives - in work, sex, politics, love, power, and life stules. An anthology of articles*. Warner Paperback Library.

Kenny, A. 1963, *Action, Emotion and Will*, Routledge & Kegan Paul, London.

King, S. 2000, *On Writing: A Memoir of the Craft*, Hodder & Stoughton, London.

Krohn, B. 2000, *Hitchcock at Work*, Phaidon Press Limited, London.

Lacey, N. (2005), *Introduction to Film*, Belgrave McMillan, New York.

Lehman, E. 2000, "North by Northwest: An interview with Ernest Lehman", *Creative Screenwriting*, vol. 7, issue 6, pp. 47–53.

Lucey, P. 1996, *Story Sense: Writing Story and Script for Feature Films and Television*, McGraw-Hill, London.

MacGrath, D., & MacDermott, F. 2003, *Screencraft: Screenwriting*, Mies, Switzerland: RotoVision SA.

MacKendrick, A. 2004, *On Film-making: An Introduction to the Craft of the Director*, Faber and Faber Limited, New York.

Mamet, D. 1991, *On Directing Film*, Penguin Group Inc., New York.

Maras, S. 2009, *Screenwriting: History, Theory and Practice*, Wall Flower Press, London.

McGilligan, P. 2003, *Alfred Hitchcock: A Life In Darkness and Light*, HarperCollins Publishers, New York.

McKee, R. 1999, *Story: Substance, Structure, Style and the Principles of Screenwriting*, Methuen Publishing Limited, London.

Mehta, D. (2006, July 26). *Psycho: Hitchcock and the Politique Des Auteurs*. Brattle Theatre Film Notes, http://www.brattleblog.brattlefilm.org/2006/07/28/psycho-hitchcock-and-the-politique-des-auteurs-30/

Millard, K. 2013, "Writing with light: The screenplay and photography", *Journal of Screenwriting*, vol. 4, no. 2, pp. 123–134.

Montagu, I. 1980, "Working with Hitch", *Sight & Sound*, vol 49, pp.189–193.

Moore, B. (Ed.) (1999) *The Australian Oxford Dictionary*. South Melbourne: Oxford University Press.

Moral, T. L. 2013, *Alfred Hitchcock's Moviemaking Master Class: Learning about Film from the Master of Suspense*, electronic book, Michael Wiese Productions, Los Angeles.

Moritz, C (2001), *Scriptwriting for the Screen*, Routledge, London.

Mukerjee, M. 2011 *Churchill's secret war : the British Empire and the ravaging of India during World War II.* Sydney: Read How You Want.

Neill, A. 1996, "Empathy and (Film) Fiction", in D. Bordwell & N. Carroll (eds.), *Post-Theory,* The University of Wisconsin Press, Madison, WI, pp. 175–194.

Oxford Dictionary (n.d.) *Oxford Learner's Dictionaries.* Retrieved November 20, 2022 from https://www.oxfordlearnersdictionaries.com/definition/english/medium_2.

Perez, G. (2001). 'Imperfection'. *Senses of Cinema* (online journal), issue 16. Retrieved May 5, 2008, from http://www.sensesofcinema.com/contents/books/01/16/cassavetes_imperfection.html.

Plantinga, C. 1999, "The Scene of Empathy and the Human Face on Film", in C. Plantinga and G. E. Smith (eds.), *Passionate Views: Film, Cognition and Emotions,* The Johns Hopkins University Press, Baltimore, MD, pp. 239–255.

Plantinga, C. 2009a, *Moving Viewers: American Film and the Spectator's Experience,* University of California Press, Berkeley.

Prinz, J. 2007, *The Emotional Construction of Morals,* Oxford University Press, Oxford.

Proferes, N. T. 2005, *Film Directing Fundamentals: See your Film before Shooting* 2nd edn., Focal Press, Oxford.

Proferes, N. T. 2005, *Film Directing Fundamentals: See your Film before Shooting* 2nd edn., Focal Press, Oxford.

Raubicheck, W. & Srebnick, W. 2011, *Scripting Hitchcock: Psycho, The Birds, and Marnie*. University of Illinois Press, Chicago, IL.

Sainsbury, P. 2002, "Visions, Illusions and Delusions", Paper presented at the Australian Screen Directors Association Conference 2002, Sydney.

Sarris, A. 1962, "Notes on the Auteur Theory in 1962," *Film Culture* no. 27 (Winter 1962/63), pp. 1–8.

Schmenner, W. & Granof, C. (eds.) 2007, *Casting a Shadow: Creating the Alfred Hitchcock Film*, Mary and Leigh Block Museum of Art and Northwestern University Press, Evanston, IL.

Schmenner, W. 2007, "Creating the Alfred Hitchcock Film", in W. Schmenner & C. Granof (eds.), *Casting a Shadow: Creating the Alfred Hitchcock Film*, Mary and Leigh Block Museum of Art and Northwestern University Press, Evanston, IL, pp. 3–14.

Seger, L. 1994, *Making a Good Script Great*, Samuel French Trade, Hollywood.

Smith, M. 1995, *Engaging Characters: Fiction, Emotion and the Cinema*, Clarendon Press, Oxford.

Smith, S. 2000, *Hitchcock: Suspense, Humour and Tone*, British Film Institute, London.

Thompson, K. 1999, *Storytelling in the New Hollywood: Understanding Classical Narrative Techniques*, Harvard University Press, Cambridge, MA.

Truffaut, F. (1977), *A Kind Word for Critics*, Harper's Magazine, October, pp. 95-100.

Truffaut, F. 1979, "Hitchcock—His True Power Is Emotion", *The New York Times*, 4 March, viewed 15 May 2014, <http://partners.nytimes.com/library/film/030479hitch-life-award.html>.

Truffaut, F. 1984, *Hitchcock*, Touchstone Books, New York.

Tudor, A. (1974), *Theories of Film*, Martin Secker & Warburg Ltd, London.

Vogler, C. 1992, *The Writer's Journey: Mythic Structure for Storytellers & Screenwriters*, Michael Wiese Productions, Studio City, CA.

Vorderer, P. & Knobloch, S. 2000, "Conflict and Suspense in Drama", in D. Zillman & P. Vorderer (eds.), *Media Entertainment: The Psychology of its Appeal*, Lawrence Erlbaum Associates, Inc., Mahwah, NJ, pp. 56–68.

Walker, F. 2014, *Maralinga: The Chilling Expose of our Secret Nuclear Shame and Betrayal of our Troops and Country*, Hachette, Sydney.

Warner Brothers Entertainment 2012, *North by Northwest: Inside the Script*, electronic book, Warner Bros. Digital Publishing.

Zillman, D. 1980, "Antatomy of Suspence", in P. H. Tannenbaum (ed.), *The Entertainment Functions of Television*, Lawrence Erlsbaum, Mahwah, NJ.

Zillmann, D. 1996, "The Psychology of Suspense in Dramatic Exposition", in P. Vorderer, W. J. Wulff, & M. Friedrichsen (eds.), *Suspense: Conceptualizations, Theoretical Analyses, and Empirical Explorations*, Lawrence Erlbaum Associates, Mahwah, NJ, pp. 199–231.

Index

39 Steps, The 14, 33–34, 61, 80, 100, 136, 157–158, 179–180, 189, 203, 233, 277–278

Abbott and Costello Meet Frankenstein 189

action. See character action, genre, action

aesthetic emotion 182, 230–231

alignment 43–45, 48, 58, 92, 103, 125, 149, 157, 162, 252–254, 259, 264, 271

All that Heaven Allows 178

Allen, Richard 92, 99, 156, 185

American Beauty 103

American Werewolf in London, An 173

Angel and the Badman 34

anticipation 92–94, 98, 100, 103, 109–110, 124, 255

Apartment, The 3, 68

archetypical film experiences 174, 176–177, 189, 191

Aristotle 65, 83–84

assimilation 90, 145–147

auteur theory 198–200, 281

author 198–199, 201, 212, 222, 224–225

Avatar 173

Baby Driver 68

Baraka 184

Barthes, Roland 84

Batman Begins 36

Beauty and the Beast 102

Bicycle Thieves 42–43, 144, 274

Birds, The 167, 208–209, 281

Blackmail 62, 159

Blade Runner 80–81

Blue Velvet 178

Bordwell, David 93–95, 170, 182

Boyle, Robert 18, 210

Branigan, Edward 20, 230–231

Bringing up Baby 172

Buckland, Warren 92, 230

Campbell, Joseph 131. See Also *Hero's Journey, The*

Capra, Frank 250–251

Carroll, Noël 97, 144–146, 148, 230–232

Chaplin, Charles 186, 188

character action 18–21, 25–26, 28–30, 35, 39–40, 42, 46–48, 51–53, 56–57, 65–67, 69, 71–72, 74, 77–79, 83–86, 89–90, 93–96, 101, 113, 115, 122–123, 126–130, 132, 138–139, 145, 153–154, 156–157, 161, 165, 183, 186–188, 225, 228, 232, 240, 246, 250–252, 271

character context 12, 96–98, 122–124, 126, 132, 138, 148

character identification 11–12, 14, 16, 18, 47–48, 52–54, 56, 58, 67, 71, 138–139, 148

character schema 39–40, 46, 48, 53, 55–56, 84, 93, 95–96, 123, 127, 138, 140, 145, 151–154, 159–162, 165, 176, 187, 189, 250–251, 278, 280

character strategy 25, 27, 56, 68–69, 71–72, 251

character type 61, 64, 189, 191

Charade 234, 237

Chatman, Seymour 85

Chicken Run 42

Christmas Carol, A 41

cognitive 8, 20–21, 23, 39–40, 46, 67, 77–78, 86, 96–98, 122, 127–128, 136–140, 143, 145–146, 152–154, 160, 165, 168, 189, 192, 224–225, 227 conflict 13, 28–38, 42–43, 59–60, 62–64, 71, 79–81, 91–95, 99–101, 104–105, 107, 109–112, 116–117, 124, 132–133, 148–151, 154–155, 159–162, 177–178, 184, 186–187, 191, 229, 262, 273–274

Dances with Wolves 173

dialogue 128–130, 132, 200–201, 207–208, 212, 214–215, 219–220, 223–224, 244–249, 271–272, 280

Doctor Zhivago 275

dramatic hook 113–115, 121

dramatic irony 59, 101–102, 105–107, 110–111, 125–126, 130, 133, 137, 148, 179, 181–182, 188, 191, 331, 333, 341

dramatic structure 5, 79, 81, 109, 112, 117, 120–121

dramaturgy 24, 83

duality of actions 12, 66–67, 122

Egri, Lajos 35, 84–85, 95, 101

emotional affect 7, 14, 18, 27, 60, 62, 66, 77, 95–97, 137–138, 145, 147, 149, 152, 154, 156, 189, 230, 249

emotional context 138

empathy 147–149, 151

enscription 126, 251

expectation 3, 26–27, 29–30, 34–35, 40–41, 44–45, 59, 65–67, 69, 90, 92, 100, 102, 105, 109, 114, 131, 133, 138, 140, 166–170, 173, 175, 177, 189–190, 212, 274,

276

external conflict 35, 38, 178

Fantastic Mr Fox 42

Fawlty Towers 186

fiction emotions 150–151, 183, 233

fiction identification 13, 47–48, 92, 137, 140, 144–145, 147–149, 151–152, 154, 160–162, 166, 174–176, 231–232, 236, 275

First Blood 178

flaws 59–60, 64

focalisation 20, 92, 229–231, 233, 252

Ford, John 199

Foreign Correspondent 223

Foster-Harris, William 32, 56, 62–63

Frenzy 129, 211

Full Monty, The 27

genre 13, 114, 138, 140, 166, 168–177, 182, 189–191, 274–275, 277

    action 177–181, 189, 191

    art-house 183–184, 189, 191

    comedy 172–174, 176, 185–189, 191

drama 177–178, 189, 191

  horror 177, 182–183, 189

  mystery 179–181, 189, 191

  subgenre 189

  thriller 181, 189, 191, 197

Gladiator 172

goal 24–38, 40, 43, 46, 48, 53, 55–57, 61–64, 67–69, 71–72, 79–81, 84–85, 91–96, 98, 105, 109–110, 112, 116, 121, 123, 145, 148, 151, 153–155, 158–161, 180–181, 183, 189

goal hypothesis 93–96, 153

Godfather, The 171

Gold Rush, The 188

Great Escape, The 45, 183

Groundhog Day 173

Halloween 181

Harry Potter and the Chamber of Secrets 233

Hateful Eight, The 104

Hauser, Frank 27, 66, 91

Hero's Journey, The 4, 86

His Girl Friday 172

Hitchcock, Alfred 6, 17–18, 33, 42–45, 58, 62, 77, 90–92, 100–103, 124, 127–129, 135–137, 143, 156, 159, 166, 179–181, 184–185, 195–198, 200, 202–203, 208–213, 215, 217–223, 226–229, 243–246, 248, 278–280, 281

identification 11–14, 16, 18, 20, 46–48, 52–54, 56, 58, 67, 71, 92, 137–140, 144–149, 151–154, 156, 160–162, 166, 174–176, 231–232, 236, 251–252, 275

identity 12, 23, 28–33, 38–39, 46–48, 53–54, 56, 65, 71–72, 97

illusion of consciousness 28, 30

immediate emotions 149, 151

inciting incident 110, 114, 118, 121, 192

Inside-out 7–13, 32, 39, 53, 65, 67, 70, 78–79, 88, 90, 95, 106, 123, 126–127, 131, 137, 145, 150, 160, 203, 224, 246, 283

internal conflict 33–38, 154

Iron Giant, The 70

It Happened One Night 171, 250

Johnstone, Keith 187

King, Steven 77

knowledge 99, 105–107, 124, 133, 147, 149, 151, 170, 179

Lady Eve 188

Lady Vanishes, The 180, 197

Lifeboat 211

Little Red Riding Hood 41

Lodger, The 195–197

Lucey, Paul 56

MacGuffin 179–181

MacKendrick, Alexander 5, 28, 79, 86

Magnolia 46, 183

Mamet, David 25, 91, 226

Man Who Knew Too Much, The 208, 220, 223, 281

Man with the Golden Arm, The 57

Maras, Steven 202, 214–215, 223–224

Marnie 209

McKee, Robert 2, 86

Meet John Doe 250–252

methods 90, 197, 203, 209, 211, 213, 219–220, 246, 282–283

mindsets 10–15, 19, 21, 23, 51, 78, 122–123, 132, 139, 177, 203, 208, 227, 251, 271

montage 127–128, 132, 210, 226–228, 241, 243, 250–252

Montagu, Ivor 195–196

moral hypothesis 94, 98, 153–155

motive 26–28, 30–31, 35–38, 40, 53, 55–58, 60–61, 64, 69, 72, 84, 95, 153–155, 180–181, 196, 256, 265

Mr. Deeds Goes to Town 250

Murder on the Orient Express 104

Mutiny on the Bounty 102

Naked 282

narrative 6, 10–11, 13, 18–19, 51, 54, 79–81, 83, 85–87, 92, 97, 100, 109–111, 113, 133, 136–139, 148, 150, 156, 162, 179, 184–185, 203, 208, 210, 213–215, 219–221, 224, 245–246, 272, 278–280

Nashville 46

North by Northwest 14, 43, 51, 58, 61, 95–96, 100, 103, 111, 117, 125, 136, 149, 154, 160, 165, 181, 189, 209, 279

Notorious 33, 58, 180, 248

object problem 214–215

orchestration 95

Outside-in 9

Plantinga, Carl 97, 145–146, 150

plot template 4–5, 10, 86–87, 89

Pocahontas 173

principles 2–3, 5, 8–9, 11, 15, 23, 65, 67, 83, 95, 201, 226, 282–283

protagonist 3, 18–20, 26, 32–33, 35–36, 38, 41–48, 51–52, 54, 61, 63–65, 68, 71–73, 80, 84, 86, 89, 91–92, 96, 102, 104, 110, 112, 114, 117, 121, 131, 137, 144–145, 147–148, 154, 156–159, 162, 168, 178–179, 181, 183, 187, 189, 191, 240, 251, 273–274

Psycho 3, 44–45, 57–58, 127, 156–157, 212, 227, 281

psychology 8, 18–19, 26, 36–37, 39–40, 47, 53–59, 63–64, 68–72, 94, 130, 178, 186, 188, 191, 283

Raiders of the Lost Ark 35, 46, 113–114, 178

Rear Window 58, 135, 210

responsive emotions 149, 151

Romeo and Juliet 36, 59, 62, 159–160

rules 2, 5, 10–11, 23, 283, 308

Sabotage 45

Saboteur 61, 189, 198

scene objective 25–26, 30, 38, 40, 56–57, 66–72, 74, 85, 94–95, 101, 116–121, 137, 144–145, 148, 151, 153–154, 156, 158, 183, 196, 229, 231–233, 251, 257

schema. See character schema

scripting 203, 215

Secrets & Lies 282

Seger, Linda 24

Sequencing 4, 86–87

setting 272–277

Seven 36

Shadow of a Doubt 211

shared suspense 100–101, 105, 107, 111, 125–126, 133, 178, 181–182, 191

Shawshank Redemption 68

Silence of the Lambs, The 117

Sixth Sense, The 103

Smiling Lieutenant, The 130

Some Like It Hot 188

Stagecoach 154–155, 171

Star Wars 110, 173

status 186–189, 191, 218

Strangers on a Train 209

strategy. See character strategy

Strictly Ballroom 273

subjective treatment 228–230, 233–234, 236–237, 240–241, 243, 250, 252, 257, 271

suppression suspense 104–105, 107, 125, 133, 179, 181–182, 191 surprise 102–103, 105, 111, 166, 168

suspense 6, 12, 43, 45, 91–95, 98–107, 109–111, 121, 123–126, 132–133, 137, 148–150, 156, 166, 178–179, 181–182, 185–186, 188–189, 191, 197–198, 212, 234

suspense hypothesis 93–95, 98

Suspicion 58

Thelma and Louise 173

themes 5, 7, 14, 52, 62, 79–81, 131–132, 157–160, 162, 170, 183–184, 197, 274–278

Thing, The 104

Titanic 29, 42, 102

Tootsie 33, 60

Toy Story 188

Truffaut 17, 43, 124, 136, 156–157, 171, 180, 281

Vertigo 7, 103, 229

villain 19, 35, 42–43, 58, 64, 95, 103, 105–106, 125, 154, 156, 166, 187, 233–234, 251

wants and needs 32–33, 35–38, 59–64, 69, 74, 79–81, 87, 112, 119, 155, 251

Wilder, Billy 130

Witness for the Prosecution 96

writer-director approach 13, 202, 208, 213, 217

Young and Innocent 197

Appendix One

Analysis of North by Northwest

The opening credits, created by Saul Bass and accompanied by music from Bernard Hermann, provide an engaging introduction to the film. The images of cosmopolitan city life set up the environment for our protagonist, who is an advertising man. Hitchcock's cameo appearance occurs in this sequence when a bus door closes as he attempts to embark.

The audience starts in the world of Roger O. Thornhill and shows all the superficiality of someone in his business. In Thornhill's everyday life, he is required to lie for his job and shows no reluctance for deception when he lies to a man waiting for a taxi. Due to Cary Grant's charming portrayal, this leaves a mixed impression of the man who is set up as the protagonist. His superficiality in these opening seconds can be contrasted to the sincerity and hurt he feels for Eve Kendall later in the film. He will grow as a result of his journey.

The fusion of humour with a thriller creates an entertaining mix for the audience. The first gag takes seconds to arrive: "Say hello to the missus"; "We're not talking".

Grant's timing and comic touches play well in this first scene as expositional information is communicated to the audience. Within just over two minutes, Hitchcock has communicated the necessary information about the character (i.e. exposition), and the adventure is set to begin. This opening is a prime example of how efficient and effective Hitchcock is in telling his stories.

The first surprise occurs when two men suddenly abduct Thornhill. Omniscient narration is used with POV shots to show the spies mistakenly thinking Thornhill is George Kaplan, which sets our protagonist off on his adventure. A mystery is set up with high-stakes questions: why is he being kidnapped? Who are these villains? Can he escape alive? When the two gangsters kidnap Thornhill, they take him to a mansion owned by Townsend. Thornhill's desire to escape the situation conflicts with the villains' desire to get information from Kaplan (who they think he is). Of course, the audience expects he will escape and all the questions answered in due time, but it is the obstacles that Roger Thornhill faces that *identify* the viewer with him.

Thornhill's drunk-driving escapade is *shared suspense*, with conflict developed due to his drunkenness while driving and his desire to escape the henchmen. This situation is mixed with the humour provided by Grant's comic facial expressions. The scene is the climax of the first sequence, where he escapes the two henchmen and is arrested for drunk driving. The police act as Roger's saviour and not as an obstacle, which they become later due to the 'double pursuit' (i.e. the spies and police wanting to capture him).

The scene in the police station is humorous, more than dramatic, as the stakes are not high (i.e. drunk driving, not murder). Thornhill's mother adds humour as he tries to prove his outlandish story. This scene lends some relief after his abduction and escape.

For Thornhill, things become more and more absurd when he and the police visit Townsend's house to find his (supposed) wife delivering a story accounting for Roger's drunkenness and stolen car. This scene, rather than explaining occurrences, makes the situation even more obtuse and disorienting for the audience. The mystery is played for humour as Thornhill unsuccessfully attempts to convince the police that he was abducted. It is only in the last shot of the scene, where the henchman is shown in the garden, that Hitchcock tells us that this is a cover-up and Thornhill is still in deep water. The mystery turns to suspense as the audience becomes aware of the danger facing Thornhill.

Thornhill's *strategy* is to find Kaplan at the hotel and solve the mystery of mistaken identity. Thornhill's *objective* is to prove his innocence, something he will be actively doing for most of the film. This situation is exacerbated by his mother, who provides a comic foil to the protagonist and an obstacle, as she has little faith in Roger. Surprisingly, Thornhill is identified as the elusive George Kaplan at the hotel, only to be phoned by the henchmen in Kaplan's room, setting up a short chase scene. After escaping the henchmen, Thornhill finds Townsend at the United Nations to prove to everyone that he is telling the truth. The climax to this sequence occurs with the stabbing of the diplomat and a signature extreme high shot of Roger running from the UN building. Townsend's death is a shock, and the surprise launches Thornhill into a high-stakes game of cat and mouse.

Roger Thornhill, in a very similar scenario to *The 39 Steps*, is wanted for a murder he did not commit. A double pursuit, where the spies and police are after Thornhill, isolates him and develops strong sympathy from the audience. So far, the film has presented an almost absurd situation which is unexplained. The First scene in the third sequence gives the audience an explanation of what has happened to Roger up to this point. It sets up the suspense for most of the film as the viewers are given information that Thornhill is not. The mystery has been solved, and *dramatic irony* replaces it, as Thornhill is unaware that he is chasing a non-existent decoy agent in George Kaplan.

How will he evade the police when he is on "every front page in America"? At this point in the story, the central conflict for Roger is evading the police. Questions about how Roger will clear his name are asked. His *strategy* is to find George Kaplan in Chicago, who viewers have just been told at the Intelligence Agency doesn't exist. At the train station, he is identified and pursued onto the train. On board the train to Chicago, he meets Eve Kendall and the film sets up his second *goal*, to find romantic love. He is infatuated with Eve, and she with him. The police stop the train during the journey to Chicago, and Eve must once more apparently help Roger by hiding him in her compartment. The audience feels anxiety for Roger as he must survive and complete his *goal* as a wanted murderer.

Roger asks the question the audience is thinking: "Why are you so good to me?" Throughout the film, the character of Eve Kendall turns from ally to obstacle and back to ally again. This sequence ends by showing the first shift from ally to obstacle for Roger. Her alignment with the villains is also an obstacle to Roger's secondary *goal*, 'to find romantic love'. Roger has trusted Eve to avoid capture from the police, setting up yet another question as to why she is aiding him. The climax occurs when the audience knows the villains are on the same train, and Roger needs to escape. Eve helps

Roger avoid the authorities, only to send him to a worse situation in the following sequence.

The scene in the Chicago train station is emotionally conflicted for the audience, as they perceive Eve as betraying Roger. She is torn between her duty and feelings for Roger when she instructs him to meet Kaplan. The audience is completely aware of her betrayal, while Thornhill trusts her and follows the directions.

The crop duster scene is one of Hitchcock and cinema's most famous and enduring sequences and offers an excellent example of 'pure cinema'. The scene is constructed through a process of asking questions of the audience. Firstly, Roger is dropped off at a remote rural crossroad to meet the mysterious George Kaplan. Where is Kaplan? When cars pass, they tease the audience, as we expect henchmen to appear. Finally, an old man waiting for a bus (who could have been Kaplan/henchmen?) notices a plane crop duster where there aren't any crops. How will Roger escape the plane? The scene's climax occurs when the plane explodes after hitting an oil tanker. These questions and the building of suspense are achieved visually through the film's narration.

Roger returns to Chicago, and while trying to find Kaplan, he unwittingly sees Eve at the same hotel. On realising Kaplan has already checked out, he goes to Eve's hotel room. Why is she so happy to see him alive when she attempted to send him to his death? What does he expect from Eve? When Eve tries unsuccessfully to distance herself from him in her hotel room, she wants to save his life.

On following Eve to an auction house, Roger is surrounded by Vandamm's henchmen and can't escape (How will he escape?). The climax occurs in the auction house when the thugs surround Roger. Drama turns to comedy as he uses the auction house as his way out alive by disrupting proceedings and forcing the police to come and arrest him. After getting arrested, he meets the Professor (part of the CIA) and becomes fully aware of his situation. This sequence is more *shared suspense* than *dramatic irony*; even though he is still searching for Kaplan, he is aware of the villains as much as the audience.

Thornhill's *goal* to find romantic love is further developed in this sequence. The scene at an airport with the Professor is when the audience and Roger learn that Eve is a double agent and that her feelings towards Roger aren't fake. The viewer expects Roger to save Eve and are not disappointed. At the airport, Thornhill is given all the information that the audience has been privy to (making the rest of the film *shared suspense*), with the additional knowledge that Eve is a double agent. Once again, Roger's journey is turned on its head, and he is left with another surprise (and not the last). By the end of the sequence, Roger's name is clear, and his active *goal* is achieved. He now must save her, and this becomes his primary focus for the remainder of the film.

The news that Eve is a double agent is the first of three surprises, while the next two surprises occur in the next sequence. The first scene is shocking for the audience as Eve shoots Roger! Though the audience knows Roger is helping Eve, they don't know their plan, and when in a cafe he gets shot, it raises a question: Has Thornhill been killed? Shortly after, the answer becomes clear when Roger climbs out of the wagon completely uninjured. This twist is planned to 'kill off' Kaplan. The third surprise occurs straight after the shooting when Eve informs Roger that she will depart with Vandamm. Once Roger is confined to the hospital, the viewer poses another question: how will he escape his confines and save Eve from Vandamm? The answer to this question thrusts the viewer into the final and most dramatic sequence of the film.

This final sequence is tense and continually builds, leading Roger and Eve into more perilous situations. Roger goes to Vandamm's house and must rescue Eve. How will he do this? This sequence builds, and Roger moves from precarious situations in Van Dam's house to being trapped on Mount Rushmore. After Roger sees Leonard has told Van Dam about the fake shooting, Eve's life is dependent on Roger's success in his rescue. The villains who are fully armed are the obstacle during this sequence. "Whatever you do, don't get on that plane!" Roger's words emphasise the dramatic problem they have. Hitchcock fully milks this situation as he shows Eve and Van Dam walking to the plane, Eve's suitcase being left behind, and Eve stepping onto the plane as a gunshot sounds.

The classic chase across the face of Mount Rushmore was the starting point for the story's development (as is discussed in Part Two) and the ending chase for the film. Eve and Roger find themselves surrounded by the villains and are eventually caught. All seems lost as Roger struggles to pull Eve to safety and pleads for help from Leonard. Leonard stands on Roger's hand, though the audience somehow expects Roger to prevail (and he does). This final sequence is full of suspense and action—more than once, Roger finds himself in impossible situations and succeeds. The resolution, like the exposition at the beginning, is brief and effective, showing "Mrs Thornhill" jumping into bed and cutting to a train entering a tunnel.

Appendix Two

Creative Practice

This section relates to my practice as outlined in Part Four.

Historical Characters

The historical figures involved in the non-fiction account of the British nuclear tests provide a solid starting point for creative practice. These people will be divided into two groups, antagonists and helpers, to differentiate their roles within the larger structure and highlight their role concerning the protagonist's journey—i.e. antagonists oppose the protagonist's goal, while the helpers help him to achieve his goal.

Antagonists

Prime Minister Robert Menzies founded the Liberal Party in 1945 and had the longest continuous term in power in Australian politics between 1949 and 1966. According to Labour MP Eddie Ward, he "had a brilliant military career cut short by the outbreak of war". When Robert Menzies won his first federal election in December 1949, he promised to ban the Communist Party, a referendum he later lost. He was extremely pro-Britain—spending considerable time in London during office—and agreed to the British request for testing on Australian soil without consulting cabinet colleagues or asking if there were any possible health risks to the population. He stated that "no conceivable injury to life, limb or property could emerge from the test" (Walker 2014, p. xiii).

British scientist William Penney was the head of the atomic programme in Australia. He was a charismatic individual, insisting that he be called Bill rather than Professor, Doctor, or Sir William—or even Lord Penney, which he became after his work was completed. The reality was that Penney did not want Australians to know the extent to which the tests were poisoning the environment, as was indicated in a secret memo to Sir Frederick Brundrett at the UK Ministry of Defence: "We think it likely that the Australians will ask us for filters which have been flown at Mosaic and Buffalo. While I am not keen on giving them samples, I do not see how we can refuse. I am recommending that, if they ask us, we give them a little piece of the filters, but we wait a few days so that some of the isotopes have decayed a good deal" (Walker 2014, p. 81).

Penney needed a scientist who would allow all the tests, not ask any difficult questions, and argue for the importance of the programme for Australia's national security. The British chose one of their own in Professor Ernest Titterton. He was a British physicist who previously worked on the Manhattan Project—the nuclear research and testing programme in the US—and, in 1950, was invited by Mark Oliphant to be the inaugural chair of atomic physics at the Australian National University. Menzies placed Titterton as head of the safety commission for the British test programme. Titterton continually argued that "the whole operation was carried out with no risk to life or property on the mainland or elsewhere", even though all evidence suggests otherwise (Walker 2014, p. 104).

Frederick Lindemann, who would later become the first and only Viscount Cherwell, was an aristocratic scientist and British PM Winston Churchill's advisor. He was elitist and held radical beliefs—such as eugenics, extreme racial beliefs, and contempt for the working classes. Cherwell had a fierce hatred of Nazi Germany even though he was born in Baden-Baden, Germany, and studied in Darmstadt and Berlin. He also hated homosexuals (though he never married and was always accompanied by his valet). Churchill held Cherwell as a guru-like figure, supported his political ambitions, and once commented on his reliance on Lindemann by saying, "Love me, love my dog, and if you don't love my dog, you damn well can't love me" (Mukerjee 2011, p. 62). Lord Cherwell made a secret, unannounced visit to Emu Fields to witness an explosion, which Penney found both embarrassing and annoying.

Helpers

Australia's leading nuclear expert at the time was Adelaide-born Mark Oliphant. He was one of the first physicists in the world to show that an atom bomb was feasible and was part of the team working on the Manhattan Project. However, Oliphant was not highly regarded by the British because he was appalled by the bombing of Japan and only supported developing nuclear power for peaceful purposes. He was a personal friend of whistle-blower Hedley Marston.

Australian biochemist Hedley Marston was arrogant, overbearing, and skilled at taking credit for the work of his junior researchers, though he would turn on the charm for anyone who could advance his career. He gained international respect by discovering that cobalt had important benefits for the health of sheep. Marston revealed through the testing of animal thyroids that the nuclear tests were contaminating large parts of the country. Marston wrote to his friend Mark Oliphant that the Maralinga test was a "quasi scientific pantomime under the cloak of secrecy and evasive lying by government authorities about the hazard of fallout. Apparently, the people of Whitehall and Canberra think the people of northern Australia to be expendable" (Walker 2014, p. 190). Marston wrote a report accusing the safety committee of lying to the Australian people. This report was rejected for publication by the *Australian Journal of Biological Sciences* due to pressure from Titterton. Marston was branded a "Red Commie" by his fellow scientists in a concerted effort to discredit him personally.

Jack Tunny was a mining prospector in remote outback country near Kuridala, Queensland (about 100 kilometres south of Cloncurry). He told a newspaper reporter about surprising readings on his Geiger counter: "This morning I measured the ground around the camp and it registered a normal count of fifteen. But when rain began to fall I tested it as it came off the roof and the counter leaped to 2000" (Walker 2014, p. 101). He contacted Clem Watson, a uranium miner at Mt Isa, who immediately confirmed the radioactivity. The story hit front pages around the country: "Atomic Rain in Qld" was the headline in the *Adelaide Advertiser*. Luke Van Houdt, an electronics technician, had a similar experience in Brisbane on the same night. He recalled the radioactive rain making his Geiger counter go "off its rocker." Within an hour of informing his boss about the readings, a car turned up, and men in overcoats and hats took the Geiger counter and other evidence away.

Eighteen-year-old British airman Patrick Connolly told the media he saw four Aboriginal bodies in a crater at Maralinga. When in the 1970s he spoke to a Perth newspaper about radiation sickness from Maralinga, two men from ASIO visited him and told him to keep his "mouth shut" or he would be deported (Walker 2014, p. 163).

Treatment

The story begins with a black-and-white newsreel, which sets up the year, country, and Cold War setting. The mention of the British nuclear testing foreshadows the conspiracy and events later in the film.

Our British protagonist, Henley Farthing, enters the film as he arrives in Australia by plane. Humour as he stumbles sets the tone: this is a fun experience with laughs, and in a similar vein to *The 39 Steps* and *North by Northwest*, it is a fantasy. At the hotel, we are greeted with more humour as Henley meets Bill Haddin (a drunken British compatriot), as well as imperialist attitudes, which again foreshadow the British nuclear tests. Henley also meets other colleagues, heading to Sydney's Chinatown for dinner. Up to this point, humour has played an essential role as the only question (i.e. hypotheses) asked so far is about Henley avoiding Bill. From here on, the dramatic questions and excitement will begin.

At the offices of ASIO (an intelligence agency), we meet two government bureaucrats who introduce a mole wanting to let the Australian public in on the truth about 'Totem'. This scene is meant to be humorous but also references the nuclear tests and the controlling attitudes of governments. The subsequent scene shows two agents following the mole through the streets of Sydney. *Shared suspense* is built by this simple scene, as the mole (Jeff) attempts to avoid the agents.

Jeff meets a party of four (including Henley) and ends up having dinner with them. The two agents have seen Jeff in the restaurant, creating more *shared suspense*. Henley receiving the trinket from Jeff in the toilet is the event that instigates his involvement in the conspiracy. What is this trinket? A mystery has been set up, and we expect these questions eventually to be answered.

Henley discovers a key in the trinket before receiving a phone call late at night. Jeff asks Henley to meet someone at Luna Park. The audience learns that Jeff has a gun to his head, which raises the conflict significantly. This information develops *dramatic irony* for the next scene at Luna Park.

Henley arrives at Luna Park and meets the agent. A third unknown man is introduced, asking another question and developing more conflict. The handover of the trinket occurs on a ghost train ride and is a mixture of excitement, tension and laughs for the audience as the agent comically tries to frighten Henley. He warns Henley about the man with a wooden leg, which is a set-up for events in the next scene at the police station. When the third man starts firing, Henley is literally on a thrilling ride. After the agent is shot, his dying word is "Penny". Henley ends up looking guilty of murder as he departs the scene. Two policemen catch him. This scene ends with humour, as a boy wants to do the ride again!

Henley is clearly out of his depth in jail at the police station, suspected of murder. *Dramatic irony* is set up once more as the audience is made aware that the foreign man also in his cell has a wooden leg. This man calling Henley "comrade" is a cliché, but hopefully in a humorous way. This movie is a fantasy, and though historical events will kick in through the second half of the picture, my aim now is to make Henley a fugitive, set up all the story's mysteries, and have fun while doing it. When the two men escape the jail, Henley moves into a different world, where he will be a fugitive. The visuals of the contrasting black and white streets and the noir-ish underground tunnel are the transitions to a new world. This chase through the streets and tunnel is *shared suspense*, with occasional humour.

Henley starts the new day as a fugitive. How will he clear his name? His active *objective* is set up. What is the purpose of this key, which everyone seems to want? A mystery also needs to be solved. Henley's name is on the front page of a newspaper, isolating him and raising the conflict. It is in the paper that he sees 'Penney' and realises that the British nuclear tests may have something to do with the key.

Once Henley realises that the key is for a deposit box in Adelaide, his next move is to the central station to catch a train. The station and train are critical to the protagonists' journey in *The 39 Steps* and *North by Northwest*. The challenge as a writer was to think up situations on the train which are original to keep the remake as different as possible.

Henley hides by working in the train's catering carriage and serves customers at the bar. A salesman with one of the first transistor radios disagrees about technology with a priest drinking at the bar. The radio foreshadows the technology being developed for nuclear tests. The central tension comes from the salesman's son, who wants more ice cream and indicates to Henley that he has recognised him from the front cover of a newspaper.

After Henley has slept in the stock carriage, *shared suspense* is produced through a chase scene with the police. The chase ends up on the rooftop, lending more conflict and drama. Henley falls as the train slows down and manages to hide from the police. When the train leaves, he is abandoned in the middle of the outback. How will he get back to civilisation? While he is marching through the scrub, everything seems lost. Some humour occurs with the lizard waking him. At his most desperate (his *objective* is to survive), he hears the sound of Dixie jazz (a surprise)!

Jack is a prospector and helps Henley in his darkest hour. Both characters are isolated souls, with Jack wanting to find friendship (which he is successful with and develops a response emotion). The outback scenes provide relief from the hectic scenes of Henley on the run. Henley experiences the outback flora and fauna first-hand and gets an appreciation of the amount of life that exists in the outback. This point has relevance later to the British nuclear tests, which treated the outback as 'empty'. The radioactive rain prompts Henley back on his quest to clear his name.

In Adelaide, Henley and Jack meet Rachel, who will become a key player in the story. She wants justice to prevail and find romantic love (i.e. the same as Pamela in *The 39 Steps*) and helps retrieve the deposit box from the bank. There is meant to be humour and tension in Henley dressing up and pretending to be someone else. The drive-by shooting as they leave the bank is a shock, leading to Henley being captured by the communists.

Henley once again meets the man with the wooden leg. This scene is highly dramatic through *shared suspense* and is also meant to be fun as the Russian is a caricature. The audience expects Henley to escape somehow. Henley's escape is very much like Hannay's escape from the police station in *The 39 Steps*: Hannay is surrounded by police and handcuffed; the next shot shows him jumping out the window and running. This situation is an example of dramatic logic and keeping the story moving, trumping the story logic of a situation (as discussed as a feature of *The 39 Steps* genre). I decided to move back to the ASIO office and let them tell the audience of Henley's fortuitous escape.

John Marsdon is based on the real-life person, Henley Marsdon (yes, I borrowed his first name for the protagonist). In real life, he was a whistle-blower about the effects of the tests whom the government discredited for his actions. In the next couple of scenes, the audience learns about the tests and their effects on the environment. Tension is kept for the viewers, knowing that ASIO is watching Marsdon. Mark Oliphant, who is at his lab, was a real person and a real-life advocate against the testing. The scene at the lab closes the first half of the film and sets up the second half, where Rachel and Henley decide to travel to Maralinga to uncover the lies.

Things start poorly for the couple and only get worse. Rachel realises Henley is wanted by the law (developing conflict for their mission), and he must reveal his true intention of travelling to Maralinga. The fighting of the couple plays humorously as they get lost in the outback. Interestingly, the 'outback' could nearly be considered a character, as I have set it up earlier in the film, and it provides the conflict for Henley and Rachel achieving their goal.

The outback also takes them to the Aboriginal community, which the test has decimated. This situation develops high conflict for these people as well as sympathy.

Planes indeed dropped cough lollies to the communities affected by the tests (what were they thinking?). I wanted to show the results of the tests first-hand, as it is the most dramatic way of telling the story and can't be defended by any argument. Henley, who studied Aboriginal culture in London, now gets a first-hand experience of reality. The theories of his studies about this culture versus the reality of these people mirror the attitudes of the British and Australian government decision-makers with the concept of having a bomb and the effects on the environment of producing one.

Henley and Rachel travel in a station wagon with two very sick children to a hospital at Cooper Pedy. Cooper Pedy is where they meet another 'aid' to their journey: an old man and his dog. He asks Henley if he wants to buy Rachel a precious stone, referring to the possibility of their romantic relationship (their passive *goals*). The audience should be starting to expect that the couple will begin to bond as the story continues. I also hope the audience finds humour in how the old man acts and calls his car Doris Day.

When the couple gets caught by soldiers and taken to Maralinga, it all seems lost. William Penney tells Henley that he is a free man and that the government wants the key and plans back. This scene closes his active *goal* to clear his name but triggers his passive *goal* of romantic love. Rachel is not given such good news by Penney and is kept under watch for her stay at Maralinga. This scene is equivalent to the airport scene in *North by Northwest*, where Roger Thornhill is told by the Professor he is not wanted anymore, and therefore, his passive goal for romantic love kicks in. The rest of the film plays as *shared suspense*, where the audience experiences events with the characters.

There is a short scene with the character of Lord Cherwell, who was a real-life person and one of Churchill's close confidants. The scene reflects the reality of the situation as the top decision-makers were Politicians and often didn't make decisions based on the science or effects of the tests. It also gives another side to William Penney's role in the nuclear tests.

After witnessing some conflict between Australian and British troops, Henley is woken in the middle of the night by a young soldier with proof of atrocities. This proof aligns more with Rachel's *goal*, but Henley naturally attempts to help fulfil her want. He also gets a first-hand look at the test bombs but also must avoid the guards. Henley sneaking about the military camp creates tension. On finding an airmen suit, he changes for a disguise, only to have the real airmen looking for their suits. High tension is resolved when Henley knocks out one of the airmen. At the film's beginning, it would have been unthinkable for him to do such a thing. Due to his journey and experiences, he has changed and now has become a man of action. This progression is a vital set-up for the fight on the aeroplane later.

On being mistaken for the real airman, Henley witnesses Lord Cherwell thanking the men for volunteering to fly through the atomic cloud. This scene is based on real accounts, where airmen unwittingly volunteered to fly through the cloud after the explosion to test radiation levels.

Henley explores the site and finds Rachel. Henley has a plan but must wait for the impending blast, so the soldiers are occupied. The blast is dramatised by showing different perspectives of the explosion. Henley and Rachel dash for an aircraft about to take off. The start of this scene until the pair lands in Sydney represents the climax of the film.

On the plane, Henley heroically fights the pilot as the aircraft heads directly for the cloud. Rachel manages to steer the plane up through the cloud and grab the gun. On capturing the pilot, there is a slight relief from the suspense as Henley and Rachel decide what to do. The moment when the pilot has bailed, and they realise their petrol reserves are limited leads to high conflict and shared suspense. Henley (as the audience expects) manages to land the plane in Sydney just in time.

In Sydney, after avoiding the police at the airport, Henley heads for the Australian Safety Authority while Rachel goes to the media. Henley meets Ernest Titterton, who (in real life) failed in his job to report contamination for political reasons. He was considered extremely lucky by the Royal Commission investigating the tests not to be formally charged. As was also the case in real life, the media did not report any stories given to them about the tests. Henley's conversation with Titterton draws the story to a close.

I decided against having Henley and Rachel come together at the end because I found it too predictable and clichéd. I thought it better to leave their relationship open by suggesting further adventures (perhaps a sequel).

I hope the single image of the crater with the bodies gives the audience an uncomfortable moment to dwell on the atrocities that occurred.

The final scene in England hints at the next chapter in this sorry story about the British tests. In real life, the authorities collected the bones of deceased infants without permission from grieving parents, intending to test the effect of the radiation on the human inhabitants of the continent.

This closure is not typical for *The 39 Steps* genre, but I felt the material called for such an ending.